EVERYMAN,
I WILL GO WITH THEE,
AND BE THY GUIDE,
IN THY MOST NEED
TO GO BY THY SIDE

The Mabinogion

Translated by Gwyn Jones and Thomas Jones
with an Introduction by Gwyn Jones
and a Preface by John Updike

EVERYMAN'S LIBRARY

168

This book is one of 250 volumes in Everyman's Library
which have been distributed to 4500 state schools
throughout the United Kingdom.
The project has been supported by a grant of £4 million
from the Millennium Commission.

ISBN 1-85715-168-2

A CIP catalogue record for this book is available from the
British Library

Published by Everyman Publishers plc,
Gloucester Mansions, 140A Shaftesbury Avenue,
London WC2H 8HD

Distributed by Random House (UK) Ltd.,
20 Vauxhall Bridge Road, London SW1V 2SA

CONTENTS

PREFACE

Imagine a reader confronted seven or eight hundred years from now with a collection of modern short stories. Beyond the solvable puzzles posed by terminology and machinery and usages long obsolete, there would loom the larger difficulty of appropriate readerly reaction. In our unmediated evocations of twentieth-century happenstance, dealing with sexual relations and career disappointments and social embarrassments, heavy with dialogue and the revelations of childhood and ending with epiphanic moments of self-knowledge or of terse spoken farewell, all lightly larded with descriptions of nature the characters pass through or furniture they sit on or television shows they half-heartedly watch – in all this, what was meant, the future reader must ask himself, to be surprising, to be in its small surprise amusing, to deviate interestingly from normal expectation, to be, in brief, *news*, telling the vanished inhabitant of today's long-settled dust what he did not quite know before, broadening and enlightening his sensibility with the delicate shocks of art?

The narrative art depends upon an interplay with a cultured audience saturated in certain presumptions and previous artistic experiences. The sexual explicitness, for instance, so liberating and enlightening as it limned heroines from Joyce's Molly Bloom to Nabokov's Lolita, is now, I believe, a little baffling to younger readers – the flash of boldness has lost its background of repression and reticence. The cleansing verbal directness and starkness of Hemingway, or for that matter of Eliot and Imagism, needed, for their tonic effect to be felt, a setting of less purposeful styles blithely accepted by a readership comfortable with more padding; and this effect is more easily felt than the distinctions among the various later minimalisms practiced by, say, Raymond Carver, Donald Barthelme, Angela Carter and Kurt Vonnegut. These writers wrote out of a certain late twentieth-century mood of burn-out, of humorous anti-romanticism; how much 'point' will be left when that mood has evaporated?

All of which is to say that we feel, reading *The Mabinogion*, as if we are dancing with a partner who hears a distinctly different music. The speed of the telling leaves us frequently lagging well behind. The incidents come toward us like the thirteen Irish ships at the beginning of 'Branwen Daughter of Llŷr' – 'with an easy swift motion'. In this particular story, which is singled out by the translators in their introduction for 'that effect of illumination and extension of time and space which lies beyond the reach of all save the world's greatest writers', marvel succeeds marvel and cruelty is heaped on cruelty at a pace that seems, to a contemporary inner ear, headless and abrupt. Where a modern author would make much of, say, Branwen's (at the least) conflicted feelings as she is unceremoniously pledged to the Irish visitor Matholwch and bedded by him, we are given instead data of kinship and the surprising aside that Bendigeidfran, the King of the Island of the Mighty, has 'never been contained within a house'. It falls to the villain, Efnisien, to defend his sister's honor, as he perceives it, by mutilating the horses of their Irish guests, cutting off their lips and ears and even eyelids – an insult that is repaired by a lavish bestowal of replacement horses and other gifts, which include a magic cauldron that can restore a corpse to life, with all powers but that of speech. Branwen is happy in Ireland, and bears Matholwch a child, Gwern. But rumors of the insult done Matholwch when abroad circulate and cause an uprising 'till there was no peace for him unless he avenge the disgrace'. Unaccountably, Branwen, an innocent bystander to her brother's wicked deed, is condemned to the castle's kitchen and boxed on the ear every day by the butcher. By means of a magical bird she smuggles word back to her kinsmen of her plight; they arrive in Ireland by using the body of their huge king as a bridge across the river Llinon. Efnisien, at a parlay which seems to be going well, commits another atrocity by thrusting Gwern, named as the new King of Ireland, into the fire. The narrator grants Efnisien the gift of anticipatory remorse: before roasting Gwern he reflects, 'By my confession to God an enormity the household would not think might be committed is the enormity I shall now commit.' When the Irish are using the magic cauldron to revive their army (hidden in sacks that Efnisien has presciently crushed with his hands), the fitfully Christian mischief-maker says in his heart, 'Alas, God, woe is me that I should be the cause of this heap of the men of the Island of the Mighty', and gets himself tossed into the cauldron, which he bursts. The havoc is near total: Branwen, though blameless, cries, 'Woe is me that ever I was born: two good islands have been laid waste because of me', and heaves a great sigh and lets her heart break. The giant Bendigeidfran bids his surviving troop of seven men to cut off his head and bury it in London with its face toward France. On their way, however, the men are beguiled for seven years by the singing of three birds, and then for eighty years more they tarry in a palace where all memory of sorrow is erased. At last they open a door which has been sealed, and memory of their sorrows floods upon them, and they complete their errand, burying the head on White Mount, where it guards the island against plague.

What freight did such a caravan of marvels carry for its auditors? They inhabited a world where the naming of places was still in progress; psychology had not yet replaced geography as an orienting science. What we are is, to an extent, *where* we are, and what links of loyalty, to political entities embodied in kings and chieftans, hold us in place. In a world without technological change, history is genealogy; the tale of Branwen ends with the Irish race reduced to five pregnant women, who bear sons who mate, when mature, 'one by one with the other's mother', and thus repopulate an island still divided, commemoratively, into five provinces. Courtesy is for ceremonial occasions; beyond the roaring hearth and loaded table of formal hospitality and truce there reigns a continual carnage, as mechanical and innocent as the chirruping mayhem of a video game. We can recognize from comic books consumed in childhood the rigid lineaments of a superhero like 'Peredur the Son of Efrawg', who as he hits his stride throws men in batches of a hundred to the ground, and scorns the assistance of a loyal hundred, lest 'I would have no more fame than any one of you', in slaying the tearful Worm. As *The Mabinogion* progresses from the mythic to the merely fabulous, the middle ages of tourneys and fair maidens replaces the dark ages of genocidal tribal battle and sturdy queens treated like serving wenches. The warrior society dons the plumes of courtly love; the sociable arts are cultivated – 'there was not a fault at court so great as their being men so poor at conversation' – and roll-calls and heraldic specifics clutter an Arthurian elaboration like 'The Dream of Rhonabwy'.

Dreams, irrepressibly erotic in content, are, with place-names and heroic genealogies, a possible means of orientation for the dwellers in the world of these tales. 'The Dream of Macsen Wledig' depicts a maiden sitting in a chair of red gold, who rises and embraces the dreaming emperor, and has him sit with her in a chair that, dreamily, is 'no straiter for them both than for the maiden alone', as elastic as a vagina. Like tumescences during sleep are the visions the heroes have of their destined ladies; when Owein beholds the Lady of the Fountain, 'he was fired with love of her, till each part of him was filled therewith'. Math, Son of Mathonwy, conjures a woman out of flowers, as if of sheer velvety and odorous sensation, and she, thus conjured, is herself susceptible; when she first sights Gwydion, 'there was no part of her that was not filled with love of him ... Nor did they delay longer than that night ere they embraced each other.' Such instant mutual gratifications extend into romance the unceremonious beddings of older, gruffer tales; what the audiences must have received from their minstrels was, like perusers of modern magazine advertisements, images to aspire to – images of a superior existence, of elaborately colored costumes and resplendent armor, of travels and gallantry, of visions, blurring into the sleeping part of life, that lifted their attention away from the squalor, fear and brutality common around them.

Fiction seeks to concoct imaginary lives more clearly significant than our own. The elements of fantasy and symbolism that arouse interest are less prominent in classic novels than in these bardic tales, but nevertheless give those novels, and much popular fiction still, an educational and communal motive lacking in that contemporary fiction whose sole excuse for being is the implicit claim that this is how things are. We should know, of course, how things are – how else can we appraise and negotiate reality? – but the singers or authors of the tales mistitled *The Mabinogion* were concerned with how things *were*, in that pre-time when names were bestowed and giants engendered races, a pre-time still in our own fibers. Legend blends with reality's live underside of dream and wish-fulfillment. Here, wishes *are* horses and beggars *do* ride. The old tales drink from the spring wherein fact has not yet been filtered from fancy, and remind us that any narrator begins by believing that he has something marvellous to tell. An appetite for the marvellous comes with the first childish comprehensions, as a mode of acclimatization to the marvel of being alive.

John Updike

JOHN UPDIKE, novelist, short-story writer, poet and critic, is perhaps most famous for the four 'Rabbit' novels (published in Everyman's Library Contemporary Classics as *Rabbit Angstrom*). His novels have won the Pulitzer Prize, the National Book Award, the National Book Critics Circle Award and the Howells Medal.

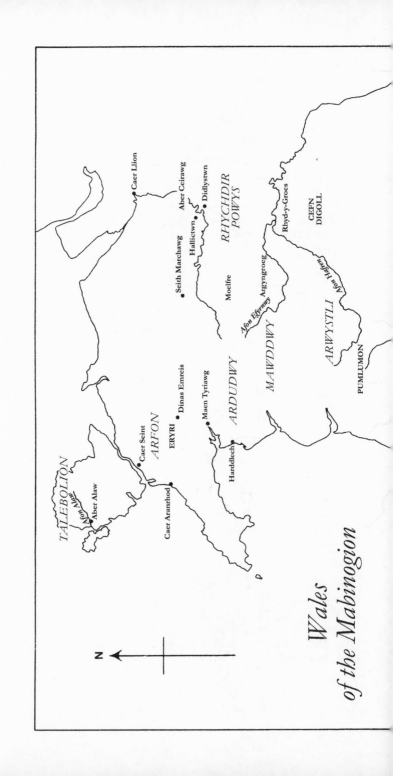

Wales
of the Mabinogion

N

TALEBOLION
Afon Alaw
Aber Alaw

Caer Seint
ARFON
ERYRI
Caer Aranrhod
Dinas Emreis
Maen Tyriawg
ARDUDWY
Harddlech

Caer Llion
Aber Ceirawg
Didlystwn
Seith Marchawg
Hallictwn
RHYCHDIR
POWYS
Moelfre
Afon Efyrnwy
Argyngroeg
Rhyd-y-Groes
CEFN
DIGOLL
MAWDDWY
ARWYSTLI
Afon Hafren
PUMLUMON

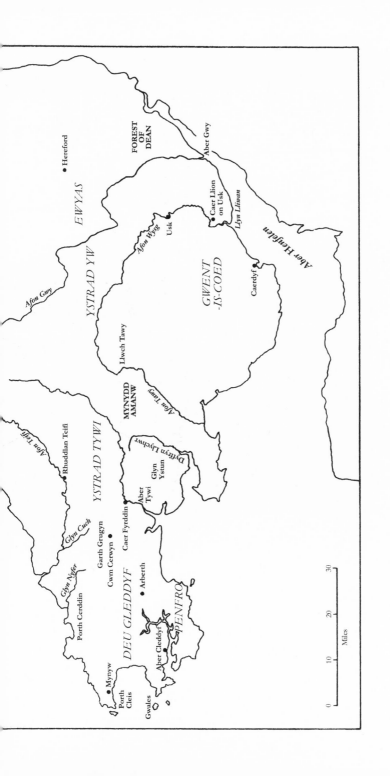

The Lands
of the
Mabinogion

N

PEN BLATHAON

MYNNYDD BANNAWG
Allt Clwyd

GODODDIN

RHEGED

Caer Efrawg

Afon Llinon

IRELAND

GWYNEDD
POWYS

CEREDIGIAWN
DYFED *DEHEUBARTH*
MORGANWG
GWENT
Aber Henfelen

LLOEGYR

Caer Loyw
London

Baddon

SUMMER COUNTRY

DEVON

CORNWALL Celli Wig

0 25 50 75 100
Miles

LLYDAW

INTRODUCTION

The eleven prose tales upon which the title 'Mabinogion' has been at once happily and arbitrarily bestowed are among the finest flowerings of the Celtic genius and, taken together, a masterpiece of our medieval European literature. Their excellence has been long, if intermittently, celebrated, and their influence deeply felt and widely recognized. The stories have been preserved in two Welsh manuscript collections, the White Book of Rhydderch (*Llyfr Gwyn Rhydderch*), written down about 1300–25, and the Red Book of Hergest (*Llyfr Coch Hergest*), of the period 1375–1425. The White Book is preserved in the National Library of Wales, Aberystwyth, the Red Book in the Library of Jesus College, Oxford. In addition, MSS. Peniarth 6, 7, 14 and 16 (all in the National Library of Wales) contain portions of various of the stories, some of them written down a hundred years before the White Book. Certain of the stories must have been known in their present (that is, their latest) redaction well before the time of the earliest of these manuscripts. The likeliest date for the Four Branches would appear to be early in the second half of the eleventh century; *Culhwch and Olwen* is earlier still – its orthography, glosses, vocabulary and syntax, and its glimpses of a more primitive social code, take parts of it back a further hundred years; and no one doubts that much of the subject matter of these stories is very old indeed, coeval maybe with the dawn of the Celtic world. But paradoxically the title 'Mabinogion', by which the stories are now collectively known, is a modern one. It was used by Lady Charlotte Guest as the title of her translations from the Red Book of Hergest and of the *Hanes Taliesin* (first found in a sixteenth-century copy). She understood it to be the plural of *mabinogi*, to which in common with the Welsh scholars of her time she attributed an incorrect meaning. But the word *mabynnogyon* occurs once only in the manuscripts, and it is as certain as such things can be that it is a scribal error of a common enough kind. In any case, the term *mabinogi* can apply only to the Four Branches of *Pwyll, Branwen*,

Manawydan and *Math*, and not to the other contents of the White Book or the Red. Thus Lady Guest's title was really a misnomer twice over; but it has proved so convenient (rather like the Old Icelandic *Edda*), and is now so well established in use, that it would be the sheerest pedantry to replace it with a clumsier if more correct alternative.

The eleven stories of the *Mabinogion* present a remarkable diversity within their medieval pattern. They fall into obvious groups: the Mabinogi proper, composed of the Four Branches of *Pwyll*, *Branwen*, *Manawydan* and *Math*; the two short pieces, *The Dream of Macsen Wledig* and *Lludd and Llefelys*; the incomparable and unclassifiable *Culhwch and Olwen*, the earliest Arthurian tale in Welsh; *The Dream of Rhonabwy*, a romantic and sometimes humorously appreciative looking-back by favour of the author's dream convention to the heroic age of Britain; and the three later Arthurian romances proper, *The Lady of the Fountain*, *Peredur* and *Gereint Son of Erbin*, with their abundant evidence of Norman-French influences.

This diversity should not, however, tempt us to overlook a substantial unity – a unity which is imposed both by their subject matter and their social and literary milieu. The matter is primarily mythology in decline and folktale, though it is unlikely that the story-tellers were themselves often, if ever, aware of this. But that such personages as Bendigeidfran, Rhiannon, Math and Mabon son of Modron, to name but a few, are in both the literary and mythological sense of divine origin, is so conclusively to be proved from the *Mabinogion* itself, from the rich and extensive Irish analogues, and from our knowledge of the myth-making and myth-degrading habits of our remote world-ancestors, that the theme needs no development at our hands. Euhemerized though such personages are, they remain invested with a physical and moral grandeur which amply bespeaks their god-like state and superhuman nature. The evidences of a pervading mythology are neither so numerous nor so striking in the later romances, but these too are seldom far from folktale. Other Arthurian elements common to all or most of the tales are those styled onomastic, the attempts to explain place-names, and the historical, in so far as the references to Arthur and the heroic story of non-divine origin may be called historical.

That Wales had its bards is a circumstance known to most. So too that the bards celebrated their patrons in verse. That oftentimes these bards were also story-tellers whose medium was prose or prose and verse is an item of knowledge as well authenticated though rather less widely diffused. The eleven tales of the *Mabinogion* are not the only examples of their craft which have survived, and the craft flourished during no shorter period than from the sixth century to the fifteenth. We know that the *cyfarwydd*'s, or story-teller's, stock-in-trade included many elaborate saga-cycles in which prose was the medium of narrative and description, and verse, often of the *englyn* type, of monologue and dialogue. Other tales were entirely in prose, and we are encouraged to guess at their number when we remember that the Irish *ollamh* was required, as a professional qualification, to know three hundred and fifty such. The triads and later verse, as well as 'authorities' like Nennius and Geoffrey of Monmouth, suggest that the Welsh story-tellers yielded to none in amplitude of material. Their tales were delivered orally, and centuries passed before some of them were committed to writing. They had thus no fixed and inviolable form, but took shape and colour from a hundred minds, each with its human disposition to variance and mutability. The *locus classicus* for the art and practice of these court story-tellers is in *Math* which informs us how, when Gwydion and his eleven companions set off for Rhuddlan Teifi, to trick Pryderi, they travelled in the guise of bards. ' "Why," said Pryderi, "gladly would we have a tale from some of the young men yonder." "Lord," said Gwydion, "it is a custom with us that the first night after one comes to a great man, the chief bard shall have the say. I will tell a tale gladly." Gwydion was the best teller of tales in the world. And that night entertained the court with pleasant tales and story-telling till he was praised by every one in the court, and it was pleasure for Pryderi to converse with him.' What tales Gwydion told, like what songs the Syrens sang, are not beyond all conjecture. They 'admit a wide solution' by such relics and fragments of Celtic tradition as have survived the steep mortality of the years. And so, natural and pious as it is to lament our lost heritage of story, we contemplate with the more pride and affection such treasures as are so happily preserved for us in the White Book and the Red.

If now we turn to a necessarily brief consideration of the eleven tales themselves, we unhesitatingly assign pride of place to the Four Branches of the Mabinogi. There has been no lack of attempts to explain the term *mabinogi*, but by common consent of Welsh scholars today it is derived from the word *mab* (youth), and is equated in meaning with the Latin *infantia* and the French *enfance*. It meant first 'youth', then a 'tale of youth', then a 'tale of a hero', and finally little more than 'tale' or 'story'. Thus a Branch of the Mabinogi is a 'portion of the story'. The reader of the Four Branches in their latest redaction may well wonder of what hero's story they are branches, and here we must rely on Professor W. J. Gruffydd's discussion of the whole problem in his *Math vab Mathonwy*, Cardiff, 1928. Briefly, Gruffydd argues (we think convincingly) that originally all four branches were concerned with the birth, exploits, imprisonment and death of Pryderi. Numerous accretions and misunderstandings have obscured this original conception, and in particular the exploits of Pryderi have yielded place to new material. In the second and third branches the children of Llŷr dominate, and in the fourth the children of Dôn, while the story of Lleu (his conception, youthful exploits, and exile by transformation) must originally have been a story in its own right. The process of accretion and modification is readily accounted for if we remember that the *cyfarwydd* had to deal with a great bulk of traditional material, and not with a series of canonical texts. The author of the Four Branches, and by 'author' we mean the man who gave them the shape in which they are now preserved, was the heir of bards and story-tellers unnumbered. The traditional material on which they had worked for many, many centuries, accreting, rejecting, explaining, forgetting, goes back to the earliest creative impulses of the Celtic world, and far from its being surprising that great changes took place, the wonder would be had they not. Something of change, something of similarity, may be gathered from the lines in the obscure poem beginning *Golychafi gulwyd*, to be found in the Book of Taliesin, and probably a monologue of Taliesin's in an early (ninth century?) version of the *Hanes*.

> I sang before the sons of Llŷr in Ebyr Henfelen ...
> I was in the battle of Goddeu
> With Lleu and Gwydion;
> They transformed the trees of the world and irises.
> I was with Brân in Ireland,
> I saw when Morddwyd Tyllon was slain ...
> Perfect is my chair in Caer Siddi,
> The plague of old age oppresses not him who is in it;
> Manawyd and Pryderi know it.

And yet again, in the poem beginning *Ren rymawyr* we may read:

> Gwydion son of Dôn, of mighty powers,
> Who made by magic a woman from flowers,
> Who brought swine from the South ...
> Who conjured up horses
> And ... saddles

If now we tabulate the contents of the Four Branches as we have them, and then discuss, even briefly, certain aspects of the saga of Pryderi and what for our present purpose may be called its contamination, the extraordinary complexity of the material will be apparent.

THE FOUR BRANCHES OF THE MABINOGI[1]

1st Branch, *Pwyll*
    Pwyll's descent to Annwn.
    The meeting of Pryderi's parents.
    Pryderi's birth.
    Pryderi's disappearance.
    His mother's penance (*Calumniated Wife* theme).
    Pryderi's restoration.

[1]The table of contents is taken from Gruffydd, *Math vab Mathonwy*, Cardiff, 1928, pp. 326–7.

2nd Branch, *Branwen*

    Events leading to Branwen's marriage with Matholwch.

    Branwen's penance (*Calumniated Wife* theme).

    Branwen's vindication.

    Brân's prowess in Ireland.

    Death of Brân.

    Death of Branwen.

    The episode of the Head (*Otherworld* theme).

3rd Branch, *Manawydan*

    Marriage of Manawydan and Rhiannon.

    The spell under which Pryderi and Rhiannon disappear.

    Restoration of Pryderi and Rhiannon.

4th Branch, *Math vab Mathonwy*

    The Story of *The King and his Prophesied Death*.

    The Story of *The Unfaithful Wife*.

    The stealing of the swine from Dyfed.

    The Death of Pryderi.

In the paragraphs that follow it is not suggested that every detail is capable of an infallible demonstration, that the review of themes and arguments is complete, or that a different explanation of parts of the Four Branches cannot be reasonably offered. The processes of literary composition are in their nature remote from mathematical proof, and the vast and fertile field of folktale is notoriously one in which the searcher can find almost anything he pleases. But Gruffydd's main conclusions are hardly to be shaken.

In the first section of *Pwyll* we recognize the story of how the king of the Otherworld changes place with an earthly king, in order that he may beget a wonder-child on an earthly mother. But the story as we have it tells rather of the king of Dyfed's sojourn in Annwn, and of his loyalty and chastity there. Consequently no child is begotten, either in Dyfed or Annwn, and a fresh start must be made. And so it happens, in the second section, that Rhiannon appears before Pwyll one day, not without the trappings of magic (the special quality of Gorsedd Arberth, the wonderful horse, and as we know from *Branwen* and *Culhwch and Olwen* she possesses magic birds), and they become man and wife. At this point the story is powerfully affected by the later theme of the Calumniated Wife (the Constance legend). Rhiannon is delivered by Pryderi, but her infant son is spirited away (in an earlier recension no doubt by his Otherworld father), and she herself is punished as though she had slain him. Next comes the episode in Gwent Is-Coed, where Teyrnon successfully protects his colt and on the selfsame occasion finds a child left at his door. Here we may well be confronted with a major confusion, if Teyrnon (*Tigernonos*) really is the Great King, and Rhiannon (*Rigantonia*) the Great Queen, who is to be equated with Modron (*Matrona*) the Great Mother, the father and mother respectively of Mabon (*Maponos*) the Great Son, with whom Pryderi is identified or at least confused. In any case, the boy is restored to his mother Rhiannon by Teyrnon, and Teyrnon having been his father till that time, Pryderi is placed in fosterage with Pendaran Dyfed, who it is tempting to believe was the original Lord of Dyfed with whose wife the King of the Underworld slept.

So much for the First Branch, the *compert* or Conception (as the Irish heroic tales would call it) of Pryderi. What of the Second, the *macgnímartha* or Youthful Exploits? Practically nothing is left: only the bare mention of Pryderi as one of the seven men who escaped from Ireland. The children of Llŷr have otherwise completely ousted him. There may possibly have been a separate mabinogi of Gwern; more obvious is the addition of Irish material, by oral transmission: the Cauldron, the Iron House, and the house made for Brân.

The Third Branch, what the Irish would call the *indarba* or Banishment, is altogether clearer. Pryderi's imprisonment in the Otherworld *caer* (stronghold) and his deliverance thence by Manawydan's guile are as plain as words can make them. So too the fall of mist, the desolation, the infertility which oppress the land of Dyfed on two occasions, and the destruction of Manawydan's crops by Llwyd son of Cil Coed, suggest that we here have to deal with a myth like that of Persephone, daughter of Demeter the Earth Mother, whose abduction by Dis in the fields of Enna robbed earth of its increase and joy. The sojourn of Manawydan and Pryderi and their wives in Lloegyr, and afterwards of Manawydan and Cigfa, and their betaking them to crafts, may be a version of the later and widespread Eustace legend, in which a great gentleman loses his wealth and must maintain himself by the work of his hands, without embitterment, and above all without any attempt to be revenged on his enemies. Such a legend could well become attached to the person of Manawydan, because the early form of his name, Manawyd, so closely resembles the word for an awl, *mynawyd*. Inevitably he becomes one of the Three Gold Shoemakers of the Island of Britain.

The confusion and complexity of the Fourth Branch, *Math*, are extreme. There is an unmistakable indication of the original *aided* or Death of Pryderi, for in the contest at Maen Tyriawg (the modern Maentwrog, north of Harlech) 'by dint of strength and valour and by magic and enchantment Gwydion conquered, and Pryderi was slain'. But the main actors in *Math* are the children of Dôn, and it can hardly be doubted that the Death of Pryderi is little more than incidental to the tale of Lleu Llaw Gyffes. Lleu is the hero of a story of the *King with the Prophesied Death* type. There is a king of whom it is prophesied that he shall be slain by his grandson; he has a daughter, and in order to circumvent the prophecy he must ensure that his daughter is never touched by man. But a means is found to outwit him, his daughter bears a male child, and in the fullness of time this child, perhaps unwittingly, slays his grandfather. The version of this tale found in *Math*, for all its changes, is still recognizable. But persons and motives have been altered decisively. Now it is the virginity of Math's footholder, not his daughter, which must be protected, and when she has been raped she is allowed to disappear from the story, and her son with her. It is Aranrhod daughter of Dôn who is delivered of the fateful child Lleu, and it is the mother, Aranrhod, and not the grandfather, Math, who labours to prevent the working out of the prophecy. Math's destiny is nowhere mentioned, and Aranrhod's hostility to her son is rationalized to shame at his illegitimate birth and incestuous begetting. Hereafter Lleu's story is mingled with a version of *The Unfaithful Wife*. His mother has sworn on him a destiny that he shall never have mortal woman to wife, so Math and Gwydion, enchanters both, conjure a wife for him out of flowers. This wife betrays him, and her lover comes near to killing him, but eventually Lleu kills the lover, presumably in the way in which in the earlier story he kills his grandfather. The wife's punishment is to be transformed into an owl.

The pattern of story set forth in the preceding paragraphs is necessarily a simplified one, but it will suggest to the reader not unacquainted with the substance and processes of folklore something of the successive redactions which occurred between the original saga of Pryderi and the Four Branches as we now have them. A further rich source of addition is the so-called onomastic tale, the fanciful explanation of the name of a place or person. Sometimes a new tale develops in the course of such an explanation, but for the most part the narrator adapts a tale already in existence. Thus the place-name 'Talebolion' in *Branwen* probably means 'End of the Ridges' or 'End of the Chasms' (the intermediate *-e-* an old orthographical form of the definite article *y*), but the narrator interprets it as *tal ebolion*, 'Payment of Colts', and provides an incident to 'explain' why it was so called. Numerous examples of such a process are to be found, and not only in the Four Branches; the explanation of the name Culhwch and of place-names which occur in the account of the hunting of Twrch Trwyth come to mind from *Culhwch and Olwen*; and Caer Fyrddin and Llydaw from *The Dream of Macsen Wledig*. Here and there we find an onomastic tale which has not been fully understood as such by the narrator. In *Math*, for instance, we read how Blodeuedd and her maidens fled to the mountains before the men of Gwynedd. In their fear they walked backwards (to look out for their pursuers), and so fell into a lake where they were all drowned, save Blodeuedd. This rather awkward episode seems to have been designed to explain the name Llyn-y-Morynion ('Maidens' Lake'), but we miss the expected tag, 'And for that reason was the lake called Llyn-y-Morynion.' It is likely that a close study of the tales, the Four Branches and *Culhwch and Olwen* in particular, would reveal many other such imperfectly understood onomastic stories.

But no story ever lived in the hearts of men because folklorists define its motifs and historians hazard its pre-natal vicissitudes. It is time to speak, though briefly, about the excellence of the

Four Branches as literature. That the final redactor, the 'author' of *Pwyll, Branwen, Manawydan* and *Math* in their present form, was a great artist no competent judge has ever denied. The natural turn of his mind was towards harmony and proportion; he brought a considerable degree of unity into the most diverse material; one senses in him at all times sanity and the spacious mind. He wrote the finest Welsh prose of his age, a grand master who never for one sentence intrudes the veil of style between the reader and what is read. Technically, we enjoy almost without awareness his perfect assurance: a skilled management of dialogue, an impressive reserve and control, a command of phrase which allowed him to move easily from tenderness to cruelty, from the grave to the grotesque, from pathos to the sublime, and a sustained yet delicately varied pace of narration. Second, though it is the tendency of folktale to deal with types, our author had a fine feeling for character. The children of Llŷr and the sons of Dôn are in their origin gods, but how consummately he gives them manhood, womanhood. Rhiannon, half contemptuous of, half pitying the lying women who accuse her of destroying her son; the impetuousness of the youthful Pryderi contrasted with the middle-aged caution of Manawydan before the magic *caer* (so admirably sustained in Manawydan's attitude towards the jealous craftsmen of Lloegyr and his bargaining with the bishop); Blodeuedd, who betrayed Lleu Llaw Gyffes with Gronw Bebyr, and 'under pretence of importunity of love' drew from him, like Delilah from Samson, the secret of how he might be slain – he never fails to explore their individual quality. And third, his vision of life must be stressed, clear, sincere, and noble. He has pondered long the destiny of mankind, its griefs and triumphs, its mystery and pain. Sometimes he touches heights at which comparison and comment are futile. He did so in the superb sentences which describe the death of Branwen; and later in the same story, in his account of the sojourn at Gwales in Penfro and the opening of the third door that looked on Cornwall and Aber Henfelen, he achieved that effect of illumination and extension of time and space which lies beyond the reach of all save the world's supreme story-tellers. That we know nothing of him personally, save that, as appears from the internal evidence of his masterpiece, he was a man of Dyfed and shaped his great work at the beginning of the second half of the eleventh century, is of little or no significance. Our concern with him is as artifex of a monument more lasting than brass, a classic of European literature, a glory of the Celtic world.

The two shorter pieces, *The Dream of Macsen Wledig* and *Lludd and Llefelys*, fall together in the mind rather by virtue of their brevity than for any correspondences of subject or treatment. *Macsen* is a joy, with its firm outlines, good proportions, high finish, and delicate yet glowing workmanship. Its one flaw is the none-too-skilful onomastic addition which tells of Cynan's exploits in Brittany. Macsen is the Spanish-born Magnus Maximus, who served with Theodosius in the British wars and rose to high military command in this island; in 383 he invaded Gaul to oust Gratian, then emperor of Rome, and after Gratian's assassination and the flight of Valentinian became master of Italy, but was himself put to death in 388 by Theodosius, at Aquileia. The excursion of Elen's brothers to Rome is historically on a par with Arthur's expedition thither, as related by Geoffrey of Monmouth and Malory, but the story shows a strong and indeed nostalgic interest in the old Roman grandeur, and the (exaggerated) contribution to it of British fighting men. *Lludd and Llefelys* is an attractive little folktale which calls for no particular comment. Its account of the dragons stirs echoes of Nennius; one judges it a late representative of a class of magical tales of rather wider appeal than the mingled subtlety and precision of the Four Branches.

The author of the Four Branches, we have said, was an artist who concealed his art. Not so the author of *Culhwch and Olwen*, who deploys with gusto every resource of language and style to heighten the colour and deepen the character of the fantastic and primitive world his creatures inhabit. It is a world in which birds and beasts are as important as men, a world of hunting, fighting, shapeshifting and magic. Immemorial themes of folktale are here: the jealous stepmother, the swearing of a destiny, asking a boon, the fulfilment of tasks, the helping companions, the oldest animals, the freeing of the prisoner, the hunting of the Otherworld beast, all strung along the controlling thread of Culhwch's winning the giant's daughter to wife – itself one of the oldest themes of all. The zest of this unknown story-teller still hits one like a bursting wave; there is magnificence in his self-awareness and virtuosity. One feels how he rejoiced in being equal to all his occasions: the gallant picture of young Culhwch and his steed, the bombast of Glewlwyd Mighty-grasp, the poetic beauty of the episode of the oldest animals, the savage grotesquery of Ysbaddaden Chief Giant, the headlong rush of the hunting of Twrch Trwyth, the lyricism of the description of Olwen. Now he is bare, hard, staccato; now he luxuriates with adjectives, compounds, puns even. It is not surprising that his story is rather loosely held together: his delight in its parts has affected its unity. Twice there appears to be an attempt to bind the diverse elements together, but each time on the dubious principle that the wider you throw your net the more surely you bring things together. When Culhwch first goes to Arthur's court, the narrator supplies a list of personages which is at once an index to cycles of lost story and a glimpse into his own teeming imagination; and second, at the court of Ysbaddaden, he finds place for a list of some forty tasks, presumably each one of them the hook on which a story might be hung. Arthur's warriors and Ysbaddaden's demands are each a mytho-heroic assemblage, and one reads them with the sensation that here, tantalizingly glimpsed, is a vast rolling panorama of lost Celtic story. Less than half the tasks are fulfilled, and of those, three do not figure in Ysbaddaden's list. It is probable that the list of tasks has been extended and not the accomplishments reduced. The personages of Arthur's court, surely the oddest retinue of any court in the world, and the list of tasks, would between them justify almost any wanderings of an author's furious fancies, but we are left with the impression of a conception too great for one man's powers. Unless indeed we have to do with a mutilated version of a masterpiece. What is left, however, is unique, a native saga hardly touched by alien influences, exciting and evocative, opening windows on great vistas of the oldest stuff of folklore and legend. After the Four Branches, it is the one story of the *Mabinogion* whose loss would not be made good by any other product of the medieval art of story-telling.

INTRODUCTION

This is not the place to discuss the historical and pseudo-historical references to Arthur to be found in the *Historia Brittonum* associated with the name of Nennius, and in the *Annales Cambriae*. But it would be an omission not to stress that *Culhwch and Olwen* is a document of the first importance for a study of the sources of the Arthurian legend. The Arthur it portrays is, of course, remarkably unlike the gracious, glorious emperor of later tradition, whether exemplified in the literatures of France, Germany or England, or for that matter in the concluding Arthurian romances of the present volume, subject as they have been to Norman-French influences. But when we recall that Arthur was not a French, German or English, but a British king, it is not unreasonable to emphasize the significance of British (which in this connexion means Welsh) material relating to him. British material, that is, uncontaminated by the Cycles of Romance, though necessarily affected by the vast complex of Celtic myth and legend. It consists for the most part of some exceptionally difficult poems, and of *Culhwch and Olwen* itself. In one of the poems, the so-called *Preideu Annwfyn* from the thirteenth-century Book of Taliesin (p. 54), we hear of Arthur's raids in his ship Prydwen upon eight *caers* in the Otherworld.

> Perfect was the imprisonment of Gweir in Caer Siddi,
> According to the Tale of Pwyll and Pryderi;
> No one before him went to it . . .
> Three freights of Prydwen went we into it,
> Save seven, none came back from Caer Siddi.

In the second verse there is mention of the Cauldron of the Head of Annwn, which 'boils not the food of a coward'.

> And when we went with Arthur . . .
> Save seven, none came back from Caer Feddwyd.

In the fifth we read of the Ych Brych, the 'Speckled Ox' of *Culhwch and Olwen*.

> And when we went with Arthur, sad journey,
> Save seven, none came back from Caer Fandwy.

xxix

And so to the last verse:

> When we went with Arthur, sad contest,
> Save seven, none came back from Caer Ochren.

In this context belongs the poem beginning *Golychafi gulwyd*, which has been quoted from earlier, and the poem beginning *Pa gur* from the thirteenth-century Black Book of Carmarthen – though the poem is considerably older than the manuscript itself. In *Pa gur* we find Arthur seeking entry into a 'house' of which Glewlwyd Mighty-grasp is porter.

> A. What man is porter?
> G. Glewlwyd Mighty-grasp.
>   What man asks it?
> A. Arthur and Cei Wyn.
> G. Who goes along with thee?
> A. The best men in the world.
> G. Into my house thou shalt not come
>   Unless thou disclose them (?).
> A. I shall disclose them,
>   And thou shalt see them.

And so Arthur names his followers: Mabon son of Modron, Cysteint son of Banon, Gwyn Godyfrion, Manawydan son of Llŷr ('of profound counsel'), Mabon son of Mellt, Anwas the Winged, Llwch Windy-hand, Bedwyr Four-teeth and Llacheu. As in *Culhwch and Olwen* pride of place is given to Cei and his exploits. Here too he is the great warlock-warrior.

> Cei pleaded with them
> While he slew them three by three . . .
> Though Arthur was but playing,
> Blood was flowing
> In the hall of Wrnach
> Fighting with a hag . . .
> An army was vanity
> Compared with Cei in battle . . .
> When he drank from a horn
> He would drink as much as four;
> Into battle when he came
> He slew as would a hundred.
> Unless God should accomplish it,

Cei's death would be unattainable.
Cei Wyn and Llacheu
They used to make battles
Before the pangs of the blue spears ...
Cei pierced nine witches.
Cei Wyn went to Môn
To kill lions.
Polished was his shield
Against Palug's Cat ...
Nine score warriors
Would fall as food for her ...

Clearly these poems and *Culhwch and Olwen* are much of a piece. They tell of the same people, and the events described are of a kind too. The account in *Preideu Annwfyn* of Arthur's sea-voyage to the Otherworld, and the mention of the *peir pen annwfyn*, remind one strongly of the account in the prose tale of Arthur's sea-voyage to fetch the cauldron of Diwrnach from Ireland; and the portion of *Branwen* which recounts Bendigeidfran's expedition to Ireland, the uses of the Cauldron of Rebirth, and the return of seven men to Wales, Pryderi being one of them, is a parallel which challenges the imagination. The feats attributed to Arthur's followers in the Glewlwyd dialogue would not be out of place in *Culhwch and Olwen*: the slaying of hags, monsters, witches. Cei and Bedwyr are consistent characters throughout, the former bearing little resemblance to the discourteous and ineffective buffoon of later romance. And what of Arthur himself? His nature is unmistakable: he is the folk hero, a beneficent giant, who with his men rids the land of other giants, of witches and monsters: he undertakes journeys to the Otherworld to rescue prisoners and carry off treasures; he is rude, savage, heroic and protective. And already he is attracting to himself the myths of early gods and the legends of early heroes. In other words, he is at the centre of British story; he is the very heart of it, both for his fame as *dux bellorum* and protector of Roman Britain against all its invaders (the historical and pseudo-historical Arthur), and for his increasingly dominating role in Celtic folklore and legend. It is remarkable how much of this British Arthur has survived in the early twelfth-century *Historia* of Geoffrey of

Monmouth and the mid-fifteenth-century *Morte Darthur* of Malory. Arthur setting off with Kaius and Bedeuerus to slay the swine-eating Spanish giant, and bursting out laughing when the monster crashes like a torn-up oak, or his battle with the beard-collecting Ritho, are cases in point. The growth may be traced both backwards and forwards. Behind the royal features in Geoffrey and Malory may be discerned the ruder lineaments of the folk hero; in the folk hero of *Culhwch and Olwen* one observes adumbrations of king and emperor. This is one of the three chief glories of this astonishing tale: its importance as a well-head of Arthurian romance. The other two are its richness as a repository of early British story and its brilliance as prose narrative. For these things it is *sui generis*, by itself, alone.

Whether a story so complicated in structure and so diffuse in episode as *Culhwch and Olwen* was ever in its entirety narrated orally, is open to question. That the intricacies of the early thirteenth-century *Dream of Rhonabwy* were expected to defy the memory of both bard and *cyfarwydd* we have the colophon (even if it is a gloss) to prove. It may not be known 'without a book'. It is an artist's piece, a succession of illuminated pages, deficient in movement and character, but a *tour de force* of close observation and description. The first set-piece, the black old hall of Heilyn Goch, is in the vein of the 'February' *histoires* of Pol de Limbourgh and Jean Foucquet; nor do their bright masterpieces of January and May out-do in loving care and brilliance of execution the pictures of the squires who interrupt Arthur and Owein at *gwyddbwyll*. The advantage, however, lies with the miniaturists, whose paints and enamels do what all the coloured words in Wales must fail to do. In detail *The Dream of Rhonabwy* is impeccable, the portraits shine like jewels, but the whole hardly equals, much less exceeds, the sum of its parts. Yet for all its elaboration, it has its roots in the native tradition of the Heroic Age. The significance of the games of *gwyddbwyll* between Arthur and Owein, like the nature and origin of Owein's ravens, has been the subject of much ingenious but unsuccessful speculation. What might have proved another difficulty the author has himself cleared up for us. For as the author of *The Dream of*

Macsen Wledig looked back with affection and respect to eternal Rome, so this later, self-conscious artist conjured up a vision of Arthur and the great men of the past, by way of comment on his own day. 'How sad I feel,' says Arthur, 'that men as mean as these keep this Island, after men as fine as those that kept it of yore.' Men as fine, that is, as Caradawg Stout-arm and Rhun son of Maelgwn Gwynedd, whom we know from history, or Goreu son of Custennin, Mabon son of Modron, Gwrhyr Interpreter of Tongues, and Gwalchmei, Gweir and Menw – old friends out of *Culhwch and Olwen* – and Owein, Peredur, and Edern son of Nudd, with whose adventures we are to grow acquainted in the three romances to come. Towards these romances the manner and matter of *The Dream of Rhonabwy* provide a natural, though unintended, transition.

In *The Lady of the Fountain*, *Peredur*, and *Gereint Son of Erbin* there is at once apparent a change of interest, purpose and fashion. Norman-French influence is strong and obvious, in background and tone and characterization, in the social and ethical code, in clothes and armour and the *realien* generally, and in the vague topography which contrasts so strongly with the precision of scene in the Four Branches and the routes marked so accurately across the pages of *Culhwch and Olwen*, of *Macsen* and *Rhonabwy*. The opening section of *Rhonabwy* is a quite striking piece of realistic description of an intensely realized setting. In place it is accurately sited in Powys; in time it belongs to the days of Madawg and Iorwoerth, the sons of Maredudd, lord of Powys, persons known to history (Madawg died in 1159, his brother six or seven years later). In all the dream-literature of the Middle Ages one cannot call to mind an author who took pains to establish his dreamer in a more credible or less comfort-able bed, or a dreamer who proceeded with more precision to his destination. But in the three romances, once a hero leaves Caer Llion on Usk, he is travelling not in Gwent or the adjoining districts of Lloegyr, but 'the bounds of the world and its wilderness'. In this, as in other ways, the Norman-French influence on Welsh story-telling was as unfortunate as it was inevitable. This is not to say that, considered as Arthurian romances, these three tales fall below the level of such tales elsewhere. They are excellent of their kind, and provide a variety of interesting episode free from the fashionable *longueurs* which make so much Arthurian romance determined reading today. It is significant too that their best passages are such as stem from the old root of native narrative: the remarkable parallel in *The Lady of the Fountain* to the vanishing of the court and later of Pryderi and Rhiannon in *Manawydan*; the *enfance* of Peredur, with its delightful incident of the two hinds, and its well-sustained folk motif of the Great Fool; the hedge of mist, the apple tree, and the horn which Gereint blew. It is probable that their charm seems less to the Welsh than to the English reader; for the former the decline from the Four Branches to *Gereint Son of Erbin* would be not unfairly expressed in the difference between Branwen and Enid, or Manawydan and Gwalchmei. In the romances lay figures move through stock adventures in unlocalized places; they entertain but have little power to move or excite. The sorrows of Branwen touch one as close after a hundred readings, but one needs sentimentality rather than sympathy to feel pity for Enid. Bendigeidfran is hurt mortally with a poisoned spear, Pryderi is borne down by main strength and magic, the enigmatic Efnisien bursts heart and cauldron alike; but the knights invariably overthrow their thousands. *Victrix causa deis placuit* ... But who for ever would wish to side with gods?

The connexion between the three Welsh prose romances and the *Yvain* (*Le Chevalier au Lion*), *Perceval* (*Conte del Graal*), and *Erec* of Chrétien de Troyes has been long and severely debated. It is part of the wider issue between the 'Continental' and the 'Welsh' schools of thought. The former has held that Wales contributed very little or even nothing of importance to the Arthurian legend as it developed in France and Germany and then England, and that the credit for the influence exerted by that legend upon the literature and culture of Europe must go to Chrétien and his disciples in France, and to Wolfram von Eschenbach, Gottfried von Strassburg, and Hartman von Aue. On the other hand, there have been many scholars to maintain that the Continental romances were derived from Welsh sources, whatever the links and transmission. There seems little room for doubt that the argument is now swinging to the 'Welsh' side, and that Chrétien's sources, little though we know of them, were derived from Welsh originals. The evidence of comparative folktale, of proper names and linguistics, and what may be reasonably if tentatively deduced from the methods of literary composition in the Middle Ages, is telling with increasing weight against the opposite view. The achievement of Chrétien and the German poets is not affected by this; their poems stand, their influence remains; their contribution to the Arthurian legend is impressive enough, though they are denied what they themselves never claimed, its origin and fountain-head.

Of the relationship between the three Welsh romances and Chrétien's poems it may be said that the romances are not translations of the *Yvain*, *Conte del Graal*, and *Erec*. It may be that they are compositions proceeding from the same ancient traditions, both oral and written, as provided Chrétien with the outlines of his stories. That the French-speaking Normans are in the direct line of transmission between Welsh tradition on the one hand and both Chrétien and the authors of the Welsh prose romances on the other, seems certain. By the twelfth century it is clear that matters Celtic were the rage in literature, and that for a variety of reasons Arthurian legend was the fashion. Arthur's dominating position in British story; Geoffrey of Monmouth's spectacularly popular *History*; the twofold advantage to the Normans of Arthur as a British, not an Anglo-Saxon, hero, with no unfortunate emotional or political connotations to his story, and the ease with which the imagination played about him rather than more defined figures like Charlemagne and Duke William; the skill of the Welsh and Bretons as story-tellers (the thing is just as true of the Icelanders), and the indubitable excellence of the stories they told: all these were elements of the supremacy. Further, the professional men of letters of the twelfth century knew their business well; they developed their material and conventionalized it at one and the same time: chivalry and courtly love, knight-errantry and faerye, religion, society and morality, mysticism and poetry – place for them all was found in the Matter of Britain, whose mighty accumulations met the diverse requirements of feather-brained page, love-sick courtier, gallant warrior, gentle lady, reverend senior, the dreamer and the man of action, the artist and the student of affairs. It displayed the pattern of society and the web and woof of human behaviour, it was remote as Broceliande and close as the nearest tilt-yard. It held a treasure for every seeker. And so, while the final miracle will always defy a logical and documented explanation, the Arthurian legend now became a priceless European inheritance, and part of the European imagination for ever. In this vast expansion of matter and significance the three Welsh prose romances now under discussion are quantitatively a humble affair. Their interest lies rather in their evidence of Welsh tradition underlying the continental expansion, and certain positive merits of narrative and construction which contrast with the deficiencies of Chrétien's story-telling. Assuredly they were popular performances, with their Norman-French characteristics imposed on the old Welsh virtues, and appealing more to their sophisticated audiences than the earlier, ruder tales of Owein, Peredur and Gereint had done. So popular indeed, that the earlier versions have yielded before them and fallen from human memory.

*

These then are the eleven stories of the *Mabinogion*. The present translation is the third into English. The pioneer in the field was Dr Owen Pughe, whose version of the first part of the tale of *Pwyll* (the episode of Pwyll and Arawn) appeared in the *Cambrian Register* for 1795, and with some slight verbal changes in the *Cambro-Briton* for February 1821. In 1829 he published a complete version of *Math Son of Mathonwy* in the *Cambrian Quarterly*. But it was left to Lady Charlotte Guest, with the help of Tegid, Carnhuanawc and others, to complete a translation of all eleven stories along with the 'Taliesin' (not found in the White Book or the

Red), and publish them in three handsome volumes during the years 1838–49. Her translation was a charming and felicitous piece of English prose, and has been justly esteemed by every succeeding generation of readers as a classic in its own right. The present translators believe themselves to be in as favourable a position to assess her merits as anyone now alive, and they cannot too emphatically pay tribute to so splendid an achievement. But the absence of texts, the lack of strict scholarship, and the ever-present sense of an undertaking *ad usum filioli* have left their tell-tale marks. Hers are beauties indeed, but too often they are not the beauties of her wonderful original. In 1887 Dr Gwenogvryn Evans and Sir John Rhŷs published a diplomatic edition of *The Text of the Mabinogion and other Welsh Tales from the Red Book of Hergest*, and in 1907 Dr Evans published a diplomatic edition of *The White Book Mabinogion*, which made available to scholars an earlier and in many ways more fundamental text along with the variants supplied by other Peniarth manuscripts. The second edition of Professor Loth's brilliant French translation, *Les Mabinogion*, Paris, 1913, was a tribute to Dr Evans's inspiring labours. Then came the second English translation, by T. P. Ellis and John Lloyd, Oxford, 1929, which restored Lady Guest's omissions, corrected her softenings, and attained a far greater accuracy of detail. It was based upon a study of all the texts, but in the present translators' opinion still left the way open for a rendering which should aim to convey literature in terms of literature and yet endure the most rigorous scrutiny of contemporary scholarship.

This new translation, now reprinted from the Golden Cockerel Press edition in folio, July 1948, is based upon the White Book of Rhydderch, as the older and truer manuscript. Its omissions, which are considerable, including as they do the whole of *The Dream of Rhonabwy* and substantial portions of other stories, have been supplied from the Red Book of Hergest. Our method can best be described as the preparation of a critical text based on the White Book, with a collation of all other MSS., and the translation of that text. We have used the diplomatic editions already referred to, of both the White Book and the Red, and consultation of the White Book manuscript has yielded a number of correct readings now incorporated in a translation for the first time. The forms of all personal and place-names have been modernized in orthography but not in phonology; we have retained the epenthetic vowel, and so far as is practicable used one form only of a name in any one tale. No translation of a Welsh classic has received warmer and more ample aid than this. There is a full account of the making of the Golden Cockerel–Everyman *Mabinogion* in the *Transactions of the Honourable Society of Cymmrodorion*, 1989, which enumerates our three main sources of support from our country's foremost scholars in this field. During 1944–48 our outstanding benefactors were Professor J. Lloyd-Jones of the National University of Ireland, and Professor Sir Ifor Williams of our sister college at Bangor, North Wales. Twenty-five years later, when Thomas Jones', illness and death threw all into sorrow, dismay and confusion during our preparation of the revised Everyman edition planned for 1974, we were profoundly grateful to our former student, colleague and friend (and thereafter the National Librarian of Wales) Professor Brynley F. Roberts, not only for a number of valuable improvements, but for a careful overseeing of the entire edition. What the unremitting support of these three experts meant in terms of confidence and applied scholarship needs no stressing. Thomas Jones, this too I need hardly add, was a scholar cast in the same heroic mould as these our Helping Companions.

To Christopher Sandford, of the Golden Cockerel Press, for his vision, care and generous spirit, we shall always feel the deepest obligation. He was the prime mover in securing the widest possible audience for what he considered his masterpiece, and it was he who ensured its appearance in Everyman's Library.

Finally, the greatest debt of all requires a separate mention. It had always seemed to either translator that without the encouragement and furtherance of his wife this work could hardly have been carried through amid the duties and distractions of four troubled years. No adequate acknowledgement is possible, but with the few words left to me it is my privilege to speak for my friend Tom as much as for myself, and repeat with fondness and pride our Dedication of July 1948: 'To ALICE AND MAIR'.

Gwyn Jones

NOTE ON THE EDITORS AND THE TEXT

———

GWYN JONES and the late THOMAS JONES were, respectively, Professor of English at Aberystwyth 1941–64 and at Cardiff 1965–76; and Professor of Welsh at Aberystwyth 1952–70. They are the authors of numerous works of scholarship in Welsh and in English, and their *Mabinogion* has, from its first appearance in 1948, been recognized as a triumph of the translator's art and a classic in its own right.

This translation of the *Mabinogion*, made by Professors Gwyn Jones and Thomas Jones of the University College of Wales, Aberystwyth, was first published in 1948 in the Golden Cock-erel Press edition-de-luxe, and appeared in Everyman's Library in 1949, since when it has been revised several times.

NOTE ON
PRONUNCIATION
OF WELSH NAMES

For the most part the pronunciation of Welsh is consistent and uncomplicated, and the notes that follow will ensure a reasonably accurate rendering of all names in the *Mabinogion*.

1. *Stress.* The stress in Welsh normally falls on the penultimate syllable of the word. In the transliterations that follow stress is indicated by italic letters.

2. *The Consonants.* As in English, except that:

   c is always the sound *k*; g is the sound in English gun; and *f* is the English *v* (*ff* = English *f*). Thus Cigfa is pronounced [*kigva*].

   h is always strongly aspirated; *r* is always strongly rolled; *rh* is pronounced *hr*: Rhiannon [hree*an*non]; *s* is always markedly sibilant, as in sun: Rhos [hros], Esni [*es*nee].

   ch is the Scottish *ch* in loch; *dd* is the *th* sound in English then or seethe; *ll* is the famous Welsh double *ll*, with the approximate sound of a strongly aspirated *hl*, or even *chl*: Lludd [hleethe].

3. *The Vowels.* All Welsh vowels are pure (i.e. monosyllabic or 'continental') sounds. They can be short or long in quantity. Thus: *a* short as in pan: Branwen [*bran*wen], or long as in palm: Brân [brahn].

   e short as in pen, or long as in French *è*: Llefelys [hle*vel*is].

   i short as in pin, or long as in marine: Iddawg [*ee*thowg].

   o short as in not: Olwen [*ol*wen], or long as in more: Môn [mohn].

   u short as in pin: Pumlumon [pim*lim*on], or long as in marine: Clud [kleed].

   y has three sounds, short as in pin: Glyn Cuch [glin keech], short as in pun, Pryderi [pru*der*ee], Yspaddaden [uspa*tha*den], or long as in Llŷr [hleer].

4. *The Diphthongs.* As a general rule, these partake of the nature of their constituent vowels. Thus:

ei, eu are pronounced like *y* in English why, and *ae* is similar: Cei [ky], Blodeuwedd [blo*dy*weth], Caer Llion [kyr *hlee*on].

aw is approximately the *ow* sound in English cow: Gwawl [gwowl], Lleu Llaw Gyffes [hly hlow *gyff*es].

oe resembles the *oy* sound in English boy: Gwent Is-Coed [gwent ees-*koyd*], Rhyd-y-Groes [hreed-uh-*groys*].

5. *w* does service as a vowel and a consonant. As a vowel it has either the short sound of *oo* in book or the long sound of *oo* in moon: Twrch Trwyth [toorch *troo*ith], Matholwch [ma*thol*ooch], Cadw [*ka*doo], Pwyll [*poo*ihl], Culhwch [*kil*hooch]. As a consonant it resembles English w: Gwawl, Gwen; but before *y* it tends to retain something of its vocalic nature: *wy* [wee or ooee]. Thus Rhonabwy, Mathonwy, Gwenhwyfar [Gwen*hooee*var], etc.

SELECT BIBLIOGRAPHY

DIPLOMATIC EDITIONS. John Rhŷs and J. Gwenogvryn Evans, *The Text of the Mabinogion and other Welsh Tales from the Red Book of Hergest*, Oxford, 1887; J. Gwenogvryn Evans, *The White Book Mabinogion*, Pwllheli, 1907.

EDITIONS OF TEXTS. Ifor Williams, *Pedeir Keinc y Mabinogi*, Cardiff, 1930; *Breuddwyd Maxen*, 3rd edn, Bangor, 1928; *Cyfranc Lludd a Llevelys*, 2nd edn, Bangor, 1932; Melville Richards, *Breudwyt Ronabwy*, Cardiff, 1948. R. L. Thomson, *Pwyll Pendeuic Dyuet*, Dublin, 1957; D. S. Thomson, *Branwen uerch Lyr*, Dublin, 1961; R. L. Thomson, *Owein*, Dublin, 1970; Rachel Bromwich and D. Simon Evans, *Culhwch ac Olwen* (testun Idris Foster), Cardiff, 1988.

STUDIES AND CONCLUSIONS. Gwilym R. Hughes and A. O. H. Jarman, ed., *A Guide to Welsh Literature*, Vol. I, Llandybie, 1974; Kenneth H. Jackson, *The International Popular Tale and Early Welsh Tradition*, Cardiff, 1961; Proinsias Mac Cana, *Branwen daughter of Llŷr*, Cardiff, 1958; *The Mabinogi*, Cardiff, 1971; W. J. Gruffydd, *Rhiannon*, Cardiff, 1953; Rachel Bromwich, A. O. H. Jarman, Brynley F. Roberts, *The Arthur of the Welsh*, Cardiff, 1991. And see the basic studies of Antti Aarne and Stith Thompson, *The Types of the Folktale. A Classification and Bibliography*, Helsinki, 1961, and Stith Thompson, *Motif-Index of Folk-Literature*, 6 vols, Copenhagen, 1955–58.

THE FOUR BRANCHES
OF THE MABINOGI

PWYLL PRINCE OF DYFED

Pwyll prince of Dyfed was lord over the seven cantrefs of Dyfed; and once upon a time he was at Arberth, a chief court of his, and it came into his head and heart to go a-hunting. The part of his domain which it pleased him to hunt was Glyn Cuch. And he set out that night from Arberth, and came as far as Pen Llwyn Diarwya, and there he was that night. And on the morrow in the young of the day he arose and came to Glyn Cuch to loose his dogs into the wood. And he sounded his horn and began to muster the hunt, and followed after the dogs and lost his companions; and whilst he was listening to the cry of the pack, he could hear the cry of another pack but they had not the same cry, and were coming to meet his own pack.

And he could see a clearing in the wood as of a level field, and as his pack reached the edge of the clearing, he could see a stag in front of the other pack. And towards the middle of the clearing, lo, the pack that was pursuing it overtaking it and bringing it to the ground. And then he looked at the colour of the pack, without troubling to look at the stag; and of all the hounds he had seen in the world, he had seen no dogs the same colour as these. The colour that was on them was a brilliant shining white, and their ears red; and as the exceeding whiteness of the dogs glittered, so glittered the exceeding redness of their ears. And with that he came to the dogs, and drove away the pack that had killed the stag, and baited his own pack upon the stag.

And whilst he was baiting his dogs he could see a horseman coming after the pack on a big dapple-grey steed, with a hunting horn round his neck, and a garment of brownish-grey stuff about him by way of a hunting garb. And thereupon the horseman drew near him, and spoke to him thus. 'Chieftain,' said he, 'I know who thou art, but I will not greet thee.' 'Why,' said he, 'perhaps thy dignity is such that it should not do so.' 'Faith,' said he, 'it is not the degree of my dignity that keeps me therefrom.' 'Chieftain,' he replied, 'what else then?' 'Between me and God,'

said he, 'thine own ignorance and discourtesy.' 'What discourtesy, chieftain, hast thou seen in me?' 'Greater discourtesy I have
not seen in man,' said he, 'than to drive away the pack that had
killed the stag and to bait thine own pack upon it. That,' said
he, 'was discourtesy, and though I will not take vengeance upon
thee, between me and God,' said he, 'I will do thee dishonour
to the value of a hundred stags.' 'Chieftain,' said he, 'if I have
done thee wrong, I will redeem thy friendship.' 'How,' he
replied, 'wilt thou redeem it?' 'According as thy dignity may be;
but I know not who thou art.' 'A crowned king am I in the land
whence I come.' 'Lord,' he replied, 'good day to thee, and from
what land is it thou comest?' 'From Annwn,'[1] answered he;
'Arawn king of Annwn am I.' 'Lord,' said he, 'how shall I win
thy friendship?' 'This is how thou shalt,' he replied. 'There is a
man whose domain is opposite to mine for ever warring against
me. That is king Hafgan, from Annwn; and by ridding me of
his oppression, and that thou easily mayest, thou shalt win my
friendship.' 'That will I do,' said he, 'gladly. But show me how
I may do it.' 'I will,' said he. 'This is how thou mayest. I will
make with thee a strong bond of friendship. This is how I will
do it: I will set thee in Annwn in my stead, and the fairest lady
thou didst ever see I will set to sleep with thee each night, and
my form and semblance upon thee, so that there shall not a
chamberlain, nor an officer, nor any other man that has ever
followed me know that thou art not I. And that,' said he, 'till
the end of a year from to-morrow, and our tryst then in this very
place.' 'Aye,' he replied, 'though I be there till the end of the
year, what guidance shall I have to find the man thou tellest of?'
'A year from to-night,' said he, 'there is a tryst between him and
me, at the ford. And be thou there in my likeness,' said he. 'And
one blow only thou art to give him; that he will not survive. And
though he ask thee to give him another, give it not, however he
entreat thee. For despite aught I might give him, as well as
before would he fight with me on the morrow.' 'Aye,' said Pwyll,
'what shall I do with my kingdom?' 'I will bring it about,' said
Arawn, 'that there shall be neither man nor woman in thy king-

1 Annwn (or Annwfn): the Celtic Hades.

dom shall know that I am not thou; and I shall go in thy stead.'
'Gladly,' said Pwyll, 'and I will be on my way.' 'Without let shall
be thy path, and nothing shall impede thee till thou arrive in my
domain, and I myself will bring thee on thy way.'

He brought him on his way till he saw the court and the
dwellings. 'There,' he said, 'the court and the kingdom in thy
power. And make for the court. There is none within that will
not know thee, and as thou seest the service therein thou wilt
know the usage of the court.'

He made for the court. And in the court he could see
sleeping-rooms and halls and chambers and the greatest show
of buildings any one had ever seen. And he went into the hall
to pull off his boots. There came squires and chamberlains to
pull them off him, and all as they came saluted him. Two
knights came to rid him of his hunting garb and to apparel him
in a robe of gold brocaded silk. And the hall was made ready.
Here he could see a war-band and retinues entering in, and the
most comely troop and the best equipped any one had seen, and
the queen with them, the fairest woman any one had ever seen,
dressed in a robe of shining gold brocaded silk. And thereupon
they went to wash and drew near the tables, and they sat in this
wise: the queen one side of him, and the earl, as he supposed,
the other side.

And he began to converse with the queen. And of all he had
ever seen to converse with, she was the most unaffected woman,
and the most gracious of disposition and discourse. And they
passed their time with meat and drink and song and carousal.
Of all the courts he had seen on earth, that was the court best
furnished with meat and drink and vessels of gold and royal
jewels.

Time came for them to go to sleep, and to sleep they went,
he and the queen. The moment they got into bed, he turned his
face to the bedside and his back towards her. From then till
morning not one word did he speak to her. On the morrow
tenderness and amiable discourse was there between them.
Whatever affection was between them during the day, not a
single night to the year's end was different from what that first
night was.

The year he spent in hunting and song and carousal, and affection and discourse with his companions, till the night the encounter should be. On that appointed night, the tryst was as well remembered by the man who dwelt furthest in the whole kingdom as by himself. And he came to the tryst, and the gentles of the kingdom with him. And the moment he came to the ford a horseman arose and spoke thus. 'Gentles,' said he, 'give good heed! It is between the two kings that this meeting is, and that between their two bodies. And each of them is a claimant against the other, and that for land and territory; and each of you may stand aside, and let the fight be between them.'

And thereupon the two kings approached each other towards the middle of the ford for the encounter. And at the first onset the man who was in Arawn's stead struck Hafgan on the centre of his shield's boss, so that it was split in two and all his armour broken, and Hafgan was his arm and his spear's length over his horse's crupper to the ground, with a mortal wound upon him. 'Ha, chieftain,' said Hafgan, 'what right hadst thou to my death? I was bringing no claim against thee; moreover I knew no reason for thee to slay me. But for God's sake,' said he, 'since thou hast begun my death, make an end.' 'Chieftain,' he replied, 'I may repent doing that which I have done to thee. Seek who may slay thee: I will not slay thee.' 'My trusty gentles,' said Hafgan, 'bear me hence. My death has been completed. I am in state to maintain you no longer.' 'Gentles mine,' said the man who was in Arawn's stead, 'take guidance, and discover who ought to be my vassals.' 'Lord,' said the gentles, 'all men should be, for there is no king over the whole of Annwn save thee.' 'Aye,' he replied, 'he who comes submissively, it is right that he be received; they that come not humbly, let them be compelled by dint of swords.'

And thereupon he received the homage of the men, and he began to subdue the land, and by mid-day on the morrow the two kingdoms were in his power. And thereupon he made for his trysting-place, and came to Glyn Cuch.

And when he came there, Arawn king of Annwn was there to meet him. Each of them welcomed the other. 'Aye,' said Arawn, 'God repay thee thy friendship. I have heard of it.' 'Aye,' he replied, 'when thou comest thyself to thy country thou wilt see what I have done for thee.' 'What thou hast done for me,' said he, 'may God repay it thee.'

Then Arawn gave to Pwyll prince of Dyfed his proper form and semblance, and he himself took his proper form and semblance; and Arawn set off for his court in Annwn, and he rejoiced to see his retinue and his war-band, for he had not seen them for a year. Yet they for their part had known nothing of his absence and felt no more novelty at his coming than of yore. That day he spent in mirth and merriment, and in sitting and conversing with his wife and gentles. And when it was more timely to seek slumber than to carouse, to sleep they went.

He got into bed, and his wife went to him. The first thing he did was to converse with his wife and indulge in loving pleasure and affection with her. And she had not been used to that for a year, and it was of that she thought. 'Alas, God,' said she, 'what different thought is there in him to-night from what has been since a year from to-night!' And she meditated a long time, and after that meditation he awoke and spoke to her, and a second time, and a third, but no answer thereto did he get from her. 'Why,' he asked, 'dost thou not speak to me?' 'I tell thee,' she said, 'for a year I have not spoken even so much in such a place as this.' 'Why now,' said he, 'we have talked closely together.' 'Shame on me,' said she, 'if since a year from yesternight, from the time we were enfolded in the bedclothes, there has been either delight or converse between us, or thou hast turned thy face towards me, let alone anything that would be more than that between us.' And then he fell a-thinking. 'O lord God,' said he, 'a man steadfast and unswerving of his fellowship did I find for a comrade.' And then he said to his wife, 'Lady,' said he, 'do not blame me. Between me and God,' said he, 'I have neither slept nor lain down with thee since a year from yesternight.' And then he told her the whole of his story. 'By my confession to God,' said she, 'strong hold hadst thou on a comrade, for warding off fleshly temptation and for keeping faith with thee.' 'Lady,' said he, 'that was my thought too when I was silent with thee.' 'Nor was that strange,' she replied.

Pwyll prince of Dyfed came likewise to his domain and land. And he began to inquire of the gentles of the land how his rule had been over them during the past year, compared with what it had been before that. 'Lord,' said they, 'never was thy discernment so marked; never wast thou so lovable a man thyself; never wast thou so free in spending thy goods; never was thy rule better than during this year.' 'Between me and God,' he replied, 'it is proper for you to thank the man who has been with you. And here is the story, even as it was' – and Pwyll related the whole of it. 'Aye, lord,' said they, 'thank God thou hadst that friendship; and the rule we have had that year, surely, thou wilt not withhold from us?' 'I will not, between me and God,' answered Pwyll.

And from that time forth they began to make strong the bond of friendship between them, and each sent to the other horses and greyhounds and hawks and all such treasures as they thought would be pleasing to the heart of either. And by reason of his sojourn that year in Annwn, and his having ruled there so prosperously and united the two kingdoms in one by his valour and his prowess, the name of Pwyll prince of Dyfed fell into disuse, and he was called Pwyll Head of Annwn from that time forth.

And once upon a time he was at Arberth, a chief court of his, with a feast prepared for him, and great hosts of men along with him. And after the first sitting Pwyll arose to take a walk, and made for the top of a mound which was above the court and was called Gorsedd Arberth. 'Lord,' said one of the court, 'it is the peculiarity of the mound that whatever high-born man sits upon it will not go thence without one of two things: wounds or blows, or else his seeing a wonder.' 'I do not fear to receive wounds or blows amidst such a host as this, but as to the wonder, I should be glad to see that. I will go,' said he, 'to the mound, to sit.'

He sat upon the mound. And as they were sitting down, they could see a lady on a big fine pale white horse, with a garment of shining gold brocaded silk upon her, coming along the highway that led past the mound. The horse had a slow even pace, as he thought who saw it, and was coming level with the mound. 'Men,' said Pwyll, 'is there any among you who knows the rider?'

'There is not, lord,' said they. 'Let one of you go and meet her,' said he, 'to find out who she is.' One arose, but when he came on to the road to meet her, she had gone past. He followed her as fast as he could on foot, but the greater was his speed, all the further was she from him. And when he saw that it was idle for him to follow her he returned to Pwyll and said to him, 'Lord,' said he, 'it is idle for any one in the world to follow her on foot.' 'Aye,' said Pwyll, 'go to the court and take the fleetest horse thou knowest and go after her.'

He took the horse and off he went. He came to the open level plain and showed his horse his spurs; and the more he pricked on his horse, all the further was she from him. Yet she held to the same pace as that she had started with. His horse flagged, and when he knew of his horse that its speed was failing, he returned to where Pwyll was. 'Lord,' said he, 'it is idle for any one to follow yonder lady. I knew of no horse in the kingdom fleeter than that, but it was idle for me to follow her.' 'Aye,' answered Pwyll, 'there is some magic meaning there. Let us go towards the court.'

They came to the court, and they spent that day. And on the morrow they arose, and that too they spent till it was time to go to meat. And after the first sitting, 'Aye,' said Pwyll, 'we will go, the company we were yesterday, to the top of the mound. And do thou,' said he to one of his young men, 'bring with thee the fleetest horse thou knowest in the field.' And that the young man did. They went towards the mound, and the horse with them. And as they were sitting down they could see the lady on the same horse, and on her the same apparel, coming along the same road. 'Behold,' said Pwyll, 'the rider of yesterday. Be ready, lad,' said he, 'to learn who she is.' 'Lord,' said he, 'that will I, gladly.' With that the rider came abreast of them. Then the young man mounted his horse, but before he had settled himself in his saddle she had gone past, with a clear space between them. Yet her pace was no more hurried than the day before. Then he put his horse into an amble, and thought that despite the easy pace at which his horse went he would overtake her; but that availed him not. He gave his horse the reins; even then he was no nearer to her than if he went at a walking pace. And the more he pricked on his horse, all the further was she from him. Yet her pace was no greater than before. Since he saw that it was idle for him to follow her, he returned and came to the place where Pwyll was. 'Lord,' said he, 'the horse can do no more than thou hast seen.' 'I have seen,' said he; 'it is idle for any one to pursue her. But between me and God,' said he, 'she had an errand to some on this plain, had obstinacy but permitted her to declare it. And we will go towards the court.'

They came to the court, and they spent that night in song and carousal, so that they were well content. And on the morrow they beguiled the day until it was time to go to meat. And when their meat was ended Pwyll said, 'Where is the company we were yesterday and the day before, at the top of the mound?' 'We are here, lord,' said they. 'Let us go to the mound,' said he, 'to sit. And do thou,' he said to his groom, 'saddle my horse well and bring him to the road, and fetch with thee my spurs.' The groom did so. They came to the mound to sit; they had been there but a short while when they could see the rider coming by the same road, and in the same guise, and at the same pace. 'Ha, lad,' said Pwyll, 'I see the rider. Give me my horse.' Pwyll mounted his horse, and no sooner had he mounted his horse than she passed him by. He turned after her and let his horse, mettled and prancing, take its own speed. And he thought that at the second bound or the third he would come up with her. But he was no nearer to her than before. He drove his horse to its utmost speed, but he saw that it was idle for him to follow her.

Then Pwyll spoke. 'Maiden,' said he, 'for his sake whom thou lovest best, stay for me.' 'I will, gladly,' said she, 'and it had been better for the horse hadst thou asked this long since.' The maiden stayed and waited, and drew back that part of her head-dress which should be over her face, and fixed her gaze upon him, and began to converse with him. 'Lady,' he asked, 'whence comest thou, and where art thou going?' 'I go mine own errands,' said she, 'and glad I am to see thee.' 'My welcome to thee,' said he. And then he thought that the countenance of every maiden and every lady he had ever seen was unlovely compared with her countenance. 'Lady,' said he, 'wilt thou tell me anything of thine errands?' 'I will, between me and God,' said she. 'My main errand was to try to see thee.' 'That,' said Pwyll, 'is to me the most pleasing errand thou couldst come on. And wilt thou tell me who thou art?' 'I will, lord,' said she. 'I am Rhiannon daughter of Hefeydd the Old, and I am being given to a husband against my will. But no husband have I wished for, and that out of love of thee, nor will I have him even now unless thou reject me. And it is to hear thy answer to that that I am come.' 'Between me and God,' replied Pwyll, 'this is my answer to thee – that if I had choice of all the ladies and maidens in the world, 'tis thou I would choose.' 'Why,' said she, 'if that is thy will, before I am given to another man, make thou a tryst with me.' 'The sooner it be,' said Pwyll, 'the better for my part; and wherever thou wilt, make the tryst.' 'I will, lord,' said she. 'A year from to-night at the court of Hefeydd I will have a feast prepared in readiness for thy coming.' 'Gladly,' he replied, 'and I will be at that tryst.' 'Lord,' said she, 'fare thee well, and remember that thou keep thy promise, and I will go my way.'

And they parted, and he went towards his war-band and his retinue. Whatever questions came from them concerning the maiden, he would turn to other matters.

Whereupon they passed the year till the appointed time, and he equipped himself as one of a hundred riders. He set off for the court of Hefeydd the Old and he came to the court, and a joyous welcome was given him; and there was much gathering of folk and rejoicing and great preparations against his coming; and all the resources of the court were dispensed at his direction. The hall was made ready, and they went to the tables. This is how they sat: Hefeydd the Old one side of Pwyll, and Rhiannon the other side; thereafter each according to his rank.

They ate and caroused and they conversed. And at the beginning of carousal after meat, they saw enter a tall auburn-haired youth of royal mien, and a garment of gold brocaded silk about him. And when he came into the high hall he greeted Pwyll and his companions. 'God's welcome to thee, friend,' said Pwyll, 'and go and sit down.' 'I will not,' said he; 'I am a suitor, and I will do my errand.' 'Do so, gladly,' said Pwyll. 'Lord,' said he, 'my errand is to thee, and it is to ask a boon of thee that I am come.' 'Whatever boon thou ask of me, so far as I can get it, it shall be thine.' 'Alas,' said Rhiannon, 'why dost thou give such an answer?' 'He has so given it, lady, in the presence of nobles,' said he. 'Friend,' said Pwyll, 'what is thy request?' 'The lady I love best thou art to sleep with this night. And it is to ask for her, and the feast and the preparations that are here, that I am come.'

Pwyll was dumb, for there was no answer he might have given. 'Be dumb as long as thou wilt,' said Rhiannon. 'Never was there a man made feebler use of his wits than thou hast.' 'Lady,' said he, 'I knew not who he was.' 'That is the man to whom they would have given me against my will,' said she, 'Gwawl son of Clud, a man rich in hosts and dominions. And because thou hast spoken the word thou hast, bestow me upon him lest dishonour come upon thee.' 'Lady,' said he, 'I know not what sort of an answer that is. I can never bring myself to do what thou sayest.' 'Bestow me upon him,' said she, 'and I will bring it about that he shall never have me.' 'How will that be?' asked Pwyll. 'I shall give into thy hand a small bag,' said she, 'and keep that with thee safe. And he will ask for the banquet and the feast and the preparations; but those things are not at thy command. And I will myself give the feast to the warband and the retinues,' said she, 'and that will be thy answer concerning that. And as for me,' said she, 'I will make a tryst with him a year from to-night, to sleep with me. And at the end of the year,' said she, 'be thou, and this bag with thee, one of a hundred horsemen in the orchard up yonder. And when he is in the midst of his mirth and carousal, do thou come in thyself, with shabby garments upon thee, and the bag in thy hand,' said she, 'and ask nothing but the bag full of food; and I will bring it about,' said she, 'that if what meat and drink are in these seven cantrefs were put into it, it would be no fuller than before. And after a great deal has been thrown therein, he will ask thee: "Will thy bag ever be full?" Answer thou: "It will not, unless a true possessor of great dominion shall arise and press the food in the bag with both his feet, and say: 'Sufficient has been put herein!'" And I will make him go and tread down the food in the bag. And when he goes, do thou turn the bag so that he goes over his head in the bag. And then slip a knot upon the thongs of the bag. And let there be a good hunting-horn about thy neck, and when he shall be tied in the bag, blow a blast on thy horn, and let that be a signal between thee and thy horse-men. When they hear the blast of thy horn, let them fall upon the court.'

'Lord,' said Gwawl, 'it were high time I had an answer to what I asked.' 'As much of what thou asked as is at my command thou shalt have,' said Pwyll. 'Friend,' added Rhiannon, 'as for the feast and the preparations that are here, I have given them to the men of Dyfed and the war-band and the retinues that are here. These I cannot permit to be given to any. But a year from to-night, a feast shall be prepared for thee in thy turn, friend, in this court, to sleep with me.'

Gwawl set off for his domain. But Pwyll came to Dyfed, and they each of them spent that year until the time set for the feast that was at the court of Hefeydd the Old. Gwawl son of Clud came to the feast that was prepared for him, and he sought the court, and a joyous welcome was given him. But Pwyll Head of Annwn came to the orchard one of a hundred horsemen, as Rhiannon had bidden him, and the bag with him. Pwyll clad himself in coarse, shabby garments, and wore big rag boots on his feet. And when he knew that they were about to begin to carouse after meat, he came on ahead to the hall; and after he had come inside the high hall he greeted Gwawl son of Clud and his company of men and women. 'God prosper thee,' said Gwawl, 'and God's welcome to thee.' 'Lord,' he replied, 'God repay thee. I have a request to thee.' 'Welcome to thy request, said he, 'and if thou ask of me a reasonable boon, gladly shalt thou have it.' 'Reasonable it is, lord,' said he; 'I ask but to ward off want. The boon I ask is this small bag full of food.' 'A modest request is that,' said he, 'and thou shalt have it gladly. Bring him food,' said he. A great many attendants arose and began to fill the bag; but for all that was put into it it was no fuller than before. 'Friend,' said Gwawl, 'will thy bag ever be full?' 'It will not, between me and God,' said he, 'for all that may ever be put into it, unless a true possessor of land and territory and dominions shall arise and tread down with both his feet the food inside the bag, and say: "Sufficient has been put herein!"' 'Brave sir,' said Rhiannon to Gwawl son of Clud, 'rise up quickly.' 'I will, gladly,' said he. And he arose and put his two feet into the bag and Pwyll turned the bag so that Gwawl was over his head in the bag, and quickly he closed the bag, and slipped a knot upon the thongs, and blew a blast on his horn. And thereupon, lo, the war-band falling upon the court, and then they seized all the host that had come with Gwawl and cast them each into his own durance. And Pwyll threw off his rags and his old rag boots and his tattered garb. And as each one of his host came inside, every man struck a blow upon the bag, and asked, 'What is here?' 'A badger,' they replied. After this fashion they played: each one of them struck a blow upon the bag, either with his foot or with a staff, and thus they played with the bag. Each one, as he came, asked, 'What game are you playing thus?' 'The game of Badger in the Bag,' said they. And then was Badger in the Bag first played.

'Lord,' said the man from the bag, 'if thou wouldst hear me – that were not the death for me, to be slain in a bag.' 'Lord,' said Hefeydd the Old, 'what he says is true. It is right and proper that thou hear him: that is not the death for him.' 'Why,' said Pwyll, 'I will do thy counsel concerning him.' 'Here is counsel for thee,' said Rhiannon then. 'Thou art now in a position in which it is proper for thee to content suitors and minstrels. Leave him there to give to all in thy stead,' said she, 'and take a pledge from him that he will never lay claim nor seek vengeance for this. And that is punishment a-plenty for him.' 'He shall have that gladly,' answered the man out of the bag. 'And gladly will I accept it,' said Pwyll, 'by the counsel of Hefeydd and Rhiannon.' 'That is our counsel,' said they. 'I accept it,' said Pwyll; 'do thou seek sureties for thyself.' 'We will answer for him,' said Hefeydd, 'until his men are free to answer for him.' And with that he was let out of the bag, and his chief men were freed. 'Demand now sureties of Gwawl,' said Hefeydd. 'We know which should be taken from him.' Hefeydd listed the sureties. 'Do thou thyself draw up thy terms,' said Gwawl. 'I am content,' said Pwyll, 'even as Rhiannon drew them up.' The sureties went on those terms. 'Aye, lord,' said Gwawl, 'I am wounded and have received great bruises, and have need of a bath; and with thy permission I will go my way. And I will leave noblemen here in my stead to answer to all who shall make request of thee.' 'Gladly,' said Pwyll, 'and do thou that.'

Gwawl set off for his domain. Then the hall was made ready for Pwyll and his retinue, and for the retinue of the court as well. And they went to sit at table; and as they sat a year from that night, they sat each one that night. They ate and caroused and time came to go to sleep. And Pwyll and Rhiannon went to their chamber, and they passed that night in pleasure and contentment.

And on the morrow in the young of the day, 'Lord,' said Rhiannon, 'arise and begin to content the minstrels, and refuse no one to-day who may desire a gift.' 'That will I gladly,' said Pwyll, 'both to-day and every day whilst this feast may last.' Pwyll arose and had silence proclaimed, to call on all suitors and minstrels to declare themselves, and had them told how all should be contented according to their wish and whim; and that was done. That feast was proceeded with, and none was denied while it lasted. And when the feast was ended, 'Lord,' said Pwyll to Hefeydd, 'with thy permission I will set out for Dyfed to-morrow.' 'Aye,' said Hefeydd, 'God speed thee. Appoint too a time and hour when Rhiannon may follow thee.' 'Between me and God,' replied Pwyll, 'we will go hence together.' 'Is that thy wish, lord?' asked Hefeydd. 'Even so, between me and God,' said Pwyll.

On the morrow they travelled towards Dyfed and made for the court of Arberth, and a feast was there in readiness for them. There came to them the full muster of the land and the dominion, of the foremost men and the foremost ladies. Neither man nor woman of these left Rhiannon without being given a memorable gift, either a brooch or a ring or a precious stone. They ruled the land prosperously that year and the next.

And in the third year the men of the land began to feel heaviness of heart at seeing a man whom they loved as much as their lord and foster-brother without offspring; and they summoned him to them. The place where they met was Preseleu in Dyfed. 'Lord,' said they, 'we know that thou art not of an age with some of the men of this country, but our fear is lest thou have no offspring of the wife thou hast; and so, take another wife of whom thou mayest have offspring. Thou wilt not last for ever,' said they, 'and though thou desire to remain thus, we will not suffer it from thee.' 'Why,' said Pwyll, 'it is not long as yet since we have been together, and many a chance may yet befall. Grant me a respite herein till the end of a year; and a year from now we will appoint a time to come together, and I will submit to your counsel.'

They appointed a time. Before the end of that time came, a son was born to him, and in Arberth was he born. And on the night that he was born women were brought to watch the boy and his mother. The women fell asleep, and the boy's mother, Rhiannon. The number of women brought into the chamber was six. They watched for part of the night; but before midnight every one there fell asleep, and towards cockcrow they awoke. And when they awoke they searched the place where they had put the boy, but there was no trace of him. 'Alas,' said one of the women, 'the boy is lost!' 'Aye,' said another, 'it would be but small vengeance to burn us or put us to death because of the boy.' 'Is there,' asked one of the women, 'any counsel in the world in this matter?' 'There is,' said another; 'I know good counsel,' said she. 'What is that?' they asked. 'There is here,' said she, 'a stag-hound bitch, with pups. Let us kill some of the pups and smear the blood on Rhiannon's face and hands, and let us throw the bones before her, and swear of her that she herself destroyed her son; and the insistence of us six will not be borne down by her on her own.' And upon that counsel they determined.

Towards day Rhiannon awoke and said, 'Women,' said she, 'where is the child?' 'Lady,' said they, 'ask not us for the child. We are nothing but blows and bruises from struggling with thee, and we are certain we never saw such fight in any woman as in thee. And it was idle for us to struggle with thee. Thou hast thyself destroyed thy son. And demand him not of us.' 'Poor creatures,' said Rhiannon, 'for the lord God who knows all things, accuse me not falsely. God who knows all things knows that accusation of me is false. And if it be fear that is upon you, by my confession to God I will protect you.' 'Faith,' said they, 'we will not bring hurt on ourselves for any one in the world.' 'Poor creatures,' said she, 'you will come to no hurt for telling the truth.' For all her words, whether fair or pitiful, she got but the one answer from the women.

With that Pwyll Head of Annwn arose, and the war-band and the hosts. And that hap could not be concealed. The story went forth throughout the land, and all the chief men heard it. And the chief men came together to make representation to Pwyll, to request him that he should put away his wife for a crime so outrageous as that she had wrought. The answer Pwyll gave was: 'No cause had they to request me that I put away my wife, save her having no offspring. But offspring I know her to have, and I will not put her away. But if she has done wrong, let her do penance for it.'

So Rhiannon summoned to her teachers and wise men. And as she preferred doing penance to wrangling with the women she took on her her penance. The penance imposed on her was to remain in that court at Arberth till the end of seven years, and to sit every day near a horse-block that was outside the gate, and to relate the whole story to every one who should come there whom she might suppose not to know it; and to those who would permit her to carry them, to offer guest and stranger to carry him on her back to the court. But it was chance that any one would permit himself to be carried. And thus she spent part of the year.

And at that time Teyrnon Twryf Liant was lord of Gwent Is-Coed, and the best man in the world was he. And in his house there was a mare, and throughout his kingdom there was neither horse nor mare more handsome than she. And every May-eve she foaled, but no one knew one word concerning her colt. One night Teyrnon talked with his wife. 'Wife,' said he, 'it is very slack of us every year to let our mare foal without our getting one of them.' 'What can be done in the matter?' asked she.

'To-night is May-eve. God's vengeance on me,' said he, 'if I do not learn what ill fate there is that takes away the colts.' He had the mare brought into a building, and took up arms, and began to keep watch for the night. And in the beginning of the night the mare cast a colt, large, handsome, and standing up on the spot. Teyrnon rose up and remarked the sturdiness of the colt, and as he was thus he heard a great commotion, and after the commotion, lo, a great claw through the window of the house and seizing the colt by the mane. Teyrnon drew his sword and struck off the arm at the elbow, so that that much of the arm together with the colt was inside with him. And with that he heard a commotion and a scream, both at once. He opened the door and rushed after the commotion. He could not see the commotion, so very black was the night. He rushed after it and pursued it. And he remembered that he had left the door open, and he returned. And at the door, lo, an infant boy in swaddling-clothes, with a sheet of brocaded silk wrapped around him. He took up the boy, and, lo, the boy was strong for the age that was his.

He closed the door and went into the chamber where his wife was. 'Lady,' said he, 'art thou asleep?' 'Not so, lord,' said she, 'I was asleep, but as thou camest in I awoke.' 'Here is a boy for thee,' said he, 'if thou wilt have him – what thou hast never had.' 'Lord,' said she, 'what tale was that?' 'Here it is, the whole of it,' said Teyrnon, and he told her all the affair. 'Why, lord,' said she, 'what sort of garments are there upon the boy?' 'A sheet of brocaded silk,' said he. 'He is the son of gentle folk,' said she. 'Lord,' said she, 'pleasure and mirth would this be to me: were it thy will, I would bring women into league with me and say that I have been with child.' 'I agree with thee gladly,' said he, 'in that.' And so it was done. They had the boy baptized with the baptism that was used then. The name that was given him was Gwri Golden-hair: what hair was on his head was yellow as gold. The boy was nursed in the court till he was a year old; and before he was one year old he was walking firmly, and he was bigger than a boy three years old who was of great growth and size. And the second year the boy was nursed, and he was as big as a child six years old. And before the end of the fourth year he would bargain with the grooms of the horses to let him take them to water.

'Lord,' said his wife to Teyrnon, 'where is the colt thou didst save the night thou didst find the boy?' 'I have made him over to the grooms of the horses,' said he, 'and charged that he be looked after.' 'Would it not be well, lord,' said she, 'for thee to have him broken in and given to the boy? For the night thou didst find the boy the colt was cast and thou didst save him.' 'I will not go against that,' said Teyrnon; 'I will permit thee to give it him.' 'Lord,' said she, 'God repay thee. I will give it him.' The horse was given to the boy, and she came to the ostlers and the grooms of the horses to bid them be careful of the horse, and for it to be broken in against the time the boy would go a-riding, and there be a tale concerning him.

Meanwhile they heard tidings of Rhiannon and her penance. Teyrnon Twryf Liant, because of the find he had made, gave ear to the tidings and inquired continually concerning them, until from many of the throng who came to the court he heard ever-renewed complaint of Rhiannon's so sad lot and punishment. Teyrnon pondered that and looked closely at the boy. And it came to his mind that in appearance he had never beheld a son and father so exceedingly alike as the boy to Pwyll Head of Annwn. The appearance of Pwyll was well known to him, for he had before that been a vassal of his. And with that, anxiety seized upon him, so very wrong it was for him to keep the boy when he knew him to be another man's son. And the first time he had privacy with his wife, he told her it was not right for them to keep the boy with them, and allow such great punishment as was for that reason on so excellent a lady as Rhiannon – and the boy the son of Pwyll Head of Annwn. And Teyrnon's wife agreed too that the boy be sent to Pwyll. 'And three things, lord,' said she, 'we shall gain thereby: thanks and gratitude for releasing Rhiannon from the punishment that is on her; and thanks from Pwyll for nursing the boy and restoring him to him; and third, if the boy prove a gentle man he will be our foster-son, and he will ever do us all the good he can.' And upon that counsel they determined.

And no later than the morrow was Teyrnon equipped, with

two more horsemen, and the boy as a fourth along with them, upon the horse which Teyrnon had given him. And they journeyed towards Arberth. It was not long before they reached Arberth. As they drew near to the court, they could see Rhiannon sitting beside the horse-block. When they had come abreast of her, 'Chieftain,' said she, 'go no further than that; I will carry each one of you to the court, and that is my penance for killing my son with my own hands and destroying him.' 'Ah, lady,' said Teyrnon, 'I do not think any one of these will go upon thy back.' 'Let him go who will,' said the boy, 'I shall not go.' 'Faith, friend,' said Teyrnon, 'nor will we.'

They went forward to the court and there was great joy at their coming. And they were beginning to hold the feast at court. Pwyll was himself come from a progress through Dyfed. They went into the hall and to wash. And Pwyll made Teyrnon welcome, and they went to sit down. This is how they sat: Teyrnon between Pwyll and Rhiannon, and Teyrnon's two companions above Pwyll, with the boy between them. When they had finished meat, at the beginning of carousal, they held discourse together. Teyrnon's discourse was an account in full of his adventure with the mare and the boy, and how the boy had been avowed by them, Teyrnon and his wife, and how they had nurtured him. 'And see there thy son, lady,' said Teyrnon. 'And whoever told lies against thee has done wrong. And when I heard of the affliction that was upon thee, it saddened me and I grieved. And I believe,' said Teyrnon, 'that there is none of all this company who will not recognize that the boy is Pwyll's son.' 'There is none,' said every one, 'who is not sure of it.' 'Between me and God,' said Rhiannon, 'I should be delivered of my care if that were true.' 'Lady,' said Pendaran Dyfed, 'well hast thou named thy son – Pryderi![2] And that best becomes him: Pryderi son of Pwyll Head of Annwn.' 'See,' said Rhiannon, 'lest his own name does not become him best.' 'What is the name?' asked Pendaran Dyfed. 'Gwri Golden-hair is the name we gave him.' 'Pryderi,' said Pendaran Dyfed, 'shall his name be.' 'That is most fitting,' said Pwyll, 'that the boy's name be taken from

2 Pryderi: Care or Thought. Pwyll: Sense.

the word his mother spoke when she received glad tidings of
him.' And thus was it determined.

'Teyrnon,' said Pwyll, 'God repay thee for rearing this boy till
the present time. And it is proper for him too, if he prove a
gentle man, to repay thee for it.' 'Lord,' said Teyrnon, 'as for the
lady that nursed him, there is not in this world a person who
feels more grief than she after him. It is well for him to remember, for my sake and that lady's, what we have done for him.'
'Between me and God,' said Pwyll, 'while I live I will maintain
thee and thy possessions, so long as I am able to maintain my
own. And if he live, more fitting is it for him to maintain thee
than for me. And if that be thy counsel, and that of these nobles,
since thou hast reared him to the present time, from now on
we will give him in fosterage to Pendaran Dyfed. And be ye
companions and foster-fathers to him.' 'That,' said every one,
'is proper counsel.' And then the boy was given to Pendaran
Dyfed, and the noblemen of the land allied themselves with
him. And Teyrnon Twryf Liant and his companions set out for
his own country and domain with love and gladness. And he
did not set off without being offered the fairest jewels and the
finest horses and the choicest dogs; but not a thing would he
have.

Then they remained in their own dominions, and Pryderi son
of Pwyll Head of Annwn was raised with care as was fit, until
he became the most gallant youth and the handsomest and the
best skilled in all manly pursuits of any in the kingdom. Thus
they passed years and years, until there came an end to the life
of Pwyll Head of Annwn and he died.

And Pryderi ruled the seven cantrefs[3] of Dyfed prosperously,
beloved by his people and by all around him. And after that he
conquered the three cantrefs of Ystrad Tywi and the four cantrefs of Ceredigiawn, and those are called the seven cantrefs of
Seisyllwch. And Pryderi son of Pwyll Head of Annwn was
busied about those conquests until it came to his mind to take a
wife. The wife he chose was Cigfa daughter of Gwyn Gohoyw,

3 cantref: like the English 'hundred', a territorial division containing a hundred
steadings, and itself divisible into two or more commots (see p. 122) for the
dispensing of law.

son of Gloyw Wallt Lydan, son of Casnar Wledig of the high-born ones of this Island.

And thus ends this branch of the Mabinogion.

BRANWEN DAUGHTER OF LLŶR

Bendigeidfran son of Llŷr was crowned king over this Island and exalted with the crown of London. And one afternoon he was at Harddlech in Ardudwy, at a court of his. And they were seated upon the rock of Harddlech overlooking the sea, and his brother Manawydan son of Llŷr with him, and two brothers on the mother's side, Nisien and Efnisien, and besides these, noblemen, as was seemly around a king. His two brothers on the mother's side were sons of Euroswydd by his mother Penarddun daughter of Beli son of Mynogan. And one of those youths was a good youth; he would make peace between the two hosts when their wrath was at the highest: that was Nisien. The other would cause strife between the two brothers when they were most loving.

And as they were seated thus, they could see thirteen ships coming from the South of Ireland, and making towards them with an easy swift motion, the wind behind them, and nearing them swiftly. 'I see ships yonder,' said the king, 'and making boldly for the land. And bid the men of the court equip themselves and go and see what their intent is.' The men equipped themselves and approached them below. When they saw the ships from near at hand, certain were they that they had never seen ships in fairer trim than they. Beautiful, seemly, and brave ensigns of brocaded silk were upon them. And thereupon, lo, one of the ships outstripping the others, and they could see a shield lifted up above the ship's deck, with the point of the shield upwards in token of peace. And the men drew near them that they might hear each other's discourse. They put out boats and came towards the land, and they greeted the king. For the king could hear them from the place where he was, upon a high rock over their heads. 'God prosper you,' said he, 'and welcome to you. Whose is this host of ships, and who is chief over them?' 'Lord,' said they, 'Matholwch king of Ireland is here, and the ships are his.' 'What would he?' asked the king. 'Does he wish to come to land?' 'Not so, lord,' said they, '– he is come on an errand to thee – unless he succeed in his errand.' 'What errand is his?' asked the king. 'He seeks to ally himself with thee, lord,' said they. 'He has come to ask for Branwen daughter of Llŷr, and if it seem good to thee he wishes to unite the Island of the Mighty with Ireland, so that they become the stronger.' 'Why,' he replied, 'let him come to land, and we will take counsel concerning that.'

That answer went to him. 'I will go gladly,' said he. He came to land, and he was made welcome, and great was the throng in the court that night, what with his hosts and those of the court. Straightway on the morrow they took counsel. What was determined in council was to bestow Branwen upon Matholwch. And she was one of the Three Matriarchs in this Island. Fairest maiden in the world was she.

And a time was set at Aberffraw, to sleep with her, and a start was made thence. And those hosts started for Aberffraw, Matholwch and his hosts in their ships, but Bendigeidfran and his hosts by land, until they came to Aberffraw. At Aberffraw they began the feast and sat them down. This is how they sat: the king of the Island of the Mighty, and Manawydan son of Llŷr one side of him, and Matholwch the other side, and Branwen daughter of Llŷr next to him. They were not within a house, but within tents. Bendigeidfran had never been contained within a house. And they began the carousal. They continued to carouse and converse. And when they perceived that it was better for them to seek slumber than to continue the carousal, to sleep they went. And that night Matholwch slept with Branwen.

And on the morrow all the host of the court arose, and the officers began to discuss the billeting of the horses and grooms. And they billeted them in every quarter as far as the sea.

And thereupon, lo, one day, Efnisien the quarrelsome man we spoke of above happening upon the billets of Matholwch's horses, and he asked whose horses they were. 'These are Matholwch's horses, king of Ireland,' said they. 'What are they doing there?' he asked. 'The king of Ireland is here and has slept with Branwen thy sister; and these are his horses.' 'And is it thus they have done with a maiden so excellent as she, and my sister at that, bestowing her without my consent! They could have put no greater insult upon me,' said he. And thereupon he set upon the horses and cut off their lips to the teeth, and their ears to their heads, and their tails to their backs, and wherever he could clutch their eyelids he cut them to the very bone. And he maimed the horses thus till there was no use could be made of the horses.

The tidings came to Matholwch. This is how they came: he was told of the maiming of his horses and their spoiling till there was no profit might be had of them. 'Aye, lord,' said one, 'insult has been wrought upon thee, and it is intended that such be done thee.' 'Faith, it is a marvel to me if they wished to insult me that they should have given me a maiden of such excellence and rank and so beloved of her kindred as they have given me.' 'Lord,' said another, 'thou seest it made plain. And there is nothing for thee to do but go to thy ships.' And thereupon he sought his ships.

The tidings came to Bendigeidfran that Matholwch was quitting the court, without asking, without leave. And messengers went to inquire of him why that was so. The messengers who went were Iddig son of Anarawd and Hefeydd the Tall. Those men overtook him and asked him what was his intent and for what reason he was going away. 'Faith,' he replied, 'had I known, I had not come hither. Full insult have I suffered; and no one had ever a less happy enterprise than I have had here. And a strange thing has come my way.' 'What is that?' they asked. 'That Branwen daughter of Llŷr should be given me, one of the Three Matriarchs of this Island, and king's daughter of the Island of the Mighty, and that I should sleep with her, and after that be insulted; and I was amazed that the intended insult was not done me before a maiden so excellent as she was given me.' 'Faith, lord, it was not with the assent of him who had authority at court,' said they, 'nor that of any of his council, that that insult was put upon thee. And though thou reckon that an insult, that affront and trick are more resented by Bendigeidfran than by thee.' 'Aye,' said he, 'I think so. But even so he cannot free me from insult thereby.'

Those men returned with that answer to the place where Bendigeidfran was, and they related to him the answer

Matholwch had spoken. 'Why,' said he, 'it is not to our advantage that he go away in enmity, and we will not let him go.' 'Well, lord,' said they, 'again send messengers after him.' 'I will,' said he. 'Arise, Manawydan son of Llŷr and Hefeydd the Tall and Unig Strong-shoulder, and go after him,' said he, 'and make known to him that he shall have a sound horse for each one of those spoiled. And along with that, as an atonement to him, he shall have a staff of silver, that shall be as thick as his little finger and as tall as himself, and a plate of gold as broad as his face. And make known to him what kind of man did that, and how it was against my will that it was done, and it was my brother on the mother's side that did it, and how it would not be easy for me to put him to death or destroy him. But let him come to see me face to face,' said he, 'and I will make peace on those terms he himself may desire.'

The messengers went after Matholwch, and they reported those words to him in friendly fashion, and he listened to them. 'Men,' said he, 'we will take counsel.' He took counsel. The counsel they thought of was: If they should reject that, they were more likely to get greater shame than get a greater reparation. And he resolved to accept it. And they came to the court in peace.

And they arranged the pavilions and the tents for them, after the fashion of arranging a hall, and they went to meat. And as they began to sit at the beginning of the feast, so sat they then. And Matholwch and Bendigeidfran began to converse. And, lo, listless and sad to Bendigeidfran the talk he had from Matholwch, whereas before this he was of constant good cheer. And he thought that the chieftain was heavy-hearted because of the smallness of the reparation he had had for the wrong done him. 'Why, man,' said Bendigeidfran, 'thou art not so good a talker to-night as the other night. And if it be because of the smallness to thy way of thinking of the reparation, thou shalt have it increased even as thou wilt, and the horses shall be made over to thee to-morrow.' 'Lord,' said he, 'God repay thee.' 'I will enhance thy reparation still further,' said Bendigeidfran. 'I will give thee a cauldron, and the virtue of the cauldron is this: a man of thine slain to-day, cast him into the cauldron, and by to-morrow he will be as well as he was at the best, save that he will not have the power of speech.' And he gave thanks for that, and felt exceeding great joy because of it.

And on the morrow his horses were made over to him as long as tamed horses lasted. And then they journeyed with him into another commot, and colts were made over to him until his tally was completed. And for that reason the name Talebolion was henceforth given to that commot.[1]

And the second night they sat together. 'Lord,' said Matholwch, 'whence came to thee the cauldron thou hast given me?' 'It came to me,' he said, 'from a man who had been in thy land; and I know not but that it was there he may have found it.' 'Who was that?' asked he. 'Llasar Llaes Gyfnewid,' he said, 'and he came here from Ireland, and his wife Cymidei Cymein-foll with him; and they escaped from the Iron House in Ireland, when it was made white-hot around them and they escaped therefrom. And it is a marvel to me if thou knowest nothing of that.'

'Lord,' said he, 'I do know; and as much as I know, I will tell thee. I was hunting in Ireland one day, on top of a mound overlooking a lake that was in Ireland, and it was called the Lake of the Cauldron. And I beheld a big man with yellow-red hair coming from the lake with a cauldron on his back. Moreover he was a monstrous man, big and the evil look of a brigand about him, and a woman following after him. And if he was big, twice as big as he was the woman; and they came towards me and greeted me. "Why," said I, "how fares it with you?" "This is how it fares with us, lord," said he; "this woman," said he, "at the end of a month and a fortnight will conceive, and the son who will then be born of that wombful at the end of the month and the fortnight will be a fighting man full armed." I took them to me to maintain them, and they were with me for a year. For that year I had them with me without grudging; from then on they were begrudged me, and before the end of the fourth month they were of their own part making themselves hated and

1 Talebolion: a name wrongly explained as tal ebolion: payment of colts. It probably means 'End of the Chasms' or 'End of the Ridges'.

unwelcome in the land, committing outrage, and molesting and harassing gentles and ladies. From then on my people rose against me to bid me part with them, and they gave me the choice, my dominions or them. I referred to the council of my country what should be done concerning them: they would not go of their own free will, nor was there need for them to go against their will, because of their fighting power. And then, in this strait, they decided to make a chamber all of iron. And when the chamber was ready, every smith that was in Ireland was summoned there, each and every possessor of tongs and hammer. And they caused charcoal to be piled as high as the top of the chamber, and they had the woman and her husband and her offspring served with ample meat and drink. And when it was known that they were drunk, they began to set fire to the charcoal against the chamber, and to blow the bellows which had been placed around the house with a man to each pair of bellows, and they began to blow the bellows till the house was white-hot around them. Then they held a council there in the middle of the chamber floor. And he waited till the iron wall was white, and by reason of the exceeding great heat he charged the wall with his shoulder and broke it out before him, and his wife after him. And none escaped thence, save him and his wife. And it was then, I suppose, lord,' said Matholwch to Bendigeidfran, 'he came over to thee.' 'Faith,' said he, 'it was then he came here and gave me the cauldron.' 'In what manner, lord, didst thou receive them?' 'I quartered them everywhere in my domain, and they are numerous and prosper everywhere, and fortify whatever place they happen to be in with men and arms, the best that any one has seen.'

That night they continued converse as long as they pleased, and song and carousal. And when they saw that it was more profitable for them to go to sleep than to sit longer, to sleep they went. And thus they spent that feast in joy; and when that was ended Matholwch set out for Ireland, and Branwen with him. Thirteen ships, moreover, set out from Aber Menei and reached Ireland. In Ireland there was great joy at their coming. Not one great man or noble lady would come to visit Branwen to whom she gave not either a brooch or a ring or a treasured royal jewel, which it was a wondrous sight to see departing. And with all this she spent that year in much good fame, and she flourished with honour and friends. And meantime it came to pass that she grew pregnant, and when the due time was past a son was born to her. This was the name given to the boy: Gwern son of Matholwch. The boy was put out to foster in the very best place for men in Ireland.

And then in the second year, lo, a murmuring in Ireland, on account of the insult which Matholwch had suffered in Wales, and the shameful trick played on him over his horses. Moreover, his foster-brothers and the men close to him taunted him therewith, and did not conceal it. And, lo, an uprising in Ireland till there was no peace for him unless he avenge the disgrace. The vengeance they took was to drive away Branwen from the same chamber with him, and compel her to cook in the court, and to cause the butcher after he had been cutting up meat to come to her and give her every day a box on the ear. And in this wise was her punishment carried out.

'Aye, lord,' said his men to Matholwch, 'set now a ban on the ships and the ferry-boats and the coracles, so that none may go to Wales, and such as come hither from Wales, imprison them and let them not go back, lest this be known.' And they determined on that.

Not less than three years they continued thus. And meantime she reared a starling on the end of her kneading-trough and taught it words and instructed the bird what manner of man her brother was. And she brought a letter of the woes and the dishonour that were upon her. And the letter was fastened under the root of the bird's wings and sent towards Wales. And the bird came to this Island. The place where it found Bendigeid-fran was at Caer Seint in Arfon, at an assembly of his one day. And it alighted on his shoulder and ruffled its feathers so that the letter was seen and it was known that the bird had been reared among dwellings.

And then the letter was taken and examined. And when the letter was read he grieved to hear of the affliction that was upon Branwen. And there and then he began to have messengers dispatched, to muster the whole of this Island. And then he had come to him the full levy of sevenscore districts and fourteen, and he complained to them in person that the affliction there was should be on his sister. And then they took counsel. The counsel that was determined on was to set out for Ireland, and leave seven men as overlords here, and Cradawg son of Brân as their chief, and their seven knights. In Edeirnon were those men left; and for that reason the name Seith Marchawg[2] was given to the township. The seven men were Cradawg son of Brân, and Hefeydd the Tall and Unig Strong-shoulder, and Iddig son of Anarawd Round-hair and Ffodor son of Erfyll, and Wlch Bone-lip and Llashar son of Llaesar Llaesgyngwyd, and Pendaran Dyfed as a young lad with them. Those seven stayed behind as seven stewards to take charge of this Island, and Cradawg son of Brân chief steward over them.

Bendigeidfran and the host of which we spoke sailed towards Ireland, and in those days the deep water was not wide. He went by wading. There were but two rivers, the Lli and the Archan were they called, but thereafter the deep water grew wider when the deep overflowed the kingdoms. And then he proceeded with all that there was of string minstrelsy on his own back and sought the land of Ireland.

And the Swineherds of Matholwch were upon the seashore one day, busied with their swine. And because of the sight they saw upon the sea, they came to Matholwch. 'Lord,' said they, 'greeting.' 'God prosper you,' said he, 'and you have news?' 'Lord,' said they, 'we have wondrous news: a forest have we seen upon the deep, in a place where we never saw a single tree.' 'That is a strange thing,' said he; 'could you see aught but that?' 'We could, lord,' said they; 'a big mountain close to the forest, and that moving, and a lofty ridge on the mountain, and a lake on each side of the ridge, and the forest and the mountain and all those things moving.' 'Why,' said he, 'there is no one here will know anything of that, except Branwen knows. Do you ask her.'

Messengers went to Branwen. 'Lady,' said they, 'what thinkest thou that is?' 'Though lady I am not,' said she, 'I know what

2 Seith Marchawg: seven riders (or seith = Latin *sancti*).

that is: the men of the Island of the Mighty on their way over, having heard of my woes and my humiliation.' 'What is the forest that was seen upon the sea?' they asked. 'The masts of ships and their yards,' said she. 'Alas,' said they, 'what was the mountain that could be seen alongside the ships?' 'Bendigeidfran, my brother, that was,' she said, 'coming by wading. There was never a ship in which he might be contained.' 'What was the lofty ridge, and the lake on each side of the ridge?' 'He,' said she, 'looking towards this island; he is angered. The two lakes on each side of the ridge are his two eyes, one on each side of his nose.'

And then all the fighting men of Ireland and of all the headlands were mustered in haste, and counsel was taken. 'Lord,' said his chief men to Matholwch, 'there is no counsel save to retreat across the Llifon,[3] a river which was in Ireland, and to leave the Llifon between thee and him, and to break down the bridge that is across the river. And there are loadstones at the bottom of the river; neither ship nor vessel can go upon it.' They withdrew across the river and broke down the bridge.

Bendigeidfran came to land and a fleet with him, towards the bank of the river. 'Lord,' said his noblemen, 'thou knowest the peculiarity of the river: none can go through it, nor is there a bridge over it. What is thy counsel as to a bridge?' said they. 'There is none,' said he, 'save that he who is chief, let him be a bridge. I will myself be a bridge,' said he. And then was that saying first uttered, and it is still used as a proverb. And then, after he had lain him down across the river, hurdles were placed upon him, and his hosts passed through over him.

Thereupon, even as he rose up, lo, the messengers of Matholwch coming to him and saluting him with greetings from Matholwch his kinsman, and showing how through his good will nothing but good should come his way. 'And Matholwch is giving the kingship of Ireland to Gwern of Matholwch, thy nephew, thy sister's son, and is investing him in thy presence, as reparation for the wrong and hurt that have been done to Branwen. And wherever thou wilt, either here

3 Llifon: Liffey.

or in the Island of the Mighty, do thou make provision for Matholwch.' 'Aye,' answered Bendigeidfran, 'if I cannot myself gain the kingship, maybe I shall take counsel concerning your message. From now on until different terms come, no answer will you get from me.' 'Why,' they replied, 'the best answer we receive, we will bring it thee, and do thou await our message.' 'I will,' said he, 'if you come quickly.'

The messengers went on their way and came to Matholwch. 'Lord,' said they, 'prepare a better answer for Bendigeidfran. He would not listen to aught of the answer we bore him.' 'Men,' said Matholwch, 'what is your counsel?' 'Lord,' said they, 'there is no counsel for thee save one. He was never contained within a house,' said they. 'Make a house,' said they, 'in his honour, so that he and the men of the Island of the Mighty may be contained in the one half of the house, and thyself and thy host in the other; and give over thy kingship to his will, and do him homage. And by reason of the honour in making the house,' said they, 'for he never had a house in which he might be contained, he will make peace with thee.' And the messengers came to Bendigeidfran with that message. And he took counsel, and in his council he determined to accept that, and that was all done by counsel of Branwen, and lest the land be laid waste she did that.

The terms of truce were drawn up, and the house was built big and roomy. But the Irish planned a ruse. The ruse they planned was to fix a peg on either side of every pillar of the hundred pillars that were in the house, and to fix a hide bag on each peg, and an armed man in every one of them. Efnisien came in ahead of the host of the Island of the Mighty, and scanned the house with fierce, ruthless looks, and he perceived the hide bags along the posts. 'What is in this bag?' said he, to one of the Irish. 'Flour, friend,' said he. He felt about him till he came to his head, and he squeezed his head till he felt his fingers sink into the brain through the bone. And he left that one and put his hand upon another, and asked, 'What is here?' 'Flour,' said the Irishman. He played the same trick on every one of them, until of all the two hundred men he had left alive but one; and he came to him and asked, 'What is here?' 'Flour, friend,' said the Irishman. And he felt about him until he came to his head, and he squeezed that one's head as he had squeezed the heads of the others. He could feel armour on that one's head. He left him not until he had killed him; and then he sang an englyn:

> There is in these bags flour of a sort:
> Champions, warriors, attackers in battle,
> Against fighters, ready for the fray.

And with that the hosts came into the house. And the men of the Island of Ireland came into the house on the one side, and the men of the Island of the Mighty on the other. And as soon as they were seated there was concord between them, and the kingship was conferred upon the boy. And then, when peace was concluded, Bendigeidfran called the boy to him. From Bendigeidfran the boy went to Manawydan, with all who saw him loving him. From Manawydan, Nisien son of Euroswydd called the boy to him. The boy went to him in friendship. 'Why,' said Efnisien, 'comes not my nephew, my sister's son, to me? Though he were not king of Ireland, gladly would I show love to the boy.' 'Let him go, gladly,' said Bendigeidfran. The boy went to him gladly. 'By my confession to God,' said Efnisien in his heart, 'an enormity the household would not think might be committed is the enormity I shall now commit.' And he arose and took up the boy by the feet and made no delay, nor did a man in the house lay hold on him before he thrust the boy headlong into the blazing fire. And when Branwen saw her son burning in the fire, she made as if to leap into the fire from the place where she was sitting between her two brothers. And Bendigeidfran grasped her with one hand, and his shield with the other. And then they all rose up throughout the house; and that was the greatest tumult that was by a host in one house, as each man caught up arms. And it was then that Morddwyd Tyllion said: 'Dogs of Gwern, beware of Morddwyd Tyllion!' And while each man reached for his arms, Bendigeidfran supported Branwen between his shield and his shoulder.

    And then the Irish began to kindle a fire under the cauldron of rebirth. And then the dead bodies were cast into the cauldron

until it was full, and on the morrow they would arise as good
fighting men as before, save that they were not able to speak.
And then when Efnisien saw the dead bodies, without room
being found anywhere for the men of the Island of the Mighty,
he said in his heart, 'Alas, God,' said he, 'woe is me that I should
be the cause of this heap of the men of the Island of the Mighty.
And shame on me,' said he, 'if I seek no deliverance therefrom.'
And he crept in among the dead bodies of the Irish, and two
bare-breeched Irishmen came to him and cast him into the cauldron as though he were an Irishman. He stretched himself out
in the cauldron, so that the cauldron burst into four pieces, and
his heart burst also.

And it was because of that that such a victory as there was
came to the men of the Island of the Mighty. Even so, there was
no victory save for the escape of seven men; and Bendigeidfran
was wounded in the foot with a poisoned spear. The seven men
who escaped were Pryderi, Manawydan, Glifieu son of Taran,
Taliesin and Ynawg, Gruddieu son of Muriel, and Heilyn son
of Gwyn the Old.

And then Bendigeidfran commanded his head to be struck
off. 'And take the head,' he said, 'and carry it to the White
Mount in London, and bury it with its face towards France.
And you will be a long time upon the road. In Harddlech you
will be feasting seven years, and the birds of Rhiannon singing
unto you. And the head will be as pleasant company to you as
ever it was at best when it was on me. And at Gwales in Penfro
you will be fourscore years; and until you open the door towards
Aber Henfelen, the side facing Cornwall, you may bide there,
and the head with you uncorrupted. But from the time you have
opened that door, you may not bide there: make for London to
bury the head. And do you cross over to the other side.'

And then his head was struck off, and they set out for the
other side, these seven, and the head with them, and Branwen
the eighth. And they came to land at Aber Alaw in Talebolion.
And then they sat down and rested them. Then she looked on
Ireland and the Island of the Mighty, what she might see of
them. 'Alas, Son of God,' said she, 'woe is me that ever I was
born: two good islands have been laid waste because of me!' And

she heaved a great sigh, and with that broke her heart. And a four-sided grave was made for her, and she was buried there on the bank of the Alaw.

And thereupon the seven men made their way towards Harddlech, and the head with them. As they journeyed, lo, there met them a troop of men and women. 'Have you tidings?' said Manawydan. 'We have not,' said they; 'save that Caswallawn son of Beli has conquered the Island of the Mighty and is a crowned king in London.' 'What has befallen Cradawg son of Brân,' they asked, 'and the seven men who were left with him in this Island?' 'Caswallawn fell upon them and slew the six men; and Cradawg broke his heart with consternation at sight of the sword slaying his men, and he not knowing who slew them. Caswallawn had apparelled him in a magic mantle, and no one could see him slay the men, but only the sword. But him Caswallawn did not wish to slay: he was his nephew, his cousin's son. And he was one of the Three Men who broke their hearts with consternation. Pendaran Dyfed, who was a young lad with the seven men, escaped into the forest,' said they.

And then they went on to Harddlech, and they sat them down and began to regale them with meat and drink; and even as they began to eat and drink there came three birds and began to sing them a certain song, and of all the songs they had ever heard each one was unlovely compared with that. And far must they look to see them out over the deep, yet was it as clear to them as if they were close by them; and at that feasting they were seven years.

And at the end of the seventh year they set out for Gwales in Penfro. And there was for them there a fair royal place overlooking the sea, and a great hall it was. And they went into the hall, and two doors they saw open; the third door was closed, that towards Cornwall. 'See yonder,' said Manawydan, 'the door we must not open.' And that night they were there without stint, and were joyful. And notwithstanding all the sorrows they had seen before their eyes, and notwithstanding that they had themselves suffered, there came to them no remembrance either of that or of any sorrow in the world. And there they passed the fourscore years so that they were not aware of having ever spent a time more joyous and delightful than that. It was not more irksome, nor could any tell of his fellow that he was older during that time, than when they came there. Nor was it more irksome having the head with them then than when Bendigeidfran had been with them alive. And because of those fourscore years it was called the Assembly of the Wondrous Head. The Assembly of Branwen and Matholwch was that wherewith they went to Ireland.

This is what Heilyn son of Gwyn did one day. 'Shame on my beard,' said he, 'if I do not open the door to know if that is true which is said concerning it.' He opened the door and looked on Cornwall and Aber Henfelen. And when he looked, they were as conscious of every loss they had ever sustained, and of every kinsman and friend they had missed, and of every ill that had come upon them, as if it were even then it had befallen them; and above all else because of their lord. And from that same moment they could not rest, save they set out with the head towards London. However long they were upon the road, they came to London and buried the head in the White Mount. And when it was buried, that was one of the Three Happy Concealments, and one of the Three Unhappy Disclosures when it was disclosed, for no plague would ever come across the sea to this Island so long as the head was in that concealment.

And that is what the tale says. That is their adventure, the men who set forth from Ireland.

In Ireland no person was left alive save five pregnant women in a cave in the Irish wilderness; and to those five women at the very same time were born five sons, and those five sons they reared until they became grown youths and bethought them of wives and desired to possess them. And then each slept one by one with the other's mother, and they ruled the country and dwelled in it, and divided it amongst them all five. And because of that division the five provinces of Ireland are still so called. And they searched the land where the battles had taken place, and they found gold and silver until they became wealthy.

And that is how this branch of the Mabinogi ends, concerning the blow to Branwen, which was one of the Three

Unhappy Blows in this Island; and concerning the Assembly of Brân, when the hosts of sevenscore districts and fourteen went over to Ireland to avenge the blow to Branwen; and concerning the feasting in Harddlech seven years; and the singing of the birds of Rhiannon, and the Assembly of the Head for fourscore years.

MANAWYDAN SON OF LLŶR

When the seven men we spoke of had buried the head of Bendigeidfran in the White Mount in London, with its face towards
France, Manawydan looked upon the town, in London, and on
his companions, and heaved a great sigh, and felt much grief
and longing within him. 'Alas, Almighty God, woe is me,' said
he, 'there is none save me without a place for him this night.'
'Lord,' said Pryderi, 'be not so unhappy. Thy cousin is king in
the Island of the Mighty, and though he has done thee wrong,
thou hast never been a claimant for land and territory. Thou art
one of the Three Ungrasping Chieftains.' 'Aye,' said he, 'yet
though that man be my cousin, it saddens me to see any one in
the place of Bendigeidfran my brother, and I cannot be happy in
the same house with him.' 'Wilt thou follow a different counsel?'
asked Pryderi. 'I had need of counsel,' said he, 'and what counsel
is that?' 'The seven cantrefs of Dyfed were left to me,' said
Pryderi, 'and Rhiannon, my mother, is there. I will bestow her
upon thee, and authority over the seven cantrefs with her. And
though thou hadst no territory save those seven cantrefs, there
are not seven cantrefs better than they. My wife is Cigfa daughter of Gwyn Gloyw,' said he, 'and though the territory is mine
in name, let the enjoyment thereof be thine and Rhiannon's; and
hadst thou ever desired territory, maybe thou mightest have
that.' 'I desire none, chieftain,' said he; 'God repay thee thy
friendship.' 'The best friendship I can show shall be thine if
thou wilt have it.' 'I will, friend,' said he; 'God repay thee. And
I will go with thee to see Rhiannon and to look on the territory.'
'Thou dost well,' he answered. 'I believe thou didst never listen
to a lady of better converse than she. What time she was in her
heyday, no lady was more comely than she; and even now thou
shalt not be ill-pleased with her looks.'

They went on their way, and however long they were upon
the road they came to Dyfed. A feast was prepared for them
against their coming, at Arberth, and Rhiannon and Cigfa had

made it ready. And then Manawydan and Rhiannon began to sit together and to converse, and with the converse his head and heart grew tender towards her, and he admired in his heart how he had never beheld a lady more graced with beauty and comeliness than she. 'Pryderi,' said he, 'I will abide by what thou didst say.' 'What saying was that?' asked Rhiannon. 'Lady,' said Pryderi, 'I have bestowed thee as wife upon Manawydan son of Llŷr.' 'And I too will abide by that, gladly,' said Rhiannon. 'Gladly will I too,' said Manawydan, 'and God repay the man who gives me his friendship as steadfastly as that.'

Before that feast ended he slept with her. 'What is left of the feast,' said Pryderi, 'do you continue with it, and I will go to tender my homage to Caswallawn son of Beli, to Lloegyr.'[1] 'Lord,' said Rhiannon, 'Caswallawn is in Kent, and thou canst continue with this feast and wait for him till he be nearer.' 'We will wait for him,' said he. And they continued with that feast, and they began to make a progress through Dyfed, and to hunt it, and to take their pleasure. And as they wandered through the country, they had never seen a land more delightful to live in, nor a better hunting ground, nor a land more abundant than that in honey and fish. And therewith such friendship grew up between those four that no one of them chose to be without the other, day or night.

And meantime he went to Caswallawn, to Oxford, to tender him his homage; and with exceeding great joy was he received there, and thanks to him for tendering him his homage.

And after his return, Pryderi and Manawydan feasted and took their ease. And they began a feast at Arberth, for it was a main court, and thence began every celebration. And after the first sitting that night, whilst the attendants were at meat, they arose and went forth and proceeded all four to Gorsedd Arberth, and a company with them. And as they were sitting thus, lo, a peal of thunder, and with the magnitude of the peal, lo, a fall of mist coming, so that no one of them could see the other. And after the mist, lo, every place filled with light. And when they looked the way they were wont before that to see the flocks and the herds and the dwellings, no manner of thing could they see: neither

1 Lloegyr: England.

house nor beast nor smoke nor fire nor man nor dwelling, but the houses of the court empty, desolate, uninhabited, without man, without beast within them, their very companions lost, without their knowing aught of them, save they four only.

'Alas, lord God,' said Manawydan, 'where is the host of the court, and our company too, save this? Let us go and look.' Into the hall they came: not a soul was there. Into the bower and the sleeping chamber they went: not a soul could they see. In mead-cellar and in kitchen there was naught but desolation.

They four set them to feasting, and they hunted and took their pleasure. And they began each one of them to wander through the land and the dominion, to see if they might descry house or habitation, but no manner of thing could they see, only wild beasts. And when they had finished their feast and their victuals, they began to live on the meat they hunted and on fish and wild swarms. And in this wise they passed a year pleasantly, and a second. And at last they grew weary.

'Faith,' said Manawydan, 'we cannot live thus. Let us make for Lloegyr and seek some craft whereby we may make our livelihood.' They made for Lloegyr and came to Hereford. And they took on them to make saddles. And Manawydan began to fashion pommels, and to colour them in the manner he had seen it done by Llasar Llaes Gygnwyd with blue-azure, and proceeded to make blue-azure even as that other had done. And for that reason it is still called *calch llasar*, because Llasar Llaes Gygnwyd made it. And of that work, so long as it might be had of Manawydan, neither pommel nor saddle was bought of a saddler throughout all Hereford; so that each of the saddlers perceived that he was deprived of his gain, and that nothing was bought of them, save when it might not be got from Mana-wydan. And with that they assembled together and agreed to slay him and his companion. But with that they received warn-ing, and took counsel whether they should quit the town. 'Between me and God,' said Pryderi, 'it is not my counsel that we quit the town, but that we slay those villeins yonder.' 'Not so,' said Manawydan, 'were we to fight with them we should get an ill name and be put in prison. It is better for us,' said he, 'to go to another town, there to earn a living.'

And then they four went to another city. 'What craft shall we take upon us?' asked Pryderi. 'We will make shields,' said Manawydan. 'Do we know anything about that?' asked Pryderi. 'We will try it,' he replied. They set to work making shields, fashioning them after the design of good shields they had seen, and applying to them the colour they had applied to the saddles. And that work prospered for them, so that never a shield was bought in the whole town save when it might not be got from them. Brisk too was their work, and the shields they made without number; and they continued in this wise until their fellow townsmen became irked with them, and agreed to try and slay them. But warning came to them, and they heard how the men were minded to make an end of them. 'Pryderi,' said Manawydan, 'these men are purposing to slay us.' 'We will not take that from the villeins. Let us fall on them and slay them.' 'Not so,' he answered, 'Caswallawn would hear of that, and his men, and we should come to grief. We will go to another town.'

They came to another town. 'What craft shall we follow?' said Manawydan. 'Whichever thou wilt of those that we know,' said Pryderi. 'Not so,' he answered, 'we will take to shoemaking; there will be no heart in shoemakers either to fight with us or forbid us.' 'I know nothing of that,' said Pryderi. 'I know it,' said Manawydan, 'and I will teach thee to stitch. And we will not trouble ourselves to dress leather, but will buy it ready dressed and will fashion our work from it.' And then he began to buy the finest cordwain he found in the town, and no other leather than that would he buy except leather for the soles; and he began to associate with the best goldsmith in the town, and had buckles made for the shoes, and the buckles gilded, and he looked on that himself until he had learnt it. And for that reason he was called one of the Three Gold Shoemakers. So long as there might be got from him either shoe or high boot, nothing was bought of a shoemaker in the whole town. The shoemakers perceived that they were losing their gain; for as Manawydan cut out the work, so Pryderi stitched it. The shoemakers came and took counsel, and in their council they agreed to slay them. 'Pryderi,' said Manawydan, 'the men are purposing to slay us.' 'Why should we take that from the thieving villeins,' said

Pryderi, 'rather than slay them all?' 'Not so,' said Manawydan, 'we will not fight with them, neither will we stay in Lloegyr any longer. Let us make for Dyfed, and go to look upon it.'

However long they were upon the road, they came to Dyfed and went on to Arberth. And they kindled fire and began to support themselves and hunt, and they spent a month thus. And they gathered their dogs about them and hunted, and were there in this wise for a year.

And one morning Pryderi and Manawydan rose up to hunt, and they made ready their dogs and went out from the court. Some of the dogs ran ahead of them and went to a small copse which was close at hand. And as soon as they went into the copse they drew back hurriedly, all bristling with fear, and returned to the men. 'Let us draw near the copse,' said Pryderi, 'to see what is in it.' They drew near the copse. As they drew near, lo, a wild boar of shining white rising up from the copse. The dogs, encouraged by the men, made at him. He then left the copse and fell back a little way from the men; and until the men were close at hand he would stand at bay against the dogs, without retreating before them, and each time the men closed in, he would fall back once more and break away. And they pursued the boar until they could see a huge lofty caer[2] all newly built, in a place where they had never seen either stone or building, and the boar making swiftly for the caer, and the dogs after him. And when the boar and the dogs had gone into the caer, they marvelled to see the caer in a place where they had never before seen any building at all. And from the top of the mound they looked and listened for the dogs. However long they remained thus, they heard not one of the dogs nor aught concerning them.

'Lord,' said Pryderi, 'I will go into the caer to seek tidings of the dogs.' 'Faith,' he replied, 'it is not good counsel for thee to go into the caer. We never saw this caer here. And if thou wilt follow my counsel, thou wilt not go inside. And it is he who cast a spell over this land caused the caer to be here.' 'Faith,' said

2 Caer: in various contexts the word denotes any fortified place: hill fort, Roman fort, or medieval castle.

Pryderi, 'I will not give up my dogs.' For all the counsel he received of Manawydan, he sought the caer.

When he came to the caer neither man nor beast nor the boar nor the dogs nor house nor habitation could he see in the caer. As it were in the middle of the caer floor, he could see a fountain with marble work around it, and on the edge of the fountain a golden bowl fastened to four chains, and that upon a marble slab, and the chains ascending into the air, and he could see no end to them. He was transported with the great beauty of the gold and with the exceeding good workmanship of the bowl, and he came to where the bowl was and laid hold of it. And as soon as he laid hold of the bowl, his two hands stuck to the bowl, and his feet to the slab on which he was standing, and all his power of speech forsook him, so that he could not utter one word. And thus he stood.

And Manawydan waited for him till near the close of day. And late in the afternoon, when he was convinced he would get no tidings of Pryderi or of the dogs, he came to the court. As he came inside, Rhiannon looked on him. 'Where,' said she, 'are thy companion and thy dogs?' 'Here,' he replied, 'is my story.' And he told it all. 'Faith,' said Rhiannon, 'a bad comrade hast thou been, but a good comrade hast thou lost.' And with that word out she went, and in the direction he told her the man and the caer were, thither she proceeded. She saw the gate of the caer open; there was no concealment on it, and in she came. And as soon as she came, she perceived Pryderi laying hold of the bowl, and she came towards him. 'Alas, my lord,' said she, 'what dost thou here?' And she laid hold of the bowl with him, and as soon as she laid hold, her own hands stuck to the bowl and her feet to the slab, so that she too was not able to utter one word. And with that, as soon as it was night, lo, a peal of thunder over them, and a fall of mist, and thereupon the caer vanished, and away with them too.

When Cigfa daughter of Gwyn Gloyw, the wife of Pryderi, saw that there was no one in the court save her and Manawydan, she made lamentation that to live was to her no better than to die. Manawydan noticed that. 'Faith,' said he, 'thou art in the wrong if through fear of me thou makest lamentation. I give

thee God for surety that thou hast not seen a comrade truer
than thou wilt find me, so long as God will that thou be this
way. Between me and God, were I in the first flush of my youth
I would keep faith with Pryderi; and for thy sake too I would
keep it. And let there be no fear upon thee,' said he. 'Between
me and God,' said he, 'thou shalt have the friendship thou
wouldst from me, so far as I can, for as long as it please God
that we be in this misery and woe.' 'God repay thee,' said she,
'that is what I thought.' And with that the maiden was cheered
and took courage on that account.

'Indeed, friend,' said Manawydan, 'this is no place for us to
stay. We have lost our dogs and can win no livelihood. Let us go
into Lloegyr; it will be easiest for us to make a living there.'
'Gladly, lord,' said she, 'and we will do that.' Together they
journeyed towards Lloegyr.

'Lord,' said she, 'what craft wilt thou take upon thee? Take
up one that is cleanly.' 'I will not,' said he, 'save shoemaking, as
I did before.' 'Lord,' said she, 'that is not to be commended for
its cleanliness to a man so skilled and of such high rank as thou.'
'That will I follow,' said he.

He began his craft, and he fashioned his work from the finest
cordwain that he found in the town. And as they had begun at
the other place, he began to buckle the shoes with gold buckles,
so that the work of all the shoemakers of the town was vain and
trivial compared with his own. And so long as there might be
got from him either shoe or high boot, nothing was bought
from the others. And thus he spent a year there, till the shoemakers grew envious and jealous of him, and warnings came to
him, and it was told him how the shoemakers had agreed to slay
him. 'Lord,' said Cigfa, 'why is this borne from the villeins?'
'Not so,' he answered. 'However, let us go to Dyfed.'

To Dyfed they made their way. Now Manawydan when he
set out for Dyfed took with him a burden of wheat, and he
made for Arberth and set up his dwelling there. And there was
nothing more delightful to him than to see Arberth and the
country he had been wont to hunt, he and Pryderi, and Rhiannon with them. He began to practise catching fish and the wild
animals in their coverts there. And thereafter he began to till,

and after that he sowed a croft, and a second, and a third. And lo, the wheat springing up the best in the world, and his three crofts thriving in like growth, so that mortal had not seen wheat finer than that.

He saw out the seasons of the year. Lo, the harvest coming. And he came to look at one of his crofts. Lo, that one was ripe. 'I will reap this to-morrow,' said he. He returned that night to Arberth. On the morrow in the grey dawn he came with intent to reap the croft. When he came there was nothing but the stalks, naked after each one of them had been broken off where the ear comes from the stalk, and the ears carried right away, and the stalks left there naked.

At this he wondered greatly, and he came to look at another croft. Lo, that one was ripe. 'Faith,' said he, 'I will reap this to-morrow.' And on the morrow he came with intent to reap it. And when he came there was nothing but the naked stalks. 'Alas, lord God,' said he, 'who is completing my ruin? And that I know, it is he who began my ruin who is completing it, and who has ruined the country along with me.'

He came to look at the third croft. When he came, mortal had not seen finer wheat, and that ripe. 'Shame on me,' said he, 'if I do not keep watch to-night. He who carried off the other corn will come to carry off this; and I will find out what it is.' And he took up his arms and began to watch the croft. And he told all that to Cigfa. 'Why,' said she, 'what hast thou in mind?' 'I will watch the croft to-night,' said he.

He went to watch the croft. And while he was about it, towards midnight, lo, the greatest commotion in the world. He looked. There was the mightiest host of mice in the world, and neither number nor measure might be set to them. And never a thing knew he before the mice were falling upon the croft, and each of them climbing up along the stalk and bending it down with it, and breaking off the ear, and making off with the ears and leaving the stalks there; and for aught he knew there was not a single stalk that had not a mouse to it. And they were making off, and the ears with them.

And then in wrath and anger he rushed in amidst the mice, but he could no more keep an eye on one of them than on the gnats or the birds in the air; but one he could see very heavy, so that he judged it incapable of any fleetness of foot. He went after that one, and caught it, and put it in his glove, and tied up the mouth of the glove with a string, and kept it with him, and made for the court. He came to the hall where Cigfa was, and brightened the fire, and hung the glove by its string upon the peg. 'What is there, lord?' asked Cigfa. 'A thief,' he answered, 'whom I found thieving from me.' 'What kind of a thief, lord, couldst thou put inside thy glove?' asked she. 'Here is the whole story,' he answered, and he told how his crofts had been laid waste for him and destroyed, and how the mice came to the last of his crofts before his very eyes. 'And one of them was very heavy, which I caught and is inside the glove, and which I will hang to-morrow. And by my confession to God, had I caught them all, I would hang them.' 'Lord,' said she, 'that was not surprising, but yet it is unseemly to see a man of such rank and dignity as thou hanging such a creature as that. And if thou didst aright thou wouldst not meddle with the creature, but let it go.' 'Shame on me,' said he, 'if I would not hang them all had I caught them; and the one I have caught I will hang.' 'Why, lord,' said she, 'there is no reason why I should succour this creature except to ward off discredit from thee. But do as thou wilt, lord.' 'If I knew of any reason in the world why thou shouldst succour it, I would abide by thy counsel concerning it,' said Manawydan, 'but as I know of none, lady, I intend to destroy it.' 'Do so gladly then,' said she.

And then he made for Gorsedd Arberth, and the mouse with him. And he planted two forks on the highest point of the mound. And while he was doing this, lo, he could see a clerk coming towards him, and on him old, poor, threadbare garments. And it was now seven years since he had set eyes on man or beast, except those four persons who had been together till two of them were lost.

'Lord,' said the clerk, 'good day to thee.' 'God prosper thee, and welcome to thee,' said he. 'Whence comest thou, clerk?' said he. 'I come, lord, from song-making in Lloegyr. And why dost thou ask, lord?' said he. 'Because for the last seven years,' said he, 'I have seen no person in this place, save four persons set apart, and thyself this very moment.' 'Why, lord,' he said, 'I am myself but now passing through this land towards my own country. And what kind of work art thou engaged on, lord?' 'Hanging a thief whom I caught thieving from me,' said he. 'What kind of a thief, lord?' asked he. 'I see a creature in thy hand like a mouse, and it ill becomes a man of such rank as thou to touch such a creature as that. Let it go!' 'I will not let it go, between me and God,' he answered. 'Thieving I caught it, and the law concerning a thief will I execute upon it: to hang it!' 'Lord,' said he, 'lest a man of such rank as thou be seen about that work, a pound which I have received as alms will I give thee – and let that creature go.' 'I will not let it go, between me and God, neither will I sell it.' 'As thou wilt, lord,' he answered; 'were it not unseemly to see a man of such rank as thou handle such a creature as that, it would not trouble me.' And away went the clerk.

As he was fixing the crossbeam upon the forks, lo, a priest coming towards him on a caparisoned horse. 'Lord, good day to thee,' said he. 'God prosper thee,' said Manawydan; 'and thy blessing.' 'The blessing of God be upon thee. And what kind of work art thou doing, lord?' 'Hanging a thief whom I caught thieving from me,' said he. 'What kind of a thief, lord?' he asked. 'A creature,' he answered, 'in the shape of a mouse. And it has thieved from me, and the doom of a thief will I execute upon it.' 'Lord,' said he, 'lest thou be seen handling that creature I will redeem it. Let it go.' 'By my confession to God, I will neither sell it nor let it go.' 'It is true, lord, it has no price set upon it. Lest thou be seen defiling thyself with that creature I will give thee three pounds – and let it go!' 'Between me and God,' said Manawydan, 'I want no price for it, save what is its due: to hang it!' 'Gladly, lord, do thy pleasure.' Away went the priest.

Then he noosed the string about the neck of the mouse. And as he was drawing it up, lo, he could see a bishop's retinue with his loads of baggage and his train, and the bishop himself making towards him. He stayed his work. 'Lord,' said he. 'What kind of work art thou engaged on?' 'Hanging a thief whom I caught thieving from me,' said he. 'Is it not a mouse,' said he,

'I see in thy hand?' 'Aye,' he replied, 'and a thief has she been to me.' 'Why,' said he, 'since I have come in at the destruction of that creature I will redeem it of thee. I will give thee seven pounds for it, and lest a man of such rank as thou be seen destroying such a worthless creature as that, let it go, and thou shalt have the money.' 'Between me and God, I will not let it go,' said he. 'Since thou wilt not let it go for that, I will give thee four-and-twenty pounds of ready money – and let it go!' 'I will not let it go, by my confession to God, for as much again,' said he. 'Since thou wilt not let it go for that,' said he, 'I will give thee all the horses thou seest in this plain, and seven loads of baggage that are here, on the seven horses they are on.' 'Between me and God, I will not,' he replied. 'Since thou wilt not have that, name its price.' 'That will I,' said he, 'that Rhiannon and Pryderi be set free.' 'That shalt thou have.' 'Between me and God, I will not.' 'What wouldst thou then?' 'That the charm and the enchantment be removed from the seven cantrefs of Dyfed.' 'That thou shalt have also – and let the mouse go!' 'I will not let it go, between me and God,' said he; 'I will know who the mouse is.' 'She is my wife; and were that not so, I should not free her.' 'How came she to me?' 'A-harrying,' he answered. 'I am Llwyd son of Cil Coed, and 'twas I cast the enchantment over the seven cantrefs of Dyfed; and to avenge Gwawl son of Clud, through friendship for him, did I cast the enchantment; and on Pryderi did I avenge the playing of Badger in the Bag on Gwawl son of Clud, when Pwyll Head of Annwn wrought that – and he wrought that at the court of Hefeydd the Old, ill-advisedly. And after hearing that thou wert a dweller in the land, my war-band came to me and asked me to transform them into mice that they might destroy thy corn. And they came the first night, my war-band alone. And the second night they came too, and they destroyed the two crofts. And the third night there came to me my wife and the ladies of the court, to ask me to transform them, and transform them I did. And she was with child. And had she not been with child, thou hadst not overtaken her. But since she was, and was caught, I will give thee Pryderi and Rhiannon, and I will remove the charm and the enchantment from Dyfed. I have now told thee who she is –

and let her go!' 'I will not let her go, between me and God,' said he. 'What wouldst thou then?' he asked. 'This,' he replied, 'is what I would have: that there never be any spell upon the seven cantrefs of Dyfed, and that none be cast upon it.' 'That shalt thou have,' said he, '– and let her go!' 'I will not let her go, between me and God,' said he. 'What wouldst thou then?' he asked. 'This,' said he, 'is what I would have: that vengeance be never taken for this upon Pryderi and Rhiannon, nor upon me.' 'All that thou shalt have. And faith, that was a shrewd stroke of thine. Hadst thou not struck on that, all the harm had lighted on thy head.' 'Aye,' said he, 'and to ward off that I made the demand.' 'And now set my wife free for me.' 'I will not set her free, between me and God, until I see Pryderi and Rhiannon with me free.' 'See, here they come,' he answered.

With that, behold, Pryderi and Rhiannon. He rose up to meet them, and greeted them, and they sat down together. 'Ah, good sir, now set my wife free for me, for thou hast now received all thou didst demand.' 'I will free her, gladly,' said he.

And then she was set free, and he struck her with a magic wand, and he changed her back into the fairest young woman that any one had seen.

'Look around thee upon the land,' said he, 'and thou wilt see all the houses and the habitations as they were at their best.' And then he rose up and looked. And when he looked, he saw all the land inhabited and complete with all its herds and its dwellings. 'In what servitude,' he asked, 'have Pryderi and Rhiannon been?' 'Pryderi would have the gate-hammers of my court about his neck, and Rhiannon would have the collars of the asses, after they had been carrying hay, about her neck. And such has been their durance.'

And by reason of that durance that story was called *Mabinogi Mynweir a Mynordd.*[3]

And thus ends this branch of the Mabinogi.

---

3 A title unintelligible to the story-teller, who has attempted an explanation of his own: mynweir he regards as a compound, myn, 'neck', and gweir, 'hay'; and mynordd as a compound, myn, 'neck', and ordd, 'hammer'. In part we can correct him; mynweir, from myn, 'neck', and gweir, 'collar', is an attested word meaning 'collar'.

MATH SON OF MATHONWY

Math son of Mathonwy was lord over Gwynedd, and Pryderi son of Pwyll was lord over one-and-twenty cantrefs in the South. Those were the seven cantrefs of Dyfed, and the seven of Morgannwg, and the four of Ceredigiawn, and the three of Ystrad Tywi.

And at that time Math son of Mathonwy might not live save while his two feet were in the fold of a maiden's lap, unless the turmoil of war prevented him. Now the maiden who was with him was Goewin daughter of Pebin of Dôl Bebin in Arfon. And she was the fairest maiden of her time of whom there was knowledge in those parts.

And he found his tranquillity at Caer Dathyl in Arfon, and he might not go the circuit of the land, save Gilfaethwy son of Dôn and Gwydion son of Dôn, his nephews, his sister's sons, and the war-band with them, would go the circuit of the land in his stead.

And the maiden was with Math at all times; and Gilfaethwy son of Dôn set his heart on the maiden and loved her so that he knew not what to do because of her; and lo, his colour and his face and his form wasting away for love of her, so that it was not easy to know him.

Gwydion his brother looked hard at him one day. 'Lad,' said he, 'what has befallen thee?' 'Why,' he answered, 'what seest thou on me?' 'I see on thee,' said he, 'that thou art losing thy looks and thy colour. And what has befallen thee?' 'Lord brother,' said he, 'what has befallen me, it is useless for me to admit to any.' 'What is that, friend?' said he. 'Thou knowest,' he replied, 'the peculiarity of Math son of Mathonwy: whatever whispering, however low, there be between men, once the wind has met it he will know of it.' 'Aye,' said Gwydion, 'thou needst not say more, I know thy thought, thou lovest Goewin.'

When he found that his brother knew his thought, he heaved the heaviest sigh in the world. 'Be quiet, friend, with thy sighing,' said Gwydion. 'It is not that way that success will be won. And I will bring about,' said he, 'since it cannot be had otherwise, the mustering of Gwynedd and Powys and Deheubarth, so that the maiden may be come at; and be thou of good heart, and I will bring it about for thee.'

And with that they went to Math son of Mathonwy. 'Lord,' said Gwydion, 'I have heard tell that there have come to the South such creatures as never came to this Island.' 'What is their name?' said he. '*Hobeu*, lord.'[1] 'What kind of animals are those?' 'Small animals, their flesh better than the flesh of oxen.' But they are small and they change names: *moch*[2] are they called nowadays. 'To whom do they belong?' 'To Pryderi son of Pwyll, to whom they were sent from Annwn, by Arawn king of Annwn.' And to this day there is kept of that name, *hanner hwch, hanner hob.*[3] 'Aye,' he replied, 'by what means will they be got from him?' 'I will go, lord, as one of twelve in the guise of bards to ask for the swine.' 'He may refuse you,' said he. 'Not bad is my plan, lord,' said he; 'I will not come back without the swine.' 'Gladly,' said he, 'go thy way.'

He went, and Gilfaethwy, and ten men with them, as far as Ceredigiawn, to the place which is nowadays called Rhuddlan Teifi. There was a court of Pryderi's there, and in the guise of bards they came inside. They made them welcome. Gwydion was placed at Pryderi's one hand that night.

'Why,' said Pryderi, 'gladly would we have a tale from some of the young men yonder.' 'Lord,' said Gwydion, 'it is a custom with us that the first night after one comes to a great man, the chief bard shall have the say. I will tell a tale gladly.' Gwydion was the best teller of tales in the world. And that night he entertained the court with pleasant tales and story-telling till he was praised by every one in the court, and it was pleasure for Pryderi to converse with him. And at the end thereof, 'Lord,' said he, 'will any one do my errand to thee better than I myself?' 'Not so,' he answered, 'a right good tongue is thine.' 'This then, lord, is my errand: to beg of thee the animals that were sent thee

1 Hobeu: hogs.
2 Moch: swine.
3 Hanner: half. Hwch: pig. Hanner hwch, hanner hob: flitch.

from Annwn.' 'Aye,' he replied, 'that would be the easiest thing in the world were there not a covenant between me and my country concerning them; that is, that they shall not go from me till they have bred double their number in the land.' 'Lord,' said he, 'I can free thee from those words. Thus can I do it: do not give me the swine to-night, and do not refuse them me. To-morrow I will show an exchange for them.'

And that night he and his companions went to their lodging to take counsel. 'Men,' said he, 'we shall not have the swine for the asking.' 'Well,' said they, 'by what plan then may they be got?' 'I shall see that they are got,' said Gwydion.

And then he betook him to his arts, and began to display his magic. And he made by magic twelve stallions and twelve greyhounds, each of them black but whitebreasted, and twelve collars and twelve leashes upon them, and any one that saw them would not know but that they were of gold; and twelve saddles upon the horses, and every part where there should be iron upon them was all of gold, and the bridles of the same workmanship.

With the horses and the dogs he came to Pryderi. 'Good day to thee, lord,' said he. 'God prosper thee,' said he, 'and welcome to thee.' 'Lord,' said he, 'here is a way out for thee from the word thou didst speak last evening about the swine, that thou wouldst not give them, and that thou wouldst not sell them. But exchange them thou mayest for that which is better. I will give these twelve horses, all caparisoned as they are, and their saddles and their bridles, and the twelve greyhounds and their collars and their leashes, as thou seest them, and the twelve golden shields thou seest yonder.' Those he had made by magic out of toadstool. 'Why,' said he, 'we will take counsel.' They found in their counsel to give Gwydion the swine, and take from him in return the horses and the dogs and the shields.

And then they took leave and started off with the swine. 'My brave lads,' said Gwydion, 'we must needs shift in haste. The spell will last but from one day till the morrow.'

And that night they journeyed as far as the uplands of Ceredigiawn, the place which for that reason is still called Mochdref. And on the morrow they pushed ahead; over Elenid they came. And that night they were between Ceri and Arwystli, in the township which is likewise for that reason called Mochdref. And thence they journeyed on, and that night they went as far as a commot in Powys which is likewise for that reason called Mochnant, and they were there that night. And thence they journeyed as far as the cantref of Rhos, and they were there that night in the township which is still called Mochdref.[4]

'Men,' said Gwydion, 'we will make for the fastness of Gwynedd with these animals. There is a marching of hosts in pursuit of us.' They made for the highest township of Arllech-woedd, and there a sty was made for the swine, and for that reason was the name Creuwryon[5] given to the township. And then after a sty had been made for the swine, they made their way to Math son of Mathonwy, as far as Caer Dathyl. And when they came there, the country was being mustered. 'What news is there?' asked Gwydion. 'Pryderi,' said they, 'is mustering one-and-twenty cantrefs in pursuit of you. Strange how very slowly you have journeyed!' 'Where are the animals you went after?' asked Math. 'A sty has been made for them in the other cantref below,' said Gwydion.

With that, lo, they could hear the trumpets and the gathering throughout the land. With that, they too equipped themselves, and went forth until they were in Pennardd in Arfon.

And that night Gwydion son of Dôn and Gilfaethwy his brother returned to Caer Dathyl, and Gilfaethwy and Goewin daughter of Pebin were put to sleep together in Math son of Mathonwy's bed; and the maidens were roughly forced out, and she was lain with against her will that night.

When they saw day on the morrow they went to the place where Math son of Mathonwy was, and his host. When they came, those men were going to take counsel on what side they should await Pryderi and the men of the South. And they too joined in council. What they determined in council was to wait in the fastness of Gwynedd in Arfon. And a stand was made in the midmost part of the two districts, Maenawr Bennardd and Maenawr Coed Alun. And Pryderi went up against them there,

4 In all these names the story-teller understands the first element, moch, as the word moch, swine. The tale here is clearly onomastic.
5 Creu: sty. Onomastic again.

and there the battle took place, and great slaughter was made on either hand, and the men of the South must needs retreat. The place they retreated to was the place which is still called Nant Call, and the pursuit was continued so far, and then there was made an immeasurable great slaughter. And then they fled as far as the place called Dôl Benmaen. And then they rallied and sought to bring about a truce, and Pryderi gave hostages against the truce. He gave Gwrgi Gwastra and three-and-twenty sons of noblemen as hostages.

And after that they travelled under truce as far as Y Traeth Mawr, but as soon as they reached Y Felenrhyd, the men on foot could not be restrained from shooting at each other. Messengers were sent by Pryderi to have the two hosts called off, and to ask that it be left to him and Gwydion son of Dôn, for it was he had caused that. The messengers came to Math son of Mathonwy. 'Aye,' said Math, 'between me and God, if it please Gwydion son of Dôn, I shall leave it gladly. Nor will I for my part compel any one to go to fight, instead of our doing what we can.' 'Faith,' said the messengers, 'it were fair, Pryderi reckons, for the man who did him this wrong to pit his body against his, and let the two hosts stand aside.' 'By my confession to God, I will not ask the men of Gwynedd to fight on my behalf, since I may myself do battle with Pryderi. I will pit my body against his, gladly.' And that answer was sent to Pryderi. 'Aye,' said Pryderi, 'nor do I ask any one to seek my redress, save myself.'

Those men were set apart and the equipping of them begun, and they fought. And by dint of strength and valour and by magic and enchantment Gwydion conquered, and Pryderi was slain. And at Maen Tyriawg, above Y Felenrhyd, was he buried, and his grave is there.

The men of the South set forth with bitter lamentation towards their own land. Nor was it strange. They had lost their lord, and many of their noblemen, and their horses, and their arms for the most part.

The men of Gwynedd went back in joy and exultation. 'Lord,' said Gwydion to Math, 'would it not be right for us to release their nobleman to the men of the South, him they gave us as a hostage against the truce? And we ought not to keep him in durance.' 'Let him be freed then,' said Math. And that youth and the hostages that were with him were freed to follow after the men of the South.

Math for his part made for Caer Dathyl. Gilfaethwy son of Dôn and the war-band that had been with him went to make the circuit of Gwynedd, as had been their custom, and they did not come to the court. Math went to his chamber and bade a place be prepared for him to recline, so that he might put his feet in the fold of the maiden's lap. 'Lord,' said Goewin, 'seek now a maiden to be under thy feet. I am a woman.' 'How is that?' 'An assault was made upon me, lord, and that openly. Nor did I bear it in quiet; there was none in the court did not know of it. They who came were thy nephews, lord, thy sister's sons, Gwydion son of Dôn and Gilfaethwy son of Dôn. And they wrought rape upon me and upon thee dishonour. And I was lain with, and that in thy chamber and thy bed.' 'Aye,' said he, 'what I can, I will do: redress for thee first, and then I too will seek redress. As for thee,' he said, 'I will take thee to wife, and the authority over my realm will I give into thy hands.'

And meantime they came not near the court, but stayed to make their circuit of the land until a ban on their meat and drink went out against them. At first they came not near him; then however they came. 'Lord,' said they, 'good day to thee.' 'Aye,' said he, 'is it to make me amends that you are come?' 'Lord, we are at thy will.' 'Had it been my will, I had not lost what I have of men and arms. My dishonour you cannot make good to me, let alone the death of Pryderi. But since you are come unto my will, I will begin punishment upon you.'

And then he took his magic wand and struck Gilfaethwy, so that he became a good-sized hind, and he seized the other quickly (though he wished to escape he could not), and struck him with the same magic wand, so that he became a stag. 'Since you are allied together, I will make you fare together, and be coupled, and of the same nature as the beasts whose guise you are in; and at the time there be offspring to them, that it be to you also. And a year from to-day come hither to me.'

At the end of the year from that same day, lo, he could hear

an uproar from under the chamber wall, and the barking of the
dogs of the court in answer to the uproar. 'Look what is without,' said he. 'Lord,' said one, 'I have looked; there are a stag
and a hind, and a fawn with them.' And thereupon he arose and
came outside. And when he came, he could see the three beasts;
the three beasts were a stag and a hind and a strong fawn. He
lifted up his magic wand. 'The one of you that has been a hind
for the past year, let him this year be a wild boar; and the one of
you that has been a stag for the past year, let him this year be a
wild sow.' And thereupon he struck them with the magic wand.
'The boy, however, I will take and have fostered and baptized.'
The name that was bestowed on him was Hyddwn. 'As for you,
go, and be the one of you a wild boar and the other a wild sow,
and the nature that is in wild swine be your nature too. And a
year from to-day be here under the wall, and your offspring
with you.'

At the end of the year, lo, they heard the barking of dogs
under the chamber wall and the mustering of the court besides
in answer to them. Thereupon he too arose and went outside.
And when he came outside he could see three beasts. The beasts
he saw were of this kind: a wild boar and a wild sow, and a well-
grown young one with them. And it was big for its age. 'Aye,'
said he, 'this one I will take to me and will have him baptized.'
And he struck him with his magic wand, so that he became a
fine boy with rich auburn hair. The name that was bestowed on
that one was Hychdwn. 'And you, the one of you that has been
a wild boar for the past year, let him this year be a she-wolf; and
the one that has been a wild sow for the past year, let him this
year be a wolf.' And thereupon he struck them with the magic
wand, so that they became wolf and she-wolf. 'And the nature
of the animals in whose guise you are, be yours too. And be here
a year from this very day, under this wall.'

That same day at the end of the year, lo, he could hear an
uproar and a barking under the chamber wall. He arose and
came outside. And when he came, lo, he could see a wolf and a
she-wolf, and a strong wolf-cub with them. 'This one I will
take,' said he, 'and have him baptized, and his name is all ready.
That is, Bleiddwn. The three sons are yours, and those three are:

> The three sons of false Gilfaethwy,
> Three champions true,
> Bleiddwn, Hyddwn, Hychdwn Hir.'[6]

– and thereupon striking them both with the magic wand, so that they were in their own flesh. 'Men,' said he, 'if you did me wrong, long enough has been your punishment. And great shame have you had, that each one of you has had young by the other. Have a bath made ready for the men, and their heads washed, and have them arrayed.' And that was done for them.

And after they were made ready they came to him. 'Men,' he said, 'you have obtained peace, and you shall have friendship. And give me counsel what maiden I shall seek.' 'Lord,' said Gwydion son of Dôn, 'it is easy to counsel thee: Aranrhod daughter of Dôn, thy niece, thy sister's daughter.'

She was fetched to him; the maiden came in. 'Maiden,' said he, 'art thou a maiden?' 'I know not but that I am.' Then he took the magic wand and bent it. 'Step over this,' said he, 'and if thou art a maiden, I shall know.' Then she stepped over the magic wand, and with that step she dropped a fine boy-child with rich yellow hair. The boy uttered a loud cry. After the boy's cry she made for the door, and thereupon dropped a small something, and before any one could get a second glimpse of it, Gwydion took it and wrapped a sheet of silk around it, and hid it. The place where he hid it was inside a small chest at the foot of his bed.

'Why,' said Math son of Mathonwy, 'I will have this one baptized' – of the rich-yellow-haired boy. 'The name I will give him is Dylan.'

The boy was baptized, and the moment he was baptized he made for the sea. And there and then, as soon as he came to the sea he received the sea's nature, and swam as well as the best fish in the sea. And for that reason he was called Dylan Eil Ton.[7] No wave ever broke beneath him. And the blow whereby his death came, his uncle Gofannon aimed. And that was one of the Three Unhappy Blows.

6 Bleidd: wolf. Hydd: stag. Hwch: pig. Hir: long, tall.
7 Dylan Eil Ton: Sea son of Wave.

As Gwydion was one day in his bed and was waking, he heard a cry in the chest at his feet. Though it was not loud, it was so loud that he heard it. He arose quickly and opened the chest; and as he opened it, he could see an infant boy thrusting his arms from the fold of the sheet and opening it apart. And he took the boy between his hands and carried him to the town, where he knew there was a woman with breasts. And he made a bargain with the woman to suckle the child. The boy was reared that year, and in a year's time they would have remarked his great size had he been two years old. And the second year he was a big boy and was able to go by himself to the court. And Gwydion himself gave heed to him when he came to the court. And the boy grew used to him and loved him better than any one. Then the boy was reared at the court till he was four years old; and it had been remarkable for a boy eight years old to be as big as he.

And one day he followed after Gwydion to go out a-walking. He made for Caer Aranrhod, and the boy with him. After he had come to the court, Aranrhod arose to meet him, to make him welcome and to give him greeting. 'God prosper thee,' said he. 'What is the boy that follows thee?' said she. 'This boy is a son of thine,' said he. 'Alas, man! What came over thee to put me to shame, and to pursue my shame, and keep it as long as this?' 'Unless thou suffer a greater shame than that I should rear a boy as fine as this, a small thing thy shame will be.' 'What is thy son's name?' asked she. 'Faith,' he said, 'there is as yet no name to him.' 'Well,' said she, 'I will swear on him a destiny, that he shall not get a name till he get it from me.' 'By my confession to God,' said he, 'thou art a wicked woman, but the boy shall have a name, even though it be vexatious to thee. And thou,' said he, ' 'tis because of him thou art angry, for that thou art not called maiden. Never again shalt thou be called maiden!' And thereupon he went away in wrath, and made for Caer Dathyl, and there he was that night.

And on the morrow he arose and took his son with him, and went to walk along the seashore between there and Aber Menei. And where he saw dulse and sea-girdle he made a ship by magic; and out of the seaweed and dulse he made cordwain, much of it, and he put colours on them so that no one had ever seen leather more lovely than that. And then he fitted a sail on the ship and came, he and the boy in the ship, to the entrance of the gate of Caer Aranrhod. And then they began to fashion shoes and to stitch them. And then they were seen from the caer. When he knew they had been seen from the caer, he took away their own semblance and put another semblance upon them, so that they would not be recognized. 'What men are in the ship?' asked Aranrhod. 'Shoemakers,' said they. 'Go and see what kind of leather they have, and what kind of work they do.'

Then they came. And when they came he was colouring cordwain, and that in gold. Then the messengers came and told her that. 'Why,' said she, 'take the measure of my foot and ask the shoemaker to make shoes for me.' He fashioned the shoes, yet not to the measure, but bigger. The shoes were brought to her. Lo, the shoes were too big. 'These are too big,' said she; 'he shall have payment for these, but let him also make some that are smaller than they.' He made others smaller by far than her foot, and sent them to her. 'Tell him not one of these shoes will go on me,' she said. That was told him. 'Why,' he said, 'I will not fashion shoes for her until I see her foot.' And that was told her. 'Aye,' said she, 'I will go to him.'

And then she came to the ship. And when she came he was cutting out, and the boy stitching. 'Why, lady,' said he, 'good day to thee.' 'God prosper thee,' said she. 'I marvel thou couldst not fit shoes to measure.' 'I was unable,' he replied; 'I shall be able now.'

And thereupon, lo, a wren alighting on board the ship. The boy aimed at it, and hit it between the sinew of its leg and the bone. She laughed. 'Faith,' said she, 'with a deft hand has the fair one hit it.' 'Aye,' he replied, 'God's curse on thee! He has now got a name, and good enough is his name. Lleu Llaw Gyffes is he from now on.'[8] And then the work vanished into dulse and seaweed; and he pursued the work no further than that. And for that reason he was called one of the Three Gold Shoemakers. 'Faith,' said she, 'thou wilt fare none the better for

8 Lleu: fair. Llaw: hand. Gyffes: deft.

being bad to me.' 'I have not been bad to thee yet,' said he. And then he released his son into his proper semblance, and took on him his own aspect. 'Well,' said she, 'I will swear on this boy a destiny that he shall never bear arms till I myself equip him therewith.' 'Between me and God,' said he, 'this springs from thy wickedness. But arms he shall have.'

Then they came towards Dinas Dinlleu. And then Lleu Llaw Gyffes was reared till he could ride every horse and till he was perfected in feature, growth and stature. And then Gwydion saw by him that he was pining for want of horses and arms, and he called him to him. 'Lad,' said he, 'we will go, thou and I, on an errand to-morrow. And be more cheerful than thou art.' 'And that will I do,' said the lad. And on the morrow in the young of the day they arose and took the seashore, up towards Bryn Arien; and at the top of Cefyn Clun Tyno they made ready on horseback and came towards Caer Aranrhod. And then they changed their semblance and made towards the gate in the guise of two young men, save that Gwydion's mien was more staid than the lad's. 'Porter,' said he, 'go in and say there are bards here from Morgannwg.' The porter went. 'God's welcome to them. Let them in,' said she. There was great joy at their coming, the hall was made ready, and they went to meat. When meat was ended, she discoursed with Gwydion of tales and story-telling. Now Gwydion was a good teller of tales.

When it was time to leave off the carousal, a chamber was made ready for them and they went to sleep. At early cockcrow Gwydion arose. And then he summoned to him his magic and his power. By the time the light of day was dawning there was a bustling to and fro and trumpets and clamour throughout the country. When day was coming on they heard a knocking at the chamber door, and with that Aranrhod bidding them open. The young lad rose up and opened; she entered and a maiden with her. 'Ah, good sirs,' said she, ''tis a bad place we are in.' 'Aye,' he replied, 'we hear trumpets and clamour; and what thinkest thou of that?' 'Faith,' said she, 'we cannot see the colour of the deep for all the ships thronging together; and they are making for the land with all the speed they can. And what shall we do?' said she. 'Lady,' said Gwydion, 'there is no other counsel for us save to close the caer upon us and to defend it as best we can.' 'Aye,' she answered, 'God repay you. Do you then prepare a defence; and here you will find arms enough.'

And with that she went after the arms. And lo, she came, and two maidens with her, and arms for two men with them. 'Lady,' said he, 'arm thou this youth, and I with the maidens will arm myself. I hear the noise of the men coming.' 'That will I, gladly.' And she armed him gladly and at all points. 'Is the arming of that youth completed?' he asked. 'It is,' she replied. 'Mine too is completed,' said he; 'let us now doff our arms; we have no need of them.' 'Alas,' said she, 'why? See the fleet around the house!' 'Lady, there is no fleet there.' 'Alas,' said she, 'what manner of mustering was it there?' 'A mustering,' he replied, 'to break thy destiny concerning thy son, and to seek arms for him. And now he has got arms, no thanks to thee for them.' 'Between me and God,' she answered, 'a wicked man art thou. And many a lad might have lost his life through the mustering thou hast brought about in this cantref to-day. And I will swear a destiny on him,' said she, 'that he shall never have a wife of the race that is now on this earth.' 'Aye,' said he, 'a wicked woman hast thou been ever, and none should further thee. But a wife he shall have all the same.'

They came to Math son of Mathonwy and made the most sustained complaint in the world against Aranrhod, and made known how he had obtained all the arms for him. 'Aye,' said Math, 'let us seek, thou and I, by our magic and enchantment to conjure a wife for him out of flowers' – and he then a man in stature, and the handsomest youth that mortal ever saw. And then they took the flowers of the oak, and the flowers of the broom, and the flowers of the meadowsweet, and from those they called forth the very fairest and best endowed maiden that mortal ever saw, and baptized her with the baptism they used at that time, and named her Blodeuedd.[9]

After they had slept together over the feast, 'It is not easy,' said Gwydion, 'for a man without territory to maintain himself.' 'Why,' said Math, 'I will give him the very best cantref for a

9 Blodeuedd: Flowers (to the story-teller).

young man to have.' 'Lord,' he asked, 'what cantref is that?' 'Cantref Dinoding,' said he. And that is nowadays called Eifyn-ydd and Ardudwy. The place in the cantref where he set up a court was the place called Mur Castell, and that in the uplands of Ardudwy. And then he settled down therein and ruled it. And every one was content with him and his rule.

And then once upon a time he went to Caer Dathyl to visit Math son of Mathonwy. The day he went to Caer Dathyl, she was stirring about the court. And she heard the blast of a horn, and after the blast of the horn, lo, a spent stag going by, and dogs and huntsmen after it, and after the dogs and the huntsmen a troop of men on foot coming. 'Send a lad,' said she, 'to learn what the company is.' The lad went and asked who they were. 'This is Gronw Bebyr, he who is lord of Penllyn,' said they. And that the lad told her.

He went after the stag, and on Cynfael river he overtook the stag and slew it. And what with slaying the stag and baiting his dogs, he was busied till the night closed in on him. And as day declined and night was drawing near, he came past the gate of the court. 'Faith,' said she, 'we shall be ill-spoken of by the chieftain for letting him go at this hour to another domain, if we do not ask him in.' 'Faith, lady,' said they, 'it is only right to ask him in.' Then messengers went to meet him and ask him in. And then he accepted the invitation gladly and came to the court, and she came herself to meet him, to make him welcome, and to give him greeting. 'Lady,' said he, 'God repay thee thy welcome.'

They changed their garb and went to sit down. Blodeuedd looked on him, and the moment she looked there was no part of her that was not filled with love of him. And he too gazed on her, and the same thought came to him as had come to her. He might not conceal that he loved her, and he told her so. She knew great joy at heart, and their talk that night was of the affection and love they had conceived one for the other. Nor did they delay longer than that night ere they embraced each other. And that night they slept together.

And on the morrow he sought to depart. 'Faith,' said she, 'thou wilt not go from me to-night.' That night too they were together. And that night they took counsel how they might stay together. 'There is no counsel for thee,' said he, 'save one: to seek to learn from him how his death may come about, and that under pretence of loving care for him.'

On the morrow he sought to depart. 'Faith, I do not counsel thee to go from me to-day.' 'Faith, since thou dost not counsel it, I will not go,' said he. 'Yet I say there is danger that the chieftain whose court it is may return.' 'Aye,' said she, 'to-morrow I will give thee leave to depart.'

On the morrow he sought to depart and she did not prevent him. 'Now,' said he, 'remember what I told thee, and speak closely with him, and that under pretence of importunity of love of him, and draw forth from him what way his death might come about.'

And that night he came home. They spent the day in talk and song and carousal. And that night they went to sleep together, and he spoke to her, and a second time, but meantime not one word did he get from her. 'What has befallen thee?' he asked; 'and art thou well?' 'I am thinking,' said she, 'that which thou wouldst not think concerning me. That is,' said she, 'I am troubled about thy death, if thou wert to go sooner than I.' 'Ah,' said he, 'God repay thee for thy loving care. But unless God slay me, it is not easy to slay me,' said he. 'Wilt thou then, for God's sake and for mine, tell me how thou might be slain? For my memory is a surer safeguard than thine.' 'I will, gladly,' said he. 'It is not easy,' said he, 'to slay me with a blow; and one must needs be a year making the spear wherewith I should be smitten, without making anything of it save when folk were at Mass on Sunday.' 'Is that certain?' said she. 'Certain, faith,' said he. 'I cannot be slain within a house,' said he, 'nor can I outside. I cannot be slain on horseback, nor can I a-foot.' 'Why,' said she, 'in what manner then couldst thou be slain?' 'I will tell thee,' said he. 'By making a bath for me on a river bank, and making a vaulted frame over the tub, and thatching it well and snugly too thereafter, and bringing a he-goat,' said he, 'and setting it beside the tub, and myself placing one foot on the back of the he-goat and the other on the edge of the tub. Whoever should smite me when so, he would bring about my death.' 'Why,' she replied, 'I thank God for that. That can be avoided easily.'

No sooner had she heard this statement than she sent it to Gronw Bebyr. Gronw laboured at making the spear, and that selfsame day at the end of a year it was ready. And that day he had her informed of it.

'Lord,' said she, 'I am wondering how that might be which thou didst once tell me of. And wilt thou show me in what manner thou wouldst stand on the edge of the tub and the he-goat, if I make ready the bath?' 'I will,' said he.

Then she sent to Gronw and bade him be under the lee of the hill which is now called Bryn Cyfergyr. That was on the bank of Cynfael river. She bade gather too all the goats she found in the cantref and had them brought to the far side of the river, facing Bryn Cyfergyr. And on the morrow she said, 'Lord,' said she, 'I have had the frame and the bath prepared, and they are ready.' 'Why,' he replied, 'gladly let us go to look at them.' They came on the morrow to look at the bath. 'Thou wilt go into the bath, lord?' said she. 'I will, gladly,' said he. He went into the bath and he bathed himself. 'Lord,' said she, 'here are the animals thou didst speak of as being called he-goats.' 'Aye,' said he, 'have one of them caught and have it fetched here.' It was fetched. Then he arose out of the bath and put on his breeks, and he placed one foot on the edge of the tub and the other on the he-goat's back. Then Gronw rose up from the hill which is called Bryn Cyfergyr, and he rose up on one knee and aimed the poisoned spear at him, and smote him in the side, so that the shaft started out of him and the head stayed in him. And then he flew up in the form of an eagle and gave a horrid scream. And after that he was seen no more.

The moment he vanished they set off for the court, and that night they slept together. And on the morrow Gronw rose up and subdued Ardudwy. After subduing the land he ruled it, so that Ardudwy and Penilyn were under his sway.

Then the tidings reached Math son of Mathonwy. Heaviness and grief Math felt within him, and Gwydion more than he by far. 'Lord,' said Gwydion, 'I shall never rest till I have tidings of my nephew.' 'Aye,' said Math, 'may God be thy strength.' And then he set out and began to go his way, and Gwynedd he traversed, and the length and breadth of Powys. When he had

traversed every part, he came to Arfon, and came to the house
of a villein in Maenawr Bennardd. He alighted at the house and
stayed there that night. The man of the house and his household
came in, and last of all came the swineherd. The man of the
house said to the swineherd, 'Fellow,' said he, 'has thy sow come
in to-night?' 'She has,' said he, 'she has just now come to the
swine.' 'What manner of journey does that sow go on?' asked
Gwydion. 'Every day when the sty is opened, out she goes. No
one can keep in touch with her, neither is it known which way
she goes more than if she went into the earth.' 'Wilt thou do
this for my sake,' asked Gwydion, 'not to open the sty until I am
on one side of the sty with thee?' 'I will, gladly,' said he.

That night they went to sleep. And when the swineherd saw
the light of day he roused Gwydion, and Gwydion rose and
arrayed himself and came with him and stood beside the sty.
The swineherd opened the sty. As soon as he opened it, lo, she
leapt forth and set off at speed, and Gwydion followed her. And
she went upstream and made for a valley which is now called
Nantlleu, and there she slowed and fed. Gwydion came under
the tree and looked to see what it was that the sow was feeding
on. And he could see the sow feeding on rotten flesh and mag-
gots. He then looked up into the top of the tree. And when he
looked he could see an eagle in the tree top. And when the eagle
shook himself the worms and the rotten flesh fell from him, and
the sow eating them. And he thought that the eagle was Lleu,
and sang an englyn:

> Grows an oak between two lakes.
> Darkly shadowed sky and glen,
> If I speak not falsely,
> From Lleu's Flowers this doth come.

With that the eagle let himself down till he was in the middle
of the tree. Then Gwydion sang another englyn:

> Grows an oak on upland plain,
> Nor rain wets it, nor heat melts;
> Nine score hardships hath he suffered
> In its top, Lleu Llaw Gyffes.

And he let himself down till he was on the lowest branch of the tree. And he sang this englyn thus:

> Grows an oak upon a steep,
> The sanctuary of a fair lord;
> If I speak not falsely,
> Lleu will come into my lap.

And he alighted on Gwydion's knee. And then Gwydion struck him with the magic wand, so that he was in his own likeness. Yet none had ever seen on man a more pitiful sight than was on him. He was nothing but skin and bone.

Then he made for Caer Dathyl, and there were brought to him there all the good physicians that were found in Gwynedd. Long before the year's end he was whole. 'Lord,' said he to Math son of Mathonwy, 'it is high time for me to have redress from him through whom I have suffered ill.' 'Faith,' said Math, 'he cannot continue thus, withholding thy redress.' 'Aye,' said he, 'the sooner I get redress the better I shall be pleased.'

Then they mustered Gwynedd and set out for Ardudwy. Gwydion travelled in the forefront and made for Mur Castell. Blodeuedd heard that they were coming, took her maidens with her and made for the mountain, and over Cynfael river they made for a court that was on the mountain. But through fear they could not proceed save with their faces looking backwards. And then, never a thing knew they before they fell into the lake, and were all drowned save she alone. And then Gwydion overtook her too, and he said to her: 'I will not slay thee. I will do to thee that which is worse; that is,' said he, 'I will let thee go in the form of a bird. And because of the dishonour thou hast done to Lleu Llaw Gyffes thou art never to dare show thy face in the light of day, and that through fear of all birds; and that there be enmity between thee and all birds, and that it be their nature to mob and molest thee wherever they may find thee; and that thou shalt not lose thy name, but that thou be for ever called Blodeuwedd.'

Blodeuwedd is 'owl' in the language of this present day. And for that reason birds are hostile to the owl. And the owl is still called Blodeuwedd.[10]

Gronw Bebyr made for Penllyn, and from there he sent envoys. The message he sent was to ask Lleu Llaw Gyffes whether he would take land or territory or gold or silver for his injury. 'I will not, by my confession to God,' said he. 'And this is the least I will accept of him, that he go to the place where I was when he aimed at me with the spear, and I in the place where he was, and let me aim a spear at him. And that is the very least I will take from him.' That was told to Gronw Bebyr. 'Aye,' said he, 'I must needs do that. My trusty gentles and my war-band and my foster-brothers, is there one of you will take the blow in my stead?' 'Faith, there is none,' said they. And because they refused to stand taking one blow for their lord, they are called, from that day to this, one of the Three Disloyal War-bands. 'Well,' said he, 'I will take it.'

And then they two came to the bank of Cynfael river. And then Gronw Bebyr stood in the place where Lleu Llaw Gyffes was when he smote him, and Lleu in the place where he himself was. And then Gronw Bebyr said to Lleu, 'Lord,' said he, 'since it was through a woman's wiles I did to thee that which I did, I beg thee in God's name, a stone I see on the river bank, let me set that between me and the blow.' 'Faith,' said Lleu, 'I will not refuse thee that.' 'Why,' said he, 'God repay thee.' And then Gronw took the stone and set it between him and the blow. And then Lleu took aim at him with the spear, and it pierced through the stone and through him too, so that his back was broken, and then was Gronw Bebyr slain. And there the stone is, on the bank of Cynfael river in Ardudwy, and the hole through it. And for that reason it is still called Llech Ronw.[11]

Then Lleu Llaw Gyffes subdued the land a second time and ruled over it prosperously. And as the tale tells, he was lord thereafter over Gwynedd.

And thus ends this branch of the Mabinogi.

---

10 Blodeuwedd: presumably 'Flower-face', no bad name for the owl.
11 Llech Ronw: Gronw's Stone.

THE FOUR INDEPENDENT
NATIVE TALES

THE DREAM OF
MACSEN WLEDIG

Macsen Wledig[1] was Emperor of Rome, and he was the handsomest and wisest of men, and the best fitted to be emperor of
all that had gone before him. And one day he held an assembly
of kings, and he said to his friends, 'To-morrow,' said he, 'I
intend to go a-hunting.' On the morrow early he set out with
his retinue and came to the valley of a river which runs down
towards Rome. He hunted the valley till it was mid-day. Moreover, there were with him two-and-thirty crowned kings, his
vassals at that time. Not for the joy of hunting did the emperor
hunt with them so long, but because he had been made a man
of such high dignity that he was lord over all those kings.

And the sun was high in heaven above their heads, and the
heat great. And sleep came upon him, and his chamberlains set
their shields about him on their spear shafts, as a ward against
the sun; they set a gold-chased shield under his head, and in
this wise Macsen slept.

And then he saw a dream. The dream that he saw was how
he was making along the river valley towards its upper reaches;
and he came to the highest mountain in the world. He thought
the mountain was as high as heaven; and as he came over the
mountain he could see how he was traversing the fairest and
most level regions that mortal had ever seen, on the far side of
the mountain. And he saw great wide rivers making from the
mountain to the sea, and he journeyed towards the sea-fords on
the rivers; however long he was journeying so, he came to the
mouth of a river, the greatest any one had seen. And he saw a
great city at the mouth of the river, and in the city a great castle,
and he saw many great towers of various colours on the castle.
And he saw a fleet at the mouth of the river, and that was the
biggest fleet that mortal had ever seen. And amidst the fleet he
saw a ship; and bigger was that by far and fairer than all the

1 Wledig, gwledig: ruler or prince.

others. And what he might see of the ship above water, one plank he saw of gold, and the next of silver. He saw a bridge of walrus-ivory from the ship to the land, and he thought how he came along the bridge on to the ship. A sail was hoisted on the ship, and away she went over sea and ocean. He saw how he came to an island, the fairest in the whole world, and after he had traversed the island from sea to answering sea, even to the uttermost bound of the island, he could see valleys and steeps and towering rocks, and a harsh rugged terrain whose like he had never seen. And from here he saw in the sea, facing that rugged land, an island. And between him and that island he saw a country whose plain was the length of its sea, its mountain the length of its woodland. And from that mountain he saw a river flow through the land, making towards the sea. And at the river mouth he could see a great castle, the fairest that mortal had ever seen, and the gate of the castle he saw open, and he came to the castle. Inside the castle he saw a fair hall. The roof of the hall he thought to be all of gold; the side of the hall he thought to be of glittering stones, each as costly as its neighbour; the hall doors he thought to be all gold. Golden couches he saw in the hall, and tables of silver. And on the couch facing him he could see two auburn-haired youths playing at gwyddbwyll.[2] A silver board he saw for the gwyddbwyll, and golden pieces thereon. The garments of the youths were of pure black brocaded silk, and frontlets of red gold holding their hair in place, and sparkling jewels of great price therein, rubies and gems alternately therein, and imperial stones. Buskins of new cordwain on their feet, and bars of red gold to fasten them.

And at the foot of the hall-pillar he saw a hoary-headed man seated in a chair of ivory, with the images of two eagles in red gold thereon. Armlets of gold were upon his arms, and many gold rings on his hands; and a golden torque about his neck, and a golden frontlet holding his hair in place; and his presence

2 Gwyddbwyll: not, as hitherto translated, chess (a battle-game), but a hunt-game, like the Icelandic *hnefatafl*. Like chess, however, it was played with a board and pieces. The king, from the centre of the board, tries to break through to the safety of the outer edge; the hunting party (without a king) endeavours to pen him in and capture him.

august. A board of gold and gwyddbwyll before him, and in his hand a rod of gold, and hard files. And he was carving men for gwyddbwyll.

And he saw a maiden sitting before him in a chair of red gold. No more than it would be easy to look on the sun when it is brightest, no easier would it be than that to look on her by reason of her excelling beauty. Vests of white silk were upon the maiden, with clasps of red gold at the breast; and a surcoat of gold brocaded silk upon her, and a mantle like to it, and a brooch of red gold holding it about her; and a frontlet of red gold on her head, with rubies and gems on the frontlet, and pearls alternately, and imperial stones; and a girdle of red gold around her; and the fairest sight to see of mortal kind.

And the maiden arose to meet him from the chair of gold, and he threw his arms around the maiden's neck, and they both sat down in the chair of gold. And the chair was not straiter for them both than for the maiden alone.

And when he had his arms around the maiden's neck, and his cheek against her cheek, what with the dogs straining at their leashes, and the shoulders of the shields coming against each other, and the spear shafts striking together, and the neighing and the stamping of the horses, the emperor awoke. And when he awoke neither life nor existence nor being was left him, for the maiden he had seen in his sleep. Not one bone-joint of his was there, not the middle of a single nail, to say nothing of a part that might be greater than that, but was filled with love of the maiden. And then his retinue said to him, 'Lord,' said they, 'it is past time for thee to take thy meat.' And then the emperor mounted his palfrey, the saddest man that mortal had ever seen, and made his way towards Rome.

And he was thus the whole week. Whenever the retinue went to drink wine and mead out of golden vessels, he went not with any of them. Whenever they went to listen to songs and entertainments, he went not with them; and nothing could be got from him save sleep. As often as he slept he could see in his sleep the woman he loved best; but when he was not sleeping he cared for naught because of her, for he knew not where in the world she was.

And one day a chamberlain spoke to him, and, chamberlain though he was, he was king of the Romani. 'Lord,' said he, 'thy men all speak ill of thee.' 'Why do they speak ill of me?' said the emperor. 'Because they get from thee neither message nor answer, such as men get from their lord. And that is the reason thou art ill-spoken of.' 'Why, man,' said the emperor, 'do thou bring around me the wise men of Rome, and I will tell why I am sad.'

And then the wise men of Rome were brought around the emperor, and he said, 'Wise men of Rome,' said he, 'a dream have I seen. And in the dream I saw a maiden. Neither life nor existence nor being is there in me for that maiden.' 'Lord,' said they, 'since thou hast entrusted us to counsel thee, counsel thee we will. And this is our counsel to thee: to send messengers for three years to the three divisions of the earth, to seek thy dream. And since thou knowest not what day, what night, good tidings may come to thee, that much hope shall sustain thee.'

Then the messengers journeyed till the end of the year, wandering the world, and seeking tidings concerning the dream. When they returned at the end of the year they knew not one word more than on the day they set out. And thereupon the emperor grieved to think that he should never get tidings of the lady he loved best.

And then said the king of the Romani to the emperor, 'Lord,' said he, 'go forth to hunt the way thou sawest thyself go, whether to the east or to the west.' And then the emperor went forth to hunt and came to the bank of the river. 'It was here,' said he, 'that I was when I saw the dream, and towards the river's upper reaches westwards was I journeying.'

And thereupon thirteen men set forth as messengers of the emperor. And before them they saw a huge mountain which they thought touched heaven. Now this was the guise in which the messengers journeyed: one sleeve there was on the cape of each one of them to his front, in token that they were messengers, so that through whatever warring land they might journey, no harm would be done them. And as they crossed that mountain, they could see wide level regions, and great wide rivers flowing through them. 'Lo,' said they, 'the land our lord saw.'

They journeyed towards the sea-fords on the rivers till they came to a great river which they saw making towards the sea, and a great city at the mouth of the river, and in the city a great castle, and great towers of various colours on the castle. They saw the biggest fleet in the world at the mouth of the river, and one ship which was bigger than any of the others. 'Lo, once more,' said they, 'the dream which our lord saw.' And in that big ship they voyaged over the sea and came to the Island of Britain. And they traversed the Island till they came to Eryri. 'Lo, once more,' said they, 'the rugged land which our lord saw.' They pressed forward till they could see Môn facing them, and till they could see Arfon likewise. 'Lo,' said they, 'the land our lord saw in his sleep.' And Aber Seint they saw, and the castle at the mouth of the river. The gate of the castle they saw open. They came into the castle. Inside the castle they saw a hall. 'Lo,' said they, 'the hall our lord saw in his sleep.' They came into the hall. They saw the two youths playing gwyddbwyll on the golden couch, and they saw the hoary-headed man at the foot of the pillar, in the ivory chair, carving the men for the gwyddbwyll. And they saw the maiden sitting in a chair of red gold.

Down on their knees went the messengers. 'Empress of Rome, all hail!' 'Ah, good sirs,' said the maiden, 'I see on you the mark of high-born men, and the badge of messengers. What mockery do you make of me?' 'No mockery, lady, do we make of thee. But the emperor of Rome hath seen thee in his sleep. Neither life nor existence has he because of thee. A choice thou shalt have of us, lady, whether to come with us, to be made empress in Rome, or the emperor to come hither and take thee to wife.' 'Ah, good sirs,' said the maiden, 'I doubt not what you tell me, nor on the other hand do I overmuch believe it. But if 'tis I whom the emperor loves, then let him come hither to fetch me.'

And by day and by night the messengers sped them back, and as their horses failed they left them and purchased others anew. And when they reached Rome they greeted the emperor and asked for their reward, and that they obtained even as they named it. 'We will be thy guide, lord,' said they, 'by sea and land, to the place where that lady is whom thou lovest best. And we know her name, her kindred, and her lineage.'

And straightway the emperor set out with his host, and those men as their guide. Towards the Island of Britain they came, over sea and ocean, and he conquered the Island from Beli son of Manogan and his sons, and drove them into the sea. And he came straight on to Arfon; and the emperor recognized the land the moment he saw it. And the moment he saw the castle of Aber Seint, 'See yonder,' said he, 'the castle wherein I saw the lady I love best.' And he came straight to the castle and into the hall, and there he saw Cynan son of Eudaf and Gadeon son of Eudaf playing at gwyddbwyll. And he saw Eudaf son of Caradawg sitting in a chair of ivory, carving pieces for the gwyddbwyll. The maiden he had seen in his sleep he saw sitting in the chair of red gold. 'Empress of Rome,' said he, 'all hail!' And the emperor threw his arms around her neck. And that night he slept with her.

And on the morrow early the maiden asked for her maiden fee, because she had been found a maid; and he asked her to name her maiden fee. And she named for her father the Island of Britain from the North Sea to the Irish Sea, and the three adjacent islands, to be held under the empress of Rome, and that three chief strongholds be made for her in the three places she might choose in the Island of Britain. And then she chose that the most exalted stronghold should be made for her in Arfon, and soil from Rome was brought there so that it might be healthier for the emperor to sleep and sit and move about. Later the other two strongholds were made for her, none other than Caer Llion and Caer Fyrddin.

And one day the emperor went to Caer Fyrddin to hunt, and he went as far as the top of Y Frenni Fawr, and there the emperor pitched his tent. And that camping-ground is called Cadeir Facsen from that day to this. Caer Fyrddin, on the other hand, was so named because the stronghold was built by a myriad men.[3]

---

3 Caer Fyrddin. The name has nothing to do with myrdd, 'myriad'. It is the old Maridunum, the modern Carmarthen.

Thereafter Elen thought to make high roads from one strong-hold to another across the Island of Britain. And the roads were made. And for that reason they are called the Roads of Elen of the Hosts, because she was sprung from the Island of Britain, and the men of the Island of Britain would not have made those great hostings for any save for her.

Seven years was the emperor in this Island. Now it was the custom of the Romans at that time, that whatever emperor should stay in foreign parts a-conquering seven years, he must remain in that conquered territory, and not be permitted to return to Rome. And then they made them a new emperor. And then that emperor drew up a letter of threat to Macsen. It was moreover no more of a letter than: IF THOU COME, AND IF EVER THOU COME TO ROME. And that letter and the tidings came all the way to Caer Llion to Macsen. And thence he in return sent a letter to the man who said he was emperor in Rome. In that letter too there was nothing save AND IF I GO TO ROME, AND IF I GO.

And then Macsen set out with his host for Rome, and France he conquered, and Burgundy, and all the countries as far as Rome, and he laid siege to the city of Rome.

A year was the emperor before the city; his taking it was no nearer than on the first day. But behind him came brothers of Elen of the Hosts from the Island of Britain, and a small host with them, and better fighters were in that small host than twice their number of the men of Rome. The emperor was told how the host was seen dismounting near his own host and pitching its tents, and never had mortal seen a host handsomer or better furnished or with braver standards for its size than that was. And Elen came to look on the host, and she recognized her brothers' standards. And then came Cynan son of Eudaf and Gadeon son of Eudaf to visit the emperor, and the emperor welcomed them and embraced them.

And then they watched the Romans assault the city. And Cynan said to his brother, 'We shall seek to assault the city more cannily than this.' And then they measured by night the height of the rampart, and they sent their carpenters to the forest, and a ladder was made for every four of their men. And when they had those ready, every day at mid-day the two emperors would take their meat, and on both sides they would cease fighting till all had finished eating. But the men of the Island of Britain took their meat in the morning, and drank till they were inspirited. And while the two emperors were at meat the Britons approached the rampart and planted their ladders against it. And forthwith they went in over the rampart. The new emperor had not time to take up arms before they fell on him and slew him, and many along with him. And three nights and three days were they subduing the men who were in the city and con-quering the castle, and another company of them guarding the city lest any of Macsen's host should come inside until they had subdued all to their will.

And then Macsen said to Elen of the Hosts: 'It is a great marvel to me, lady,' said he, 'that it was not for me thy brothers should conquer this city.' 'Lord emperor,' she answered, 'my brothers are the wisest youths in the world. Now go thyself to ask for the city, and if they are masters of it thou shalt have it gladly.' And then the emperor and Elen came to ask for the city. And then they told the emperor that taking the city and bestowing it upon him was the concern of none save the men of the Island of Britain. And then the gates of the city of Rome were opened, and the emperor sat on his throne, and all the Romans did him homage.

And then the emperor said to Cynan and Gadeon, 'Good sirs,' said he, 'I have gained possession of all my empire. And this host I give you to conquer what region of the world you will.' And then they set out and conquered lands and castles and cities, and they slew all their men, but the women they left alive. And in this wise they continued until the youths who had come with them were hoary-headed men with the length of time they had been about that conquest. And then Cynan said to Gadeon his brother, 'Which wilt thou,' said he, 'remain in this land or go to the land from whence thou art sprung?' So he determined to go to his own land, and many along with him; but Cynan and another company stayed on to live there. And they determined to cut out the tongues of the women, lest their language be corrupted. And because the women were silenced of their speech, and the men spoke on, the men of Llydaw were called Brytanieid.[4] And thence there often came, and still come from the Island of Britain, men of that tongue.

And this tale is called the Dream of Macsen Wledig, emperor of Rome. And here is an end of it.

4 The derivation of Llydaw (Brittany) implied in this sentence is from lled, 'half', and taw, 'silent'. An onomastic tale again.

LLUDD AND LLEFELYS

To Beli the Great, son of Manogan, were three sons: Lludd and
Caswallawn and Nyniaw; and according to the story a fourth
son of his was Llefelys. And when Beli died and the kingdom
of the Island of Britain fell into the hands of Lludd his eldest
son, and Lludd ruled it prosperously, he rebuilt the walls of
London and girt it about with innumerable towers; and after
that he bade the citizens build houses within it, so that there
might not be in the kingdoms houses of such splendour as
would be therein. Moreover, he was a good warrior and generous
and liberal in giving meat and drink to all who sought them.
And though he had many castles and cities he loved this one
more than any; and he dwelt in it the greatest part of the year,
and on that account it was called Caer Ludd, and at last Caer
Lundein. And it was after the coming of the foreign folk thereto
that it was called Lundein, or otherwise Lwndrys.

Best of all his brothers Lludd loved Llefelys, for a wise and
prudent man was he. And when he heard that the king of France
had died, leaving no offspring save an only daughter, and had
left the dominions in her hands, he came to Lludd his brother
to seek of him counsel and aid, and that not more for his own
advantage, but to seek increase in honour and dignity and status
for their kindred, if he might go to the kingdom of France to
seek that maiden as his wife. And straightway his brother agreed
with him, and he was pleased with his counsel in that matter.

And straightway ships were made ready and filled with armed
knights, and they set out for France. And straightway after their
coming to land they sent messengers to declare to the nobles of
France the reason for the quest he was come to seek. And by
common counsel of the nobles of France and its princes the
maiden was given to Llefelys, and the crown of the kingdom
along with her; and thereafter he ruled the land prudently and
wisely and happily, so long as his life lasted.

And after a space of time had passed, three plagues befell in the Island of Britain, whose like none in the Islands had seen before. The first of these was a certain folk that came and was called the Coranieid. And so great was their knowledge that there was no discourse over the face of the Island, however low it might be spoken, that they did not know about if the wind met it. And because of this no hurt might be done them.

The second plague was a scream which was raised every May-eve over every hearth in the Island of Britain. And that would pierce folks' hearts, and strike them with such terror that men would lose their hue and their strength and women the fruit of their wombs, and the young men and maidens would lose their senses, and all animals and trees and the earth and the waters be left barren.

The third plague was that however much might be the provision and food prepared in the king's courts, even though it were a year's provision of meat and drink, never a thing of it would be enjoyed save what was consumed the very first night.

Yet the first plague was open and manifest, but of the two other plagues there was none who knew what their meaning might be, and for this reason there was greater hope of winning deliverance from the first than there was from the second or from the third. And thereat king Lludd felt great trouble and care, since he knew not how he might win deliverance from those plagues. And he summoned to him all the nobles of his kingdom, and asked counsel of them what they should do against those plagues; and by the common counsel of his nobles, Lludd son of Beli went to Llefelys his brother, king of France (for a man great in counsel and wise was he), to seek advice from him. And then they made ready a fleet, and that in secret and in silence, lest that folk should know the reason for their mission, or any besides the king and his counsellors. And once they were ready, they went into their ships, Lludd and those he chose along with him; and they began to cleave the seas towards France.

And when those tidings came to Llefelys, since he knew not the reason for his brother's fleet, he came from the other side to meet him, and with him a fleet of vast size. And when Lludd saw that, he left all his ships out on the deep save one ship, and in that one he came to meet his brother. And he came in one other ship to meet his brother, and when they were met together each embraced the other, and each welcomed the other with brotherly affection.

And after Lludd had made known to his brother the reason for his mission, Llefelys declared that he himself knew the reason for his coming to those parts. And then they took counsel together to discuss their business in some way other than that, so that the wind might not catch their discourse, lest the Coranieid should know what they were saying. And then Llefelys had made a long horn of bronze, and through that horn they conversed; and whatever words they said one to the other through the horn, it came to each of them as nothing but hateful contrariety. And when Llefelys perceived that, and how there was a demon thwarting them and making mischief through the horn, he had wine poured into the horn, and had it washed, and by the virtue of the wine had the demon driven out of the horn. And when their talk was unhindered, Llefelys told his brother that he would give him certain insects and that he should keep some of these alive to breed, for fear lest a plague such as that should perchance come a second time, and other of the insects he should take and mash them with water; and he affirmed that was good for destroying the Coranieid folk. That is to say, when he returned home to his kingdom he should summon together all the people, his own folk and the Coranieid folk, to one assembly, under pretence of making peace between them; and when they were all assembled he should take that magic water and sprinkle it over all alike. And he affirmed that that water would poison the Coranieid folk, but would neither slay nor injure any of his own folk.

'The second plague,' said he, 'which is in thy dominion, that is a dragon, and a dragon of another foreign folk is fighting with it and striving to overcome it. And therefore,' said he, 'this dragon of yours raises a dire scream. And this is how thou canst prove it. After thou hast returned home, have the Island measured in its length and its breadth, and in the place where thou shalt find the exact point of centre, have a pit dug in that place, and then have set in that pit a tub full of the best mead that can be made, and a covering of silk over the face of the tub. And then keep watch in thine own person, and then thou shalt see the dragons fighting in the shape of monster animals. But at last they shall go in dragon-shape aloft in air; and last of all, when they shall have grown weary of their dire and frightful combat, they will fall in the shape of two little pigs upon the covering, and will make the covering sink down with them, and will drag it to the bottom of the tub, and they will drink up all the mead, and after that they will fall asleep. And then do thou straightway wrap the covering about them, and in the strongest place thou canst find in thy dominions bury them in a stone coffer, and hide them in the earth. And so long as they are in that strong place no plague shall come to the Island of Britain from elsewhere.

'The cause of the third plague,' said he, 'is a mighty man of magic who carries off thy meat and thy drink and thy provisions. And he through his magic and enchantment causes every one to fall asleep. And on that account thou must needs in thine own person keep watch over thy feasts and thy provisioning. And lest that sleep of his should overcome thee, let there be on hand a tub of cold water, and when sleep bears hard upon thee, get into the tub.'

And then Lludd returned to his country. And straightway he summoned to him each and every one of his own folk and of the Coranieid. And as Llefelys instructed him, he mashed the insects with water and sprinkled it over all alike, and there and then destroyed so the whole folk of the Coranieid, without hurt to any of the Britons.

And a while thereafter Lludd had the Island measured in its length and in its breadth, and in Oxford he found the point of centre. And in that place he had a pit dug in the ground, and in that pit he set a tub full of the best mead that might be made, and a covering of silk over the face of it, and he himself keeping watch that night. And as he was thus, he saw the dragons fighting; and when they were worn and weary they descended on top of the covering, and dragged it with them to the bottom of the tub. And when they had made an end of drinking the mead they fell asleep. And in their sleep Lludd wrapped the covering about them, and in the safest place he found in Eryri he hid them in a stone coffer. The form by which that place was known thereafter was Dinas Emreis, and before that Dinas Ffaraon Dandde. He was one of the Three Noble Youths who broke their hearts with consternation. And so ended the tempestuous scream that was in his dominion.

And when that was over, king Lludd had prepared an exceeding great feast. And when it was ready he had a tub of cold water set near at hand, and he himself in his own person kept watch over it. And while he was thus, clad in arms, about the third watch of the night, lo, he heard much rare pastime and variety of song, and drowsiness compelling him to sleep. And thereupon, lest his design be hindered, and his drowsiness overcome him, he went often into the water. And at last, lo, a man of huge stature, clad in strong heavy armour, coming in with a hamper, and as he had been wont, putting all the provisions and store of meat and drink into the hamper, and making off with it. And nothing was more wonderful to Lludd than that so much should be contained in that hamper. And thereupon king Lludd made after him, and spoke to him thus: 'Stop, stop!' said he, 'though thou hast wrought many wrongs and losses ere this, thou shalt do so no further, unless thy skill at arms show thou art stronger and braver than I.' And straightway he placed the hamper on the ground and waited for him to come up. And a terrible encounter was there between them, until sparks of fire flew from their weapons. But at length Lludd came to grips with him, and fate willed that victory should fall to Lludd, by casting down the oppressor between him and the ground. And when he had been overcome by might and by main, he asked for quarter. 'How could I give thee quarter,' asked the king, 'after the many losses and wrongs thou hast wrought me?' 'All the losses that I have ever wrought thee,' he answered, 'I will make good even to the extent I have inflicted them. And I will never do the like henceforth, and a liege man will I be to thee for evermore.' And the king accepted that of him.

And in this wise Lludd rid the Island of Britain of the three plagues. And from that time till his life's end Lludd son of Beli ruled the Island of Britain in prosperous peace.

And this tale is called the Adventure of Lludd and Llefelys. And thus it ends.

CULHWCH AND OLWEN

Cilydd son of Cyleddon Wledig wished for a wife as wellborn as himself. The wife that he took was Goleuddydd daughter of Anlawdd Wledig. After his stay with her the country went to prayers whether they might have offspring, and they got a son through the prayers of the country. But from the time she grew with child, she went mad, without coming near a dwelling. When her time came upon her, her right sense came back to her; it came in a place where a swineherd was keeping a herd of swine, and through terror of the swine the queen was delivered. And the swineherd took the boy until he came to the court. And the boy was baptized, and the name Culhwch given to him because he was found in a pig-run.[1] Nonetheless the boy was of gentle lineage: he was first cousin to Arthur. And the boy was put out to nurse.

And after that the boy's mother, Goleuddydd daughter of Anlawdd Wledig, grew sick. She called her husband to her, and quoth she to him, 'I am going to die of this sickness, and thou wilt wish for another wife. And these days wives are the dispensers of gifts, but it is wrong for thee to despoil thy son. I ask of thee that thou take no wife till thou see a two-headed briar on my grave.' That he promised her. She summoned her preceptor to her and bade him strip the grave each year, so that nothing might grow on it. The queen died. The king would send an attendant every morning to see whether anything was growing on the grave. At the end of seven years the preceptor neglected that which he had promised the queen. One day when the king was hunting, he drew near the graveyard; he wanted to see the grave whereby he was to take a wife. He saw the briar. And when he saw it the king took counsel where he might get a wife. Quoth one of the counsellors, 'I could tell of a woman would suit thee well. She is the wife of king Doged.' They

1 Culhwch: pig-run. A fanciful explanation, from hwch: pig. Compare the note on Pryderi, p. 20.

decided to seek her out. And they slew the king, and his wife they brought home with them, and an only daughter she had along with her; and they took possession of the king's lands.

Upon a day as the good lady went walking abroad, she came to the house of an old crone who was in the town, without a tooth in her head. Quoth the queen: 'Crone, wilt thou for God's sake tell me what I ask of thee? Where are the children of the man who has carried me off by force?' Quoth the crone: 'He has no children.' Quoth the queen: 'Woe is me that I should have come to a childless man!' Said the crone: 'Thou needst not say that. It is prophesied that he shall have offspring. 'Tis by thee he shall have it, since he has not had it by another. Besides, be not unhappy, he has one son.'

The good lady returned home joyfully, and quoth she to her husband, 'What reason hast thou to hide thy child from me?' Quoth the king, 'I will hide him no longer.' Messengers were sent after the boy, and he came to the court. His stepmother said to him, 'It were well for thee to take a wife, son, and I have a daughter meet for any nobleman in the world.' Quoth the boy, 'I am not yet of an age to take a wife.' Said she in reply: 'I will swear a destiny upon thee, that thy side shall never strike against woman till thou win Olwen daughter of Ysbaddaden Chief Giant.' The boy coloured, and love of the maiden entered into every limb of him, although he had never seen her. Quoth his father to him, 'How, son, why dost thou colour? What ails thee?' 'My stepmother has sworn on me that I shall never win a wife until I win Olwen daughter of Ysbaddaden Chief Giant.' 'It is easy for thee to achieve that, son,' said his father to him. 'Arthur is thy first cousin. Go then to Arthur to trim thy hair, and ask that of him as his gift to thee.'

Off went the boy on a steed with light-grey head, four winters old, with well-knit fork, shell-hoofed, and a gold tubular bridle-bit in its mouth. And under him a precious gold saddle, and in his hand two whetted spears of silver. A battle-axe in his hand, the forearm's length of a full grown man from ridge to edge. It would draw blood from the wind; it would be swifter than the swiftest dewdrop from the stalk to the ground, when the dew would be heaviest in the month of June. A gold-hilted sword on his thigh, and the blade of it gold, and a gold-chased buckler upon him, with the hue of heaven's lightning therein, and an ivory boss therein. And two greyhounds, whitebreasted, brindled, in front of him, with a collar of red gold about the neck of either, from shoulder-swell to ear. The one that was on the left side would be on the right, and the one that was on the right side would be on the left, like two sea-swallows sporting around him. Four clods the four hoofs of his steed would cut, like four swallows in the air over his head, now before him, now behind him. A four-cornered mantle of purple upon him, and an apple of red gold in each of its corners; a hundred kine was the worth of each apple. The worth of three hundred kine in precious gold was there in his foot gear and his stirrups, from the top of his thigh to the tip of his toe. Never a hair-tip stirred upon him, so exceeding light his steed's canter under him on his way to the gate of Arthur's court.

Quoth the youth, 'Is there a porter?' 'There is. And thou, may thy head not be thine, that thou dost ask! I am porter to Arthur each first day of January, but my deputies for the year save then, none other than Huandaw and Gogigwr and Llaesgymyn, and Penpingion who goes upon his head to spare his feet, neither heavenwards nor earthwards, but like a rolling stone on a court floor.' 'Open the gate.' 'I will not.' 'Why wilt thou not open it?' 'Knife has gone into meat, and drink into horn, and a thronging in Arthur's hall. Save the son of a king of a rightful dominion, or a craftsman who brings his craft, none may enter. Meat for thy dogs and corn for thy horse, and hot peppered chops for thyself, and wine brimming over, and delectable songs before thee. Food for fifty men shall come to thee in the hospice; there men from afar take their meat, and the scions of other countries who do not proffer a craft in Arthur's court. It will be no worse for thee there than for Arthur in the court: a woman to sleep with thee, and delectable songs before thee. To-morrow at tierce, when the gate is opened for the host that came here to-day, for thee shall the gate be opened first, and thou shalt sit wherever thou wilt in Arthur's hall, from its upper end to its lower.' The youth said, 'I will do nothing of that. If thou open the gate, it is well. If thou open it not, I will bring dishonour upon thy lord and ill report upon thee. And I will raise three shouts at the entrance of this gate, so that it shall not be less audible on the top of Pengwaedd in Cornwall and in the depths of Dinsel in the North, and in Esgeir Oerfel in Ireland. And every woman with child that is in this court shall miscarry, and such of them as are not with child their wombs shall turn to a burden within them, so that they may never bear child from this day forth.' Quoth Glewlwyd Mighty-grasp, 'Shout as much as thou wilt about the laws of Arthur's court, thou shalt not be let in till first I go and have a word with Arthur.'

And Glewlwyd came into the hall. Quoth Arthur to him, 'Thou hast news from the gate?' 'I have. Two-thirds of my life are past, and two-thirds of thine own. I was of old in Caer Se and Asse, in Sach and Salach, in Lotor and Ffotor. I was of old in India the Great and India the Lesser. I was of old in the contest between the two Ynyrs, when the twelve hostages were brought from Llychlyn. And of old I was in Egrop, and in Africa was I, and in the islands of Corsica, and in Caer Brythwch and Brythach, and Nerthach. I was there of old when thou didst slay the war-band of Gleis son of Merin, when thou didst slay Mil the Black, son of Dugum; I was there of old when thou didst conquer Greece unto the east. I was of old in Caer Oeth and Anoeth, and in Caer Nefenhyr Nine-teeth. Fair kingly men saw we there, but never saw I a man so comely as this who is even now at the entrance to the gate.' Quoth Arthur, 'If thou didst enter walking go thou out running. And he that looks upon the light, and opens his eye and shuts it, an injunction upon him. And let some serve with golden drinking horns, and others with hot peppered chops, so that there be ample meat and drink for him. A shameful thing it is to leave in wind and rain a man such as thou tellest of.' Quoth Cei: 'By the hand of my friend, if my counsel were acted upon, the laws of court would not be broken for his sake.' 'Not so, fair Cei. We are noble men so long as we are resorted to. The greater the bounty we show, all the greater will be our nobility and our fame and our glory.'

And Glewlwyd came to the gate and opened the gate to him. And what every man did, to dismount at the gate on the horse-block, he did not do; but on his steed he came inside. Quoth

Culhwch, 'Hail, sovereign prince of this Island! Be it no worse unto the lower half of the house than unto the upper. Be this greeting equally to thy nobles, and thy retinue, and thy leaders of hosts. May there be none without his share of it. Even as I gave thee full greeting, may thy grace and thy faith and thy glory be in this Island.' 'God's truth, so be it, chieftain! Greeting to thee too. Sit thou between two of the warriors, and delectable song before thee, and the privilege of an atheling for thee, an heir to a throne, for as long as thou shalt be here. And when I dispense my gifts to guests and men from afar, it shall be at thy hand that I so begin in this court.' Quoth the youth: 'I have not come here to wheedle meat and drink. But if I obtain my boon, I will repay it, and I will praise it. If I obtain it not, I will bear hence thine honour as far as thy renown was farthest in the four corners of the world.' Quoth Arthur, 'Though thou bide not here, chieftain, thou shalt obtain the boon thy head and thy tongue shall name, as far as wind dries, as far as rain wets, as far as sun runs, as far as sea stretches, as far as earth extends, save only my ship and my mantle, and Caledfwlch my sword, and Rhongomyniad my spear, and Wynebgwrthucher my shield, and Carnwennan my dagger, and Gwenhwyfar my wife.' 'God's truth thereon?' 'Thou shalt have it gladly. Name what thou wilt.' 'I will. I would have my hair trimmed.' 'That thou shalt have.' Arthur took a golden comb and shears with loops of silver, and he combed his head.

And he asked who he was. Quoth Arthur: 'My heart grows tender towards thee: I know thou art sprung from my blood. Declare who thou art.' 'I will: Culhwch son of Cilydd son of Cyleddon Wledig, by Goleuddydd daughter of Anlawdd Wledig, my mother.' Quoth Arthur: 'True it is. Thou art then my first cousin. Name what thou wilt, and thou shalt have it, whatever thy mouth and thy tongue shall name.' 'God's truth thereon to me, and the truth of thy kingdom?' 'Thou shalt have it gladly.' 'My claim on thee is that thou get me Olwen daughter of Ysbaddaden Chief Giant. And I invoke her in the name of thy warriors.'

He invoked his boon in the name of Cei and Bedwyr, and Greidawl Gallddofydd, and Gwythyr son of Greidawl, and

Greid son of Eri, and Cynddylig the Guide, and Tathal Frank-deceit, and Maelwys son of Baeddan, and Cnychwr son of Nes, and Cubert son of Daere, and Fercos son of Roch, and Lluber Beuthach, and Corfil Berfach, and Gwyn son of Esni, and Gwyn son of Nwyfre, and Gwyn son of Nudd, and Edern son of Nudd, and Cadwy son of Gereint, and Fflewdwr Fflam Wledig, and Rhuawn Bebyr son of Dorath, and Bradwen son of Moren Mynawg, and Moren Mynawg himself, and Dalldaf son of Cimin Cof, and the son of Alun Dyfed, and the son of Saidi, and the son of Gwryon, and Uchdryd Host-sustainer, and Cynwas Cwryfagyl, and Gwrhyr Fat-kine, and Isberyr Cat-claw, and Gallgoid the Hewer, and Duach, and Brathach, and Nerthach, sons of Gwawrddur Bow-back (from the uplands of hell these men were sprung), and Cilydd Hundred-holds, and Canhastyr[2] Hundred-hands, and Cors Hundred-claws, and Esgeir Gulhwch Gofyncawn,[3] and Drwst Iron-fist, and Glewlwyd Mighty-grasp, and Llwch Windy-hand, and Anwas the Winged, and Sinnoch son of Seithfed, and Wadu son of Seithfed, and Naw son of Seithfed, and Gwenwynwyn son of Naw son of Seithfed, and Bedyw son of Seithfed, and Gobrwy son of Echel Big-hip, and Echel Big-hip himself, and Mael son of Roycol, and Dadweir Blind-head, and Garwyli son of Gwythawg Gwyr, and Gwythawg Gwyr himself, and Gormant son of Rica, and Menw son of Teirgwaedd, and Digon son of Alar,[4] and Selyf son of Sinoid, and Gusg son of Achen, and Nerth son of Cadarn,[5] and Drudwas son of Tryffin, and Twrch son of Perif, and Twrch son of Anwas, and Iona king of France, and Sel son of Selgi, and Teregud son of Iaen, and Sulien son of Iaen, and Bradwen son of Iaen, and Moren son of Iaen, and Siawn son of Iaen, and Cradawg son of Iaen (men of Caer Dathal were they, kindred to Arthur on his father's side); Dirmyg son of Caw, and Iustig son of Caw, and Edmyg son of Caw, and Angawdd son of Caw, and Gofan son of Caw, and Celyn son of Caw, and Conyn son of Caw, and Mabsant

2 Canhastyr: Hundred-holds.
3 Gofyncawn: Reed-cutter (?).
4 Enough son of Surfeit.
5 Might son of Strong.

son of Caw, and Gwyngad son of Caw, and Llwybyr son of Caw, and Coch son of Caw, and Meilyg son of Caw, and Cynwal son of Caw, and Ardwyad son of Caw, and Ergyriad son of Caw, and Neb son of Caw,[6] and Gildas son of Caw, and Calcas son of Caw, and Hueil son of Caw (he never submitted to a lord's hand); and Samson Dry-lip, and Teliesin Chief of Bards, and Manawydan son of Llŷr, and Llary son of Casnar Wledig, and Sberin son of Fflergant king of Llydaw, and Saranhon son of Glythfyr, and Llawr son of Erw, and Anynnawg son of Menw son of Teirgwaedd, and Gwyn son of Nwyfre, and Fflam son of Nwyfre,[7] and Gereint son of Erbin, and Ermid son of Erbin, and Dywel son of Erbin, and Gwyn son of Ermid, and Cyndrwyn son of Ermid, and Hyfeidd One-cloak, and Eiddon the Magnanimous, and Rheiddwn Arwy; and Gormant son of Rica (brother to Arthur on his mother's side, his father the chief elder of Cornwall), and Llawfrodedd the Bearded, and Nodawl Cut-beard, and Berth son of Cado, and Rheiddwn son of Beli, and Isgofan the Generous, and Isgawyn son of Banon, and Morfran son of Tegid (no man placed his weapon in him at Camlan, so exceedingly ugly was he; all thought he was a devil helping. There was hair on him like the hair of a stag), and Sandde Angel-face (no one placed his spear in him at Camlan, so exceeding fair was he; all thought he was an angel helping), and Cynwyl the Saint (one of the three men that escaped from Camlan. He was the last to part from Arthur, on Hengroen[8] his horse), and Uchdryd son of Erim, and Eus son of Erim, and Henwas[9] the Winged son of Erim, and Henbeddestyr[10] son of Erim, and Sgilti Lightfoot son of Erim (three peculiarities had these men: Henbeddestyr never found man who might keep up with him, whether on horseback or on foot; Henwas the Winged, never a four-footed creature could run abreast of him the length of one acre, much less what would be farther than

6 Dirmyg: Scorn. Edmyg: Fame. Conyn: Stalk. Ardwyad: Sustainer. Ergyriad: Striker. Neb: Someone.
7 Flame son of Firmament.
8 Hengroen: Old-skin.
9 Henwas: Old Servant.
10 Henbeddestyr: Old walker.

that; Sgilti Lightfoot, when the whim to run his lord's errand
was in him, he never sought a road so long as he knew whither
he was bound; but so long as there were trees along the tops of
the trees he would go, and so long as there was a mountain on
the tips of the reeds would he go, and throughout his life never
a reed bent beneath his feet, much less did one break, so exceedingly light of foot was he); Teithi the Old son of Gwynnan,
whose dominions the sea overran, and with difficulty he himself
escaped and came to Arthur (and a peculiarity was on his knife:
from the time he came here never a haft stayed on it, and for
that reason sickness grew within him, and languor as long as he
lived; and of that he died). And Carnedyr son of Gofynion the
Old, and Gwenwynwyn son of Naf, Arthur's first fighter, and
Llygadrudd Emys,[11] and Gwrfoddw the Old (uncles of Arthur
were they, his mother's brothers), Culfanawyd son of Gwryon,
and Llenlleawg the Irishman from the headland of Gamon, and
Dyfnwal the Bald, and Dunarth king of the North, Teyrnon
Twryf Liant, and Tegfan the Lame, and Tegyr Talgellawg,
Gwrddywal son of Efrei, and Morgant the Generous, Gwystyl
son of Nwython, and Rhun son of Nwython, and Llwydeu son
of Nwython, and Gwydre son of Llwydeu by Gwenabwy daughter of Caw, his mother (Hueil his uncle stabbed him, and
thereby there was feud between Hueil and Arthur because of
the wound); Drem son of Dremidydd,[12] who saw from Celli
Wig in Cornwall as far as Pen Blathaon in Prydein,[13] when a fly
would rise in the morning with the sun; and Eidoel son of Nêr,
and Gwlyddyn the Craftsman, who built Ehangwen,[14] Arthur's
hall; Cynyr Fair-beard (Cei was said to be his son. He said to
his wife: 'If there be anything of me in thy son, maiden, cold
will be his heart ever, and there will be no warmth in his hands.
Another peculiarity will be on him: if he is my son, headstrong
will he be. Another peculiarity will be on him: when he carries
a burden, be it great or small, it will never be seen, neither from
in front nor from behind. Another peculiarity will be on him:

11 Llygadrudd: red eye. Emys: stallion.
12 Sight son of Seer.
13 Prydein here means Pictland.
14 Fair and roomy.

none will endure water and fire so well as he. Another peculiarity will be on him: there will be no servant or officer like to him'); Henwas and Hen Wyneb, and Hen Gedymddeith,[15] Gallgoig another (whatever township he came to, though there were three hundred homesteads therein, were he in need of aught, he would never leave sleep on man's eye whilst he was there); Berwyn son of Cyrenyr, and Paris king of France (and thereby the city of Paris gets its name); Osla Big-knife (who bore Bronllafn Short-broad. When Arthur and his hosts came to a torrent's edge, a narrow place on the water would be sought, and his knife in its sheath laid across the torrent. That would be bridge enough for the hosts of the Island of Britain and its three adjacent islands with their spoil); Gwyddawg son of Menestyr, who slew Cei (and Arthur then slew him and his brothers to avenge Cei); Garanwyn son of Cei, and Amren son of Bedwyr, and Eli and Myr, and Rheu Rhwydd Dyrys, and Rhun Rhuddwern, and Eli and Trachmyr, Arthur's head huntsmen, and Llwydeu son of Cel Coed, and Huabwy son of Gwryon, and Gwyn Godyfron, and Gweir Dathar the Servitor, and Gweir son of Cadellin Silver-brow, and Gweir False-valour, and Gweir White-shaft (uncles of Arthur, his mother's brothers); the sons of Llwch Windy-hand from beyond the Tyrrhene sea, Llenlleawg the Irishman and the exalted one of Britain, Cas son of Saidi, Gwrfan Wild-hair, Gwilenhin king of France, Gwitart son of Aedd king of Ireland, Garselit the Irishman, Panawr Head of the Host, Atlendor son of Naf, Gwyn the Irascible, overseer of Cornwall and Devon (one of the nine who plotted the battle of Camlan), Celli and Cuel, and Gilla Stag-shank (three hundred acres he would clear at a single leap, the chief leaper of Ireland), Sol and Gwaddyn Osol, and Gwaddyn Oddeith[16] (Sol could stand all day on one foot. Gwaddyn Osol, if he stood on top of the highest mountain in the world, it would become a level plain under his foot. Gwaddyn Oddeith, even as the hot metal when it would be drawn from the forge was the bright fire from his foot-soles when a

15 Henwas: Old Servant; Hen Wyneb: Old Face; Hen Gedymddeith: Old Comrade.
16 Gwaddyn: Sole; Gwaddyn Oddeith: Sole-blaze.

hard thing came against him. He cleared the way for Arthur on the march); Long Erwm and Long Atrwm (the day they came to a feast, three cantrefs would they seize for their needs; feasting till noon and drinking till night. When they went to sleep they would devour the heads of insects through hunger, as though they had never set tooth in food. When they went to a feast they left neither fat nor lean, neither hot nor cold, neither sour nor sweet, neither fresh nor salt, neither cooked nor raw); Huarwar son of Halwn (who asked his fill of Arthur as a boon. He was one of the three mighty plagues of Cornwall and Devon until his fill was found him. No glimmer of a smile was ever to be seen on him save when he was sated); Gwarae Golden-hair, the two whelps of the bitch Rhymhi, Gwyddrud and Gwydden the Abstruse, Sugyn son of Sugnedydd[17] (who would suck up the sea on which were three hundred ships till there remained naught but a dry strand. There was a red-hot breast fever in him); Cacamwri, Arthur's servant (show him a barn, were there a course for thirty ploughs therein, he would beat it with an iron flail till it was no better for the boards, the cross-pieces and the sidebeams than for the small oats in the mow at the bottom of the barn); Llwng and Dygyflwng, and Anoeth the Bold, and Long Eiddyl and Long Amren (two servants of Arthur were they), and Gwefyl son of Gwastad (on the day he was sad, one of his lips he would let down to his navel, and the other would be as a cowl on his head); Uchdryd Cross-beard (who would throw the bristling red beard he had on him across fifty rafters which were in Arthur's hall); Elidyr the Guide, Ysgyrdaf and Ysgudydd (two servants of Gwenhwyfar were they; as swift were their feet at their errand as their thoughts); Brys son of Brysethach from the top of the Black Fernbrake in Prydein, and Gruddlwyn the Dwarf; Bwlch and Cyfwlch and Syfwlch, sons of Cleddyf Cyfwlch, grandsons of Cleddyf Difwlch (three gleaming glitterers their three shields; three pointed piercers their three spears; three keen carvers their three swords; Glas, Glesig, Gleisad, their three dogs; Call, Cuall, Cafall, their three horses; Hwyrddyddwg and Drwgddyddwg and

17 Suck son of Sucker.

Llwyrddyddwg, their three wives; Och and Garym and Dias-
bad, their three grandchildren; Lluched and Neued and
Eisywed, their three daughters; Drwg and Gwaeth and Gwaethaf Oll, their three maid-servants;[18] Eheubryd son of Cyfwlch,
Gorasgwrn son of Nerth,[19] Gwaeddan son of Cynfelyn Half-
wit; Dwn the Valorous Chieftain, Eiladar son of Pen Llarcan,
Cynedyr the Wild son of Hetwn Silver-brow, Sawyl High-
head, Gwalchmei son of Gwyar, Gwalhafed son of Gwyar,
Gwrhyr Interpreter of Tongues (he knew all tongues), and
Cethtrwm the priest; Clust son of Clustfeinad[20] (were he to be
buried seven fathom in the earth, he would hear an ant fifty
miles off when it stirred from its couch of a morning); Medyr
son of Medredydd[21] (who from Celli Wig would hit a wren on
Esgeir Oerfel in Ireland, exactly through its two legs), Gwiawn
Cat-eye (who could cut a haw from a gnat's eye without harm-
ing the eye), Ôl son of Olwydd[22] (whose father's swine were
carried off seven years before he was born, and when he grew to
man he tracked the swine, and came home with them in seven
herds); Bidwini the bishop, who blessed meat and drink. The
gentle gold-torqued maidens of this Island: in addition to
Gwenhwyfar, the first lady of this Island, and Gwenhwyach her
sister, and Rathtyen the only daughter of Clememyl – Celemon
daughter of Cei, and Tangwen daughter of Gweir Dathar the
Servitor, Gwen Alarch[23] daughter of Cynwal Hundred-hogs,
Eurneid daughter of Clydno Eidin, Eneuawg daughter of
Bedwyr, Enrhydreg daughter of Tuduathar, Gwenwledyr
daughter of Gwaredur Bow-back, Erdudfyl daughter of Tryffin,
Eurolwyn daughter of Gwdolwyn the Dwarf, Teleri daughter of
Peul, Indeg daughter of Garwy the Tall, Morfudd daughter
of Urien Rheged, fair Gwenlliant the magnanimous maiden,

18 Late-bearer and Ill-bearer and Full-bearer, their three wives; Och and
Scream and Shriek, their three grandchildren; Plague and Want and Penury,
their three daughters; Bad and Worse and Worst of All, their three
maidservants.
19 Big-bone son of Might.
20 Ear son of Hearer.
21 Aim son of Aimer.
22 Track son of Tracker (?).
23 White Swan.

Creiddylad daughter of Lludd Silver-hand (the maiden of most majesty that was ever in the Island of Britain and its three adjacent islands. And for her Gwythyr son of Greidawl and Gwyn son of Nudd fight for ever each May-calends till the day of doom), Ellylw daughter of Neol Hang-cock (and she lived three generations), Esyllt Whiteneck and Esyllt Slenderneck – in the name of all these did Culwch son of Cilydd invoke his boon.

Arthur said, 'Ah, chieftain, I have never heard tell of the maiden thou tellest of, nor of her parents. I will gladly send messengers to seek her.' From that night till the same night at the end of a year the messengers were a-wandering. At the end of the year, when Arthur's messengers had found nothing, said the chieftain, 'Every one has obtained his boon, yet am I still lacking. I will away and take thine honour with me.' Said Cei, 'Ah, chieftain, overmuch dost thou asperse Arthur. Come thou with us. Till thou shalt say she exists not in the world, or till we find her, we will not be parted from thee.'

Then Cei arose. Cei had this peculiarity, nine nights and nine days his breath lasted under water, nine nights and nine days would he be without sleep. A wound from Cei's sword no physician might heal. A wondrous gift had Cei: when it pleased him he would be as tall as the tallest tree in the forest. Another peculiarity had he: when the rain was heaviest, a handbreadth before his hand and another behind his hand what would be in his hand would be dry, by reason of the greatness of his heat; and when the cold was hardest on his comrades, that would be to them kindling to light a fire.

Arthur called on Bedwyr, who never shrank from an enterprise upon which Cei was bound. It was thus with Bedwyr, that none was so handsome as he in this Island, save Arthur and Drych son of Cibddar, and this too, that though he was one-handed no three warriors drew blood in the same field faster than he. Another strange quality was his; one thrust would there be of his spear, and nine counter-thrusts.

Arthur called on Cynddylig the Guide. 'Go thou for me upon this enterprise along with the chieftain.' He was no worse a guide in the land he had never seen than in his own land.

He called Gwrhyr Interpreter of Tongues: he knew all tongues.

He called Gwalchmei son of Gwyar, because he never came home without the quest he had gone to seek. He was the best of walkers and the best of riders. He was Arthur's nephew, his sister's son, and his first cousin.

Arthur called on Menw son of Teirgwaedd, for should they come to a heathen land he might cast a spell over them, so that none might see them and they see every one.

Away they went till they came to a wide open plain and saw a fort, the greatest of forts in the world. That day they journeyed. When they thought they were near to the fort they were no nearer than at first. And the second and the third day they journeyed, and with difficulty did they get thereto. However, as they were coming to the same plain as it, they could see a great flock of sheep without limit or end to it, and a shepherd tending the sheep on top of a mound, and a jerkin of skins upon him, and at his side a shaggy mastiff which was bigger than a nine year old stallion. It was the way of him that never a lamb had he lost, much less a grown beast. No company had ever fared past him that he did not do it harm or deadly hurt; every dead tree and bush that was on the plain, his breath would burn them to the very ground.

Quoth Cei: 'Gwrhyr Interpreter of Tongues, go and have word with yonder man.' 'Cei, I made no promise to go save as far as thou thyself wouldst go.' 'Then let us go there together.' Quoth Menw son of Teirgwaedd: 'Have no qualms to go thither. I will cast a spell over the dog, so that he shall do harm to none.'

They came to where the shepherd was. Quoth they, 'Things are well with thee, shepherd.' 'May things never be better with you than with me.' 'Yea, by God, for thou art chief.' 'There is no affliction to do me harm save my wife.' 'Whose are the sheep thou tendest, or whose is the fort?' 'Fools of men that you are! Throughout the world it is known that this is the fort of Ysbaddaden Chief Giant.' 'And thou, who art thou?' 'Custennin son of Mynwyedig am I, and because of my wife Ysbaddaden Chief Giant has wrought my ruin. You too, who are you?' 'Messengers of Arthur are here, to seek Olwen.' 'Whew, men! God protect you! For all the world, do not that. Never a one has come to make that request that went away with his life.'

The shepherd arose. As he arose Culhwch gave him a ring of gold. He sought to put on the ring, but it would not go on him, and he placed it on the finger of his glove and went home and gave the glove to his wife. And she took the ring from the glove. 'Whence came this ring to thee, husband? 'Twas not often that thou hast had treasure-trove.' 'I went to the sea, to find sea-food. Lo! I saw a body coming in on the tide. Never saw I body so beautiful as that, and on its finger I found this ring.' 'Alas, husband, since sea does not tolerate a dead man's jewels therein, show me that body.' 'Wife, the one whose body that is, thou shalt see him here presently.' 'Who is that?' the woman asked. 'Culhwch son of Cilydd son of Cyleddon Wledig, by Goleu-ddydd daughter of Anlawdd Wledig, his mother, who is come to seek Olwen.' Two feelings possessed her: she was glad that her nephew, her sister's son, was coming to see her; and she was sad because she had never seen any depart with his life that had come to make that request.

They came forward to the gate of the shepherd Custennin's court. She heard the noise of their coming. She ran with joy to meet them. Cei snatched a log out of the wood-pile, and she came to meet them, to try and throw her arms about their necks. Cei thrust a stake between her two hands. She squeezed the stake so that it became a twisted withe. Quoth Cei, 'Woman, had it been I thou didst squeeze in this wise, there were no need for another to love me ever. An ill love, that!'

They came into the house and their needs were supplied. After a while, when all were letting themselves be busied, the woman opened a coffer alongside the hearth, and out of it arose a lad with curly yellow hair. Quoth Gwrhyr, ' 'Twere pity to hide a lad like this. I know that it is no fault of his own that is visited upon him.' Quoth the woman, 'He is all that is left. Three-and-twenty sons of mine has Ysbaddaden Chief Giant slain, and I have no more hope of this one than of the others.' Quoth Cei, 'Let him keep company with me, and we shall not be slain save together.'

They ate. Quoth the woman, 'On what errand are you come hither?' 'We are come to seek Olwen.' 'For God's sake, since none from the fort has yet seen you, get you back!' 'God knows we will not get us back till we have seen the maiden. Will she come to where she may be seen?' 'She comes hither every Saturday to wash her head; and in the bowl where she washes she leaves all her rings. Neither she nor her messenger ever comes for them.' 'Will she come hither if she is sent for?' 'God knows I will not slay my soul. I will not betray the one who trusts in me. But if you pledge your word you will do her no harm, I will send for her.' 'We pledge it,' said they.

She was sent for. And she came, with a robe of flame-red silk about her, and around the maiden's neck a torque of red gold, and precious pearls thereon and rubies. Yellower was her head than the flower of the broom, whiter was her flesh than the foam of the wave; whiter were her palms and her fingers than the shoots of the marsh trefoil from amidst the fine gravel of a welling spring. Neither the eye of the mewed hawk, nor the eye of the thrice-mewed falcon, not an eye was there fairer than hers. Whiter were her breasts than the breast of the white swan, redder were her cheeks than the reddest foxgloves. Whoso beheld her would be filled with love of her. Four white trefoils sprang up behind her wherever she went; and for that reason was she called Olwen.[24]

She entered the house and sat between Culhwch and the high seat, and even as he saw her he knew her. Said Culhwch to her, 'Ah maiden, 'tis thou I have loved. And come thou with me.' 'Lest sin be charged to thee and me, that I may not do at all. My father has sought a pledge of me that I go not without his counsel, for he shall live only until I go with a husband. There is, however, counsel I will give thee, if thou wilt take it. Go ask me of my father. And however much he demand of thee, do thou promise to get it, and me too shalt thou get. But if he have cause to doubt at all, get me thou shalt not, and 'tis well for thee if thou escape with thy life.' 'I promise all that, and will obtain it,' said he.

She went to her chamber. They then arose to go after her to the fort, and slew nine gatemen who were at nine gates without

24 Olwen: White-track (to the author, but it probably means 'Fair' or 'Beautiful').

a man crying out, and nine mastiffs without one squealing. And they went forward to the hall.

Quoth they, 'In the name of God and man, greeting unto thee, Ysbaddaden Chief Giant.' 'And you, where are you going?' 'We are going to seek Olwen thy daughter for Culhwch son of Cilydd.' 'Where are those rascal servants and those ruffians of mine?' said he. 'Raise up the forks under my two eyelids that I may see my future son-in-law.' That was done. 'Come hither to-morrow. I will give you some answer.'

They rose, and Ysbaddaden Chief Giant snatched at one of the three poisoned stone-spears which were by his hand and hurled it after them. And Bedwyr caught it and hurled it back at him, and pierced Ysbaddaden Chief Giant right through the ball of his knee. Quoth he, 'Thou cursed savage son-in-law! I shall walk the worse up a slope. Like the sting of a gadfly the poisoned iron has pained me. Cursed be the smith who fashioned it, and the anvil on which it was wrought, so painful it is!'

That night they lodged in the house of Custennin. And on the morrow with pomp and with brave combs set in their hair they came into the hall. They said, 'Ysbaddaden Chief Giant, give us thy daughter in return for her portion and her maiden fee to thee and her two kinswomen. And unless thou give her, thou shalt meet thy death because of her.' 'She and her four great-grandmothers and her four great-grandfathers are yet alive. I must needs take counsel with them.' 'So be it with thee,' said they. 'Let us go to our meat.' As they arose he took hold of the second stone-spear which was by his hand and hurled it after them. And Menw son of Teirgwaedd caught it and hurled it back at him, and pierced him in the middle of his breast, so that it came out in the small of his back. 'Thou cursed savage son-in-law! Like the bite of a big-headed leech the hard iron has pained me. Cursed be the forge wherein it was heated. When I go uphill, I shall have tightness of chest, and belly-ache, and a frequent loathing of meat.' They went to their meat.

And the third day they came to court. Quoth they, 'Ysbaddaden Chief Giant, shoot at us no more. Seek not thy harm and deadly hurt and death.' 'Where are my servants? Raise up the forks — my eyelids have fallen over the balls of my eyes — so that

I may take a look at my future son-in-law.' They arose, and as they arose he took the third poisoned stone-spear and hurled it after them. And Culhwch caught it and hurled it back, even as he wished, and pierced him through the ball of the eye, so that it came out through the nape of the neck. 'Thou cursed savage son-in-law! So long as I am left alive, the sight of my eyes will be the worse. When I go against the wind they will water, a headache I shall have, and a giddiness each new moon. Cursed be the forge wherein it was heated. Like the bite of a mad dog to me the way the poisoned iron has pierced me.' They went to their meat.

On the morrow they came to court. Quoth they, 'Shoot not at us. Seek not the harm and deadly hurt and martyrdom that are upon thee, or what may be worse, if such be thy wish. Give us thy daughter.' 'Where is he who is told to seek my daughter?' ''Tis I who seek her, Culhwch son of Cilydd.' 'Come hither where I may see thee.' A chair was placed under him, face to face with him.

Said Ysbaddaden Chief Giant, 'Is it thou that seekest my daughter?' ''Tis I who seek her.' 'Thy pledge would I have that thou wilt not do worse by me than is just.' 'Thou shalt have it.' 'When I have myself gotten that which I shall name to thee, then thou shalt get my daughter.' 'Name what thou wouldst name.'

'I will,' said he. 'Dost see the great thicket yonder?' 'I see.' 'I must have it uprooted out of the earth and burnt on the face of the ground so that the cinders and ashes thereof be its manure; and that it be ploughed and sown so that it be ripe in the morning against the drying of the dew, in order that it may be made into meat and drink for thy wedding guests and my daughter's. And all that I must have done in one day.'

'It is easy for me to get that, though thou think it is not easy.'

'Though thou get that, there is that thou wilt not get. A husbandman to till and prepare that land, other than Amaethon son of Dôn. He will not come with thee of his own free will, nor canst thou compel him.'

'It is easy for me to get that, though thou think it is not easy.'

'Though thou get that, there is that thou wilt not get.

Gofannon son of Dôn to come to the headland to set the irons. He will not do work of his own free will, save for a king in his own right, nor canst thou compel him.'

'It is easy for me to get that, though thou think it is not easy.'

'Though thou get that, there is that thou wilt not get. The two oxen of Gwlwlydd Wineu, both yoked together to plough well the rough ground yonder. He will not give them of his own free will, nor canst thou compel him.'

'It is easy for me to get that, though thou think it is not easy.'

'Though thou get that, there is that thou wilt not get. The Melyn Gwanwyn and the Ych Brych,[25] both yoked together, must I have.'

'It is easy for me to get that, though thou think it is not easy.'

'Though thou get that, there is that thou wilt not get. The two horned oxen, one of which is beyond Mynydd Bannawg,[26] and the other this side – and to fetch them together in the one plough. Nyniaw and Peibiaw are they, whom God transformed into oxen for their sins.'

'It is easy for me to get that, though thou think it is not easy.'

'Though thou get that, there is that thou wilt not get. Dost see the hoed tilth yonder?' 'I see.' 'When I first met the mother of that maiden, nine hestors of flax seed were sown therein; neither black nor white has come out of it yet, and I have that measure still. I must have that in the new-broken ground yonder, so that it may be a white head-dress for my daughter's head on the day of thy wedding-feast.'

'It is easy for me to get that, though thou think it is not easy.'

'Though thou get that, there is that thou wilt not get. Honey that will be nine times sweeter than the honey of a virgin swarm, without drones and without bees, to make bragget for the feast.'

'It is easy for me to get that, though thou think it is not easy.'

'Though thou get that, there is that thou wilt not get. The cup of Llwyr son of Llwyrion, in which is the best of all drink; for there is no vessel in the world which can hold that strong drink, save it. Thou shalt not have it of his own free will, nor canst thou compel him.'

25 Yellow-Palewhite and the Speckled Ox.
26 A mountain in Scotland, possibly the Grampians.

'It is easy for me to get that, though thou think it is not easy.'

'Though thou get that, there is that thou wilt not get. The hamper of Gwyddneu Long-shank: if the whole world should come around it, thrice nine men at a time, the meat that every one wished for he would find therein, to his liking. I must eat therefrom the night my daughter sleeps with thee. He will give it to no one of his own free will, nor canst thou compel him.'

'It is easy for me to get that, though thou think it is not easy.'

'Though thou get that, there is that thou wilt not get. The horn of Gwlgawd Gododdin to pour out for us that night. He will not give it of his own free will, nor canst thou compel him.'

'It is easy for me to get that, though thou think it is not easy.'

'Though thou get that, there is that thou wilt not get. The harp of Teirtu to entertain me that night. When a man pleases, it will play of itself; when one would have it so, it will be silent. He will not give it of his own free will, nor canst thou compel him.'

'It is easy for me to get that, though thou think it is not easy.'

'Though thou get that, there is that thou wilt not get. The birds of Rhiannon, they that wake the dead and lull the living to sleep, must I have to entertain me that night.'

'It is easy for me to get that, though thou think it is not easy.'

'Though thou get that, there is that thou wilt not get. The cauldron of Diwrnach the Irishman, the overseer of Odgar son of Aedd king of Ireland, to boil meat for thy wedding guests.'

'It is easy for me to get that, though thou think it is not easy.'

'Though thou get that, there is that thou wilt not get. I must needs wash my head and shave my beard. The tusk of Ysgithyrwyn Chief Boar I must have, wherewith to shave myself. I shall be none the better for that unless it be plucked from his head while alive.'

'It is easy for me to get that, though thou think it is not easy.'

'Though thou get that, there is that thou wilt not get. There is no one in the world can pluck it from his head save Odgar son of Aedd king of Ireland.'

'It is easy for me to get that, though thou think it is not easy.'

'Though thou get that, there is that thou wilt not get. I will not entrust the keeping of the tusk to any save Cadw of

Prydein.[27] The threescore cantrefs of Prydein are under him. He will not come out of his kingdom of his own free will, nor can he be compelled.'

'It is easy for me to get that, though thou think it is not easy.'

'Though thou get that, there is that thou wilt not get. I must needs dress my beard for me to be shaved. It will never settle unless the blood of the Black Witch be obtained, daughter of the White Witch, from the head of the Valley of Grief in the uplands of Hell.'

'It is easy for me to get that, though thou think it is not easy.'

'Though thou get that, there is that thou wilt not get. The blood will be of no use unless it be obtained while warm. There is no vessel in the world will keep heat in the liquid that is put therein save the bottles of Gwyddolwyn the Dwarf, which keep their heat from the time when the liquid is put into them in the east till one reaches the west. He will not give them of his own free will, nor canst thou compel him.'

'It is easy for me to get that, though thou think it is not easy.'

'Though thou get that, there is that thou wilt not get. Some will wish for milk, but there will be no way to get milk for every one until the bottles of Rhynnon Stiff-beard are obtained. In them no liquid ever turns sour. He will not give them of his own free will, nor can he be compelled.'

'It is easy for me to get that, though thou think it is not easy.'

'Though thou get that, there is that thou wilt not get. There is no comb and shears in the world wherewith my hair may be dressed, so exceeding stiff it is, save the comb and shears that are between the two ears of Twrch Trwyth son of Taredd Wledig. He will not give them of his own free will, nor canst thou compel him.'

'It is easy for me to get that, though thou think it is not easy.'

'Though thou get that, there is that thou wilt not get. Twrch Trwyth will not be hunted till Drudwyn be obtained, the whelp of Greid son of Eri.'

'It is easy for me to get that, though thou think it is not easy.'

'Though thou get that, there is that thou wilt not get. There

27 Cadw of Prydein: Cadw of Pictland. Cadw: to keep.

is no leash in the world may hold on him, save the leash of Cors Hundred-claws.'

'It is easy for me to get that, though thou think it is not easy.'

'Though thou get that, there is that thou wilt not get. There is no collar in the world can hold the leash, save the collar of Canhastyr Hundred-hands.'

'It is easy for me to get that, though thou think it is not easy.'

'Though thou get that, there is that thou wilt not get. The chain of Cilydd Hundred-holds to hold the collar along with the leash.'

'It is easy for me to get that, though thou think it is not easy.'

'Though thou get that, there is that thou wilt not get. There is no huntsman in the world can act as houndsman to that hound, save Mabon son of Modron, who was taken away when three nights old from his mother. Where he is is unknown, or what his state is, whether alive or dead.'

'It is easy for me to get that, though thou think it is not easy.'

'Though thou get that, there is that thou wilt not get. Gwyn Dun-mane, the steed of Gweddw (as swift as the wave is he!), under Mabon to hunt Twrch Trwyth. He will not give him of his own free will, nor canst thou compel him.'

'It is easy for me to get that, though thou think it is not easy.'

'Though thou get that, there is that thou wilt not get. Mabon will never be obtained, where he is is unknown, till his kinsman Eidoel son of Aer be first obtained; for he will be untiring in quest of him. He is his first cousin.'

'It is easy for me to get that, though thou think it is not easy.'

'Though thou get that, there is that thou wilt not get. Garselit the Irishman, chief huntsman of Ireland is he. Twrch Trwyth will never be hunted without him.'

'It is easy for me to get that, though thou think it is not easy.'

'Though thou get that, there is that thou wilt not get. A leash from the beard of Dillus the Bearded, for save that there is nothing will hold those two whelps. And no use can be made of it unless it be twitched out of his beard while he is alive, and he be plucked with wooden tweezers. He will not allow any one to do that to him while he lives, but it will be useless if dead, for it will be brittle.'

'It is easy for me to get that, though thou think it is not easy.'

'Though thou get that, there is that thou wilt not get. There is no huntsman in the world will hold those two whelps, save Cynedyr the Wild son of Hetwn the Leper. Nine times wilder is he than the wildest wild beast on the mountain. Him wilt thou never get, nor wilt thou get my daughter.'

'It is easy for me to get that, though thou think it is not easy.'

'Though thou get that, there is that thou wilt not get. Thou wilt not hunt Twrch Trwyth until Gwyn son of Nudd be obtained, in whom God has set the spirit of the demons of Annwn, lest this world be destroyed. He will not be spared thence.'

'It is easy for me to get that, though thou think it is not easy.'

'Though thou get that, there is that thou wilt not get. There is no horse in the world that will avail Gwyn to hunt Twrch Trwyth, save Du[28] the horse of Moro Oerfeddawg.'

'It is easy for me to get that, though thou think it is not easy.'

'Though thou get that, there is that thou wilt not get. Until Gwilenhin king of France come, Twrch Trwyth will never be hunted without him. It is improper for him to leave his kingdom, and he will never come hither.'

'It is easy for me to get that, though thou think it is not easy.'

'Though thou get that, there is that thou wilt not get. Twrch Trwyth will never be hunted without the son of Alun Dyfed be obtained. A good unleasher is he.'

'It is easy for me to get that, though thou think it is not easy.'

'Though thou get that, there is that thou wilt not get. Twrch Trwyth will never be hunted until Aned and Aethlem be obtained. Swift as a gust of wind would they be; never were they unleashed on a beast they did not kill.'

'It is easy for me to get that, though thou think it is not easy.'

'Though thou get that, there is that thou wilt not get. Arthur and his huntsmen to hunt Twrch Trwyth. A man of might is he, and he will not come with thee – the reason is that he is a man of mine.'

'It is easy for me to get that, though thou think it is not easy.'

28 Du: black.

'Though thou get that, there is that thou wilt not get. Twrch Trwyth can never be hunted until Bwlch and Cyfwlch and Syfwlch be obtained, sons of Cilydd Cyfwlch, grandsons of Cleddyf Difwlch. Three gleaming glitterers their three shields; three pointed piercers their three spears; three keen carvers their three swords; Glas, Glesig, Gleisad, their three dogs; Call, Cuall, Cafall, their three horses; Hwyrddyddwg and Drwgddyddwg and Llwyrddyddwg, their three wives; Och and Garym and Diasbad, their three witches; Lluched and Neued and Eisywed, their three daughters; Drwg and Gwaeth and Gwaethaf Oll, their three maid-servants. The three men shall wind their horns, and all the others will come to make outcry, till none would care though the sky should fall to earth.'

'It is easy for me to get that, though thou think it is not easy.'

'Though thou get that, there is that thou wilt not get. The sword of Wrnach the Giant; never can he be slain save with that. He will not give it to any one, neither for price nor for favour nor canst thou compel him.'

'It is easy for me to get that, though thou think it is not easy.'

'Though thou get that, there is that thou wilt not get. Wakefulness without sleep at night shalt thou have in seeking those things. And thou wilt not get them, nor wilt thou get my daughter.'

'Horses shall I have and horsemen, and my lord and kinsman Arthur will get me all those things. And I shall win thy daughter, and thou shalt lose thy life.'

'Set forward now. Thou shalt not be answerable for food or raiment for my daughter. Seek those things. And when those things are won, my daughter too thou shalt win.'

That day they journeyed till evening, until there was seen a great fort of mortared stone, the greatest of forts in the world. Lo, they saw coming from the fort a black man, bigger than three men of this world. Quoth they to him: 'Whence comest thou, fellow?' 'From the fort you see yonder.' 'Whose is the fort?' 'Fools of men that you are! There is none in the world does not know whose fort this is. It belongs to Wrnach the Giant.' 'What usage is there for a guest and far-comer alighting at this fort?'

'Ah, chieftain, God protect you! No guest has ever come thence with his life. None is permitted therein save him who brings his craft.'

They made their way to the gate. Quoth Gwrhyr Interpreter of Tongues, 'Is there a porter?' 'There is. And thou, may thy head not be thine, that thou dost ask!' 'Open the gate.' 'I will not.' 'Why wilt thou not open it?' 'Knife has gone into meat, and drink into horn, and a thronging in Wrnach's hall. Save for a craftsman who brings his craft, it will not be opened again this night.' Quoth Cei, 'Porter, I have a craft.' 'What craft hast thou?' 'I am the best furbisher of swords in the world.' 'I will go and tell that to Wrnach the Giant and will bring thee an answer.'

The porter came inside. Said Wrnach the Giant, 'Thou hast news from the gate?' 'I have. There is a company at the entrance to the gate who would like to come in.' 'Didst thou ask if they had a craft with them?' 'I did, and one of them declared he knew how to furbish swords.' 'I had need of him. For some time I have been seeking one who should polish my sword, but I found him not. Let that man in, since he had a craft.'

The porter came and opened the gate, and Cei came inside all alone. And he greeted Wrnach the Giant. A chair was placed under him. Said Wrnach, 'Why, man, is this true which is reported of thee, that thou knowest how to furbish swords?' 'I do that,' said Cei. The sword was brought to him. Cei took a striped whetstone from under his arm. 'Which dost thou prefer upon it, white-haft or dark-haft?' 'Do with it what pleases thee, as though it were thine own.' He cleaned half of one side of the blade for him and put it in his hand. 'Does that content thee?' 'I would rather than all that is in my dominions that the whole of it were like this. It is a shame a man as good as thou should be without a fellow.' 'Oia, good sir, I have a fellow, though he does not practise this craft.' 'Who is he?' 'Let the porter go forth, and I will tell his tokens: the head of his spear will leave its shaft, and it will draw blood from the wind, and settle upon the shaft again.' The gate was opened and Bedwyr entered in. Said Cei, 'A wondrous gift has Bedwyr, though he does not practise this craft.'

And there was great debate betwixt those men outside. Cei

and Bedwyr came inside. And a young lad came inside with them, the shepherd Custennin's only son. He and his comrades, who stayed close to him, crossed the three baileys as though this were a thing less than naught to them, until they came inside the fort. Quoth his comrades of Custennin's son, 'Best of men is he.' From then on he was called Goreu son of Custennin.[29] They dispersed to their lodgings that they might slay those who lodged them, without the Giant knowing.

The furbishing the sword was done, and Cei gave it into the hand of Wrnach the Giant, as though to see whether the work was to his satisfaction. Said the giant, 'The work is good, and I am content with it.' Quoth Cei, 'It is thy scabbard has damaged thy sword. Give it to me to take out the wooden side-pieces, and let me make new ones for it.' And he took the scabbard, and the sword in the other hand. He came and stood over the giant, as if he would put the sword into the scabbard. He sank it into the giant's head and took off his head at a blow. They laid waste the fort and took away what treasures they would. To the very day at the end of a year they came to Arthur's court, and the sword of Wrnach the Giant with them.

They told Arthur how it had gone with them. Arthur said, 'Which of those marvels will it be best to seek first?' 'It will be best,' said they, 'to seek Mabon son of Modron, and there is no getting him until his kinsman Eidoel son of Aer is got first.' Arthur rose up, and the warriors of the Island of Britain with him, to seek for Eidoel; and they came to Glini's outer wall, to where Eidoel was in prison. Glini stood on the rampart of the fort, and he said, 'Arthur, what wouldst thou have of me, since thou wilt not leave me alone on this crag? I have no good herein and no pleasure, neither wheat nor oats have I, without thee too seeking to do me harm.' Arthur said, 'Not to thy hurt have I come hither, but to seek out the prisoner that is with thee.' 'I will give thee the prisoner, though I had not bargained to give him up to any one. And besides this, my aid and my backing thou shalt have.'

29 Goreu: best.

The men said to Arthur, 'Lord, get thee home. Thou canst not proceed with thy host to seek things so petty as these.' Arthur said, 'Gwrhyr Interpreter of Tongues, it is right for thee to go on this quest. All tongues hast thou, and thou canst speak with some of the birds and the beasts. Eidoel, it is right for thee to go along with my men to seek him – he is thy first cousin. Cei and Bedwyr, I have hope that whatever you go to seek will be obtained. Go then for me on this quest.'

They went on their way as far as the Ouzel of Cilgwri. 'For God's sake,' Gwrhyr asked her, 'knowest thou aught of Mabon son of Modron, who was taken when three nights old from betwixt his mother and the wall?' The Ouzel said, 'When first I came hither, there was a smith's anvil here, and as for me I was a young bird. No work has been done upon it save whilst my beak was thereon every evening. To-day there is not so much of it as a nut not worn away. God's vengeance on me if I have heard aught of the man you are asking after. Nevertheless, that which it is right and proper for me to do for Arthur's messengers, I will do. There is a kind of creature God made before me; I will go along as your guide thither.'

They came to the place where the Stag of Rhedynfre was. 'Stag of Rhedynfre, here we have come to thee, Arthur's messengers, since we know of no animal older than thou. Say, knowest thou aught of Mabon son of Modron, who was taken away from his mother when three nights old?' The Stag said, 'When first I came hither, there was but one tine on either side of my head, and there were no trees here save a single oak-sapling, and that grew into an oak with a hundred branches, and the oak thereafter fell, and to-day there is naught of it save a red stump; from that day to this I have been here. I have heard naught of him you are asking after. Nevertheless I will be your guide, since you are Arthur's messengers, to the place where there is an animal God made before me.'

They came to the place where the Owl of Cwm Cawlwyd was. 'Owl of Cwm Cawlwyd, here are Arthur's messengers. Knowest thou aught of Mabon son of Modron, who was taken away from his mother when three nights old?' 'If I knew it, I would tell it. When first I came hither, the great valley you see was a wooded glen, and a race of men came thereto and it was laid waste. And the second wood grew up therein, and this wood is the third. And as for me, why! the roots of my wings are mere stumps. From that day to this I have heard naught of the man you are asking after. Nevertheless I will be a guide to Arthur's messengers until you come to the place where is the oldest creature that is in this world, and he that has fared furthest afield, the Eagle of Gwernabwy.'

Gwrhyr said, 'Eagle of Gwernabwy, we have come to thee, Arthur's messengers, to ask whether thou knowest aught of Mabon son of Modron who was taken away from his mother when three nights old?' The Eagle said, 'I came here a long time ago, and when first I came hither I had a stone, and from its top I pecked at the stars each evening; now it is not a hand-breadth in height. From that day to this I have been here, but have heard naught of him you are asking after. Save that at one faring I went to seek my meat as far as Llyn Llyw, and when I came there I sank my claws into a salmon, thinking he would be meat for me many a long day, and he drew me down into the depths, so that it was with difficulty I got away from him. And my whole kindred and I went after him, to seek to destroy him. But he sent messengers to make peace with me, and came to me in person to have fifty tridents taken out of his back. Unless he knows something of what you seek, I know none who may. Nevertheless, I will be your guide to the place where he is.'

They came to the place where he was. The Eagle said, 'Salmon of Llyn Llyw, I have come to thee with Arthur's messengers to ask whether thou knowest aught of Mabon son of Modron who was taken away from his mother when three nights old?' 'As much as I know, I will tell. With every tide I go up along the river until I come to the bend of the wall of Caer Loyw; and there I found such distress that I never found its equal in all my life; and, that you may believe, let one of you come here on my two shoulders.' And Cei and Gwrhyr Interpreter of Tongues went upon the salmon's two shoulders, and they journeyed until they came to the far side of the wall from the prisoner, and they could hear wailing and lamentation on the far side of the wall from them. Gwrhyr said, 'What man laments in this house of stone?' 'Alas, man, there is cause for him who is here to lament. Mabon son of Modron is here in prison; and none was ever so cruelly imprisoned in a prison house as I; neither the imprisonment of Lludd Silver-hand nor the imprisonment of Greid son of Eri.' 'Hast thou hope of getting thy release for gold or for silver or for worldly wealth, or by battle and fighting?' 'What is got of me, will be got by fighting.'

They returned thence and came to where Arthur was. They told where Mabon son of Modron was in prison. Arthur summoned the warriors of this Island and went to Caer Loyw where Mabon was in prison. Cei and Bedwyr went upon the two shoulders of the fish. Whilst Arthur's warriors assaulted the fort, Cei broke through the wall and took the prisoner on his back; and still he fought with the men. Arthur came home and Mabon with him, a free man.

Arthur said, 'Which of the marvels is it now best to seek first?' 'It is best to seek for the two whelps of the bitch Rhymhi.' 'Is it known where she is?' asked Arthur. 'She is,' said one, 'at Aber Deu Gleddyf.' Arthur came to the house of Tringad in Aber Cleddyf and asked him, 'Hast thou heard of her in these parts? In what shape is she?' 'In the shape of a she-wolf,' answered he, 'and she goes about with her two whelps. Often has she slain my stock, and she is down in Aber Cleddyf in a cave.'

Arthur went to sea in his ship Prydwen, and others by land to hunt the bitch, and in this wise they surrounded her and her two whelps, and God changed them back into their own semblances for Arthur. Arthur's host dispersed, one by one, two by two.

And as Gwythyr son of Greidawl was one day journeying over a mountain, he heard a wailing and a grievous lamentation, and these were a horrid noise to hear. He sprang forward in that direction, and when he came there he drew his sword and smote off the anthill level with the ground, and so saved them from the fire. And they said to him, 'Take thou God's blessing and ours, and that which no man can ever recover, we will come and recover it for thee.' It was they thereafter who came with the nine hestors of flax seed which Ysbaddaden Chief Giant had named to Culhwch, in full measure, with none of it wanting save for a single flax seed. And the lame ant brought that in before night.

As Cei and Bedwyr were sitting on top of Pumlumon on Carn Gwylathyr, in the highest wind in the world, they looked about them and they could see a great smoke towards the south, far off from them, and not blowing across with the wind. And then Cei said, 'By the hand of my friend, see yonder the fire of a warrior.' They hastened towards the smoke and approached thither, watching from afar as Dillus the Bearded was singeing a wild boar. Now, he was the mightiest warrior that ever fled from Arthur. Then Bedwyr said to Cei, 'Dost know him?' 'I know him,' said Cei; 'that is Dillus the Bearded. There is no leash in the world may hold Drudwyn the whelp of Greid son of Eri, save a leash from the beard of him thou seest yonder. And that too will be of no use unless it be plucked alive with wooden tweezers from his beard; for it will be brittle, dead.' 'What is our counsel concerning that?' asked Bedwyr. 'Let us suffer him,' said Cei, 'to eat his fill of meat and after that he will fall asleep.' Whilst he was about this, they busied themselves making tweezers. When Cei knew for certain that he was asleep, he dug a pit under his feet, the biggest in the world, and he struck him a blow mighty past telling, and pressed him down in the pit until they had entirely twitched out his beard with the tweezers; and after that they slew him outright.

And then the two of them went to Celli Wig in Cornwall, and a leash from Dillus the Bearded's beard with them. And Cei gave it into Arthur's hand, and thereupon Arthur sang this englyn:

> Cei made a leash
> From Dillus' beard, son of Eurei.
> Were he alive, thy death he'd be.

And because of this Cei grew angry, so that it was with difficulty the warriors of this Island made peace between Cei and Arthur. But nevertheless, neither for Arthur's lack of help, nor for the

slaying of his men, did Cei have aught to do with him in his
hour of need from that time forward.

And then Arthur said, 'Which of the marvels will it now be
best to seek?' 'It will be best to seek Drudwyn the whelp of
Greid son of Eri.'

A short while before this Creiddylad daughter of Lludd Silver-
hand went with Gwythyr son of Greidawl; and before he had
slept with her there came Gwyn son of Nudd and carried her
off by force. Gwythyr son of Greidawl gathered a host, and he
came to fight with Gwyn son of Nudd. And Gwyn prevailed,
and he took prisoner Greid son of Eri, Glinneu son of Taran,
and Gwrgwst the Half-naked and Dyfnarth his son. And he
took prisoner Pen son of Nethawg, and Nwython, and Cyledyr
the Wild his son, and slew Nwython and took out his heart,
and compelled Cyledyr to eat his father's heart; and because of
this Cyledyr went mad. Arthur heard tell of this, and he came
into the North and summoned to him Gwyn son of Nudd and
set free his noblemen from his prison, and peace was made
between Gwyn son of Nudd and Gwythyr son of Greidawl.
This is the peace that was made: the maiden should remain in
her father's house, unmolested by either side, and there should
be battle between Gwyn and Gwythyr each May-calends for
ever and ever, from that day till doomsday; and the one of them
that should be victor on doomsday, let him have the maiden.

And when those lords had been thus reconciled, Arthur
obtained Dun-mane the steed of Gweddw, and the leash of
Cors Hundred-claws.

After that Arthur made his way to Llydaw, and with him
Mabon son of Mellt and Gware Golden-hair, to seek the two
dogs of Glythfyr Ledewig. And when he had obtained them,
Arthur went to the west of Ireland to seek out Gwrgi Seferi,
and Odgar son of Aedd king of Ireland along with him. And
after that Arthur went into the North and caught Cyledyr the
Wild; and he went after Ysgithyrwyn Chief Boar. And Mabon
son of Mellt went, and the two dogs of Glythfyr Ledewig in his
hand, and Drudwyn the whelp of Greid son of Eri. And Arthur

himself took his place in the hunt, and Cafall, Arthur's dog, in
his hand. And Cadw of Prydein mounted Llamrei, Arthur's
mare, and he was the first to bring the boar to bay. And then
Cadw of Prydein armed him with a hatchet, and boldly and
gallantly set upon the boar and split his head in two. And Cadw
took the tusk. It was not the dogs which Ysbaddaden had named
to Culhwch which killed the boar, but Cafall, Arthur's own dog.

And after Ysgithyrwyn Chief Boar was slain, Arthur and his
host went to Celli Wig in Cornwall; and thence he sent Menw
son of Teirgwaedd to see whether the treasures were between
the two ears of Twrch Trwyth – so mean a thing would it be to
go to fight with him, had he not those treasures. However, it
was certain that he was there; he had already laid waste the third
part of Ireland. Menw went to seek them out. He saw them in
Esgeir Oerfel in Ireland. And Menw transformed himself into
the likeness of a bird and alighted over his lair and sought to
snatch one of the treasures away from him. But for all that he
got nothing save one of his bristles. The other arose in his might
and shook himself so that some of his poison caught him. And
after that Menw was never without scathe.

After that Arthur sent a messenger to Odgar son of Aedd king
of Ireland, to ask for the cauldron of Diwrnach the Irishman,
his overseer. Odgar besought him to give it. Said Diwrnach,
'God knows, though he should be the better for getting one
glimpse of it, he should not have it.' And Arthur's messenger
came back from Ireland with a nay. Arthur set out and a light
force with him, and went in Prydwen his ship, and came to
Ireland, and they made for the house of Diwrnach the Irishman.
The hosts of Odgar took note of their strength; and after they
had eaten and drunk their fill Arthur demanded the cauldron.
He made answer that were he to give it to any one, he would
have given it at the word of Odgar king of Ireland. When he
had spoken them nay, Bedwyr arose and laid hold of the cauldron and put it on the back of Hygwydd, Arthur's servant; he
was brother by the same mother to Cacamwri, Arthur's servant.
His office was always to carry Arthur's cauldron and to kindle

fire under it. Llenlleawg the Irishman seized Caledfwlch and swung it in a round and he slew Diwrnach the Irishman and all his host. The hosts of Ireland came and fought with them. And when the hosts were utterly routed Arthur and his men went on board ship before their very eyes, and with them the cauldron full of the treasures of Ireland. And they disembarked at the house of Llwydeu son of Cel Coed, at Porth Cerddin in Dyfed. And Mesur-y-Peir is there.[30]

And then Arthur gathered together what warriors there were in the Island of Britain and its three adjacent islands, and what there were in France and Brittany and Normandy and the Summer Country, and what there were of picked dogs and horses of renown. And with all those hosts he went to Ireland, and at his coming there was great fear and trembling in Ireland. And when Arthur had come to land, there came to him the saints of Ireland to ask his protection. And he granted them protection, and they gave him their blessing. The men of Ireland came to Arthur and gave him a tribute of victuals. Arthur came to Esgeir Oerfel in Ireland, to the place where Twrch Trwyth was, and his seven young pigs with him. Dogs were let loose at him from all sides. That day until evening the Irish fought with him; nevertheless he laid waste one of the five provinces of Ireland. And on the morrow Arthur's war-band fought with him: save for what evil they got from him, they got nothing good. The third day Arthur himself fought with him, nine nights and nine days: he slew of his pigs but one pigling. His men asked Arthur what was the history of that swine, and he told them: 'He was a king, and for his wickedness God transformed him into a swine.'

Arthur sent Gwyrhyr Interpreter of Tongues to seek to have word with him. Gwyrhyr went in the form of a bird and alighted above the lair of him and his seven young pigs. And Gwyrhyr Interpreter of Tongues asked him, 'For His sake who made thee in this shape, if you can speak, I beseech one of you to come and talk with Arthur.' Grugyn Silver-bristle made answer. Like wings of silver were all his bristles; what way he went through

---

30 Mesur-y-Peir. The place-name has apparently not survived. Its elements mean 'Measure of the Cauldron', but the explanation is onomastic.

wood and meadow one could discern from how his bristles glittered. This was the answer Grugyn gave: 'By Him who made us in this shape, we will neither do nor say aught for Arthur. Harm enough hath God wrought us, to have made us in this shape, without you too coming to fight with us.' 'I tell you, Arthur will fight for the comb, the razor and the shears which are between the two ears of Twrch Trwyth.' Said Grugyn, 'Until first his life be taken, those treasures will not be taken. And to-morrow in the morning we will set out hence and go into Arthur's country, and there we will do all the mischief we can.'

They set out by sea towards Wales; and Arthur and his hosts, his horses and his dogs, went aboard Prydwen, and in the twinkling of an eye they saw them. Twrch Trwyth came to land at Porth Cleis in Dyfed. That night Arthur came as far as Mynyw. On the morrow Arthur was told they had gone by, and he overtook him killing the cattle of Cynwas Cwryfagyl, after slaying what men and beasts were in Deu Gleddyf before the coming of Arthur.

From the time of Arthur's coming, Twrch Trwyth made off thence to Preseleu. Arthur and the hosts of the world came thither. Arthur sent his men to the hunt, Eli and Trachmyr, and Drudwyn the whelp of Greid son of Eri in his own hand; and Gwarthegydd son of Caw in another quarter, with the two dogs of Glythfyr Ledewig in his hand; and Bedwyr with Arthur's dog Cafall in his hand. And he ranged all the warriors on either side of the Nyfer. There came the three sons of Cleddyf Difwlch, men who had won great fame at the slaying of Ysgithyrwyn Chief Boar. And then he set out from Glyn Nyfer and came to Cwm Cerwyn, and there he stood at bay. And he then slew four of Arthur's champions, Gwarthegydd son of Caw, Tarawg of Allt Clwyd, Rheiddwn son of Eli Adfer, and Isgofan the Generous. And after he had slain those men, again he stood at bay against them there, and slew Gwydre son of Arthur, Garselit the Irishman, Glew son of Ysgawd, and Isgawyn son of Banon. And then he himself was wounded.

And the morrow's morn at point of day some of the men caught up with him. And then he slew Huandaw and Gogigwr and Penpingon, the three servants of Glewlwyd Mighty-grasp, so that God knows he had never a servant left to him in the world, save only Llaesgymyn,[31] a man for whom none was the better. And over and above those he slew many a man of the country, and Gwlyddyn the Craftsman, Arthur's chief builder. And then Arthur caught up with him at Peluniawg, and he then slew Madawg son of Teithion, and Gwyn son of Tringad son of Neued, and Eiriawn Penlloran. And thence he went to Aber Tywi. And there he stood at bay against them, and he then slew Cynlas son of Cynan and Gwilenhin king of France. Thereafter he went to Glyn Ystun, and then the men and dogs lost him.

Arthur summoned to him Gwyn son of Nudd and asked him whether he knew aught of Twrch Trwyth. He said he did not. Thereupon all the huntsmen went to hunt the pigs as far as Dyffryn Llychwr. And Grugyn Silver-bristle and Llwydawg the Hewer dashed into them and slew the huntsmen so that not a soul of them escaped alive, save one man only. So Arthur and his hosts came to the place where Grugyn and Llwydawg were. And then he let loose upon them all the dogs that had been named to this end. And at the clamour that was then raised, and the barking, Twrch Trwyth came up and defended them. And ever since they had crossed the Irish Sea, he had not set eyes on them till now. Then was he beset by men and dogs. With might and with main he went to Mynydd Amanw, and then a pigling was slain of his pigs. And then they joined with him life for life, and it was then Twrch Llawin was slain. And then another of his pigs was slain, Gwys was his name. And he then went to Dyffryn Amanw, and there Banw and Benwig were slain. Not one of his pigs went with him alive from that place, save Grugyn Silver-bristle and Llwydawg the Hewer.

From that place they went on to Llwch Ewin, and Arthur caught up with him there. Then he stood at bay. And then he slew Echel Big-hip, and Arwyli son of Gwyddawg Gwyr, and many a man and dog besides. And after that they went on to Llwch Tawy. Grugyn Silver-bristle then parted from them, and Grugyn thereafter made for Din Tywi. And he proceeded then into Ceredigiawn, and Eli and Trachmyr with him, and a multi-

31 Llaesgymyn: Slack-hewer.

tude along with them besides. And he came as far as Garth
Grugyn. And there Grugyn was slain in their midst, and he
slew Rhuddfyw Rhys and many a man with him. And then
Llwydawg went on to Ystrad Yw. And there the men of Llydaw
met with him, and he then slew Hir Peisawg king of Llydaw,
and Llygadrudd Emys and Gwrfoddw, Arthur's uncles, his
mother's brothers. And there he himself was slain.

Twrch Trwyth went then between Tawy and Ewyas. Arthur
summoned Cornwall and Devon to meet him at the mouth of
the Severn. And Arthur said to the warriors of this Island:
'Twrch Trwyth has slain many of my men. By the valour of men,
not while I am alive shall he go into Cornwall. I will pursue him
no further, but I will join with him life for life. You, do what you
will.' And by his counsel a body of horsemen was sent, and the
dogs of the Island with them, as far as Ewyas, and they beat back
thence to the Severn, and they waylaid him there with what tried
warriors there were in this Island, and drove him by sheer force
into Severn. And Mabon son of Modron went with him into
Severn, on Gwyn Dun-mane the steed of Gweddw, and Goreu
son of Custennin and Menw son of Teirgwaedd, between Llyn
Lliwan and Aber Gwy. And Arthur fell upon him, and the
champions of Britain along with him. Osla Big-knife drew near,
and Manawydan son of Llŷr, and Cacamwri, Arthur's servant,
and Gwyngelli, and closed in on him. And first they laid hold of
his feet, and soused him in Severn till it was flooding over him.
On the one side Mabon son of Modron spurred his horse and
took the razor from him, and on the other Cyledyr the Wild, on
another horse, plunged into Severn with him and took from him
the shears. But or ever the comb could be taken he found land
with his feet; and from the moment he found land neither dog
nor man nor horse could keep up with him until he went into
Cornwall. Whatever mischief was come by in seeking those
treasures from him, worse was come by in seeking to save the
two men from drowning. Cacamwri, as he was dragged forth,
two quernstones dragged him into the depths. As Osla Big-knife
was running after the boar, his knife fell out of its sheath and he
lost it; and his sheath thereafter being full of water, as he was
dragged forth, it dragged him back into the depths.

Then Arthur went with his hosts until he caught up with him in Cornwall. Whatever mischief was come by before that was play to what was come by then in seeking the comb. But from mischief to mischief the comb was won from him. And then he was forced out of Cornwall and driven straight forward into the sea. From that time forth never a one has known where he went, and Aned and Aethlem with him. And Arthur went thence to Celli Wig in Cornwall, to bathe himself and rid him of his weariness.

Said Arthur, 'Is there any of the marvels still unobtained?' Said one of the men, 'There is: the blood of the Black Witch, daughter of the White Witch, from the head of the Valley of Grief in the uplands of Hell.' Arthur set out for the North and came to where the hag's cave was. And it was the counsel of Gwyn son of Nudd and Gwythyr son of Greidawl that Cacamwri and Hygwydd his brother be sent to fight with the hag. And as they came inside the cave the hag grabbed at them, and caught Hygwydd by the hair of his head and flung him to the floor beneath her. And Cacamwri seized her by the hair of her head, and dragged her to the ground off Hygwydd, but she then turned on Cacamwri and dressed them down both and disarmed them, and drove them out squealing and squalling. And Arthur was angered to see his two servants well nigh slain, and he sought to seize the cave. And then Gwyn and Gwythyr told him, 'It is neither seemly nor pleasant for us to see thee scuffling with a hag. Send Long Amren and Long Eiddil into the cave.' And they went. But if ill was the plight of the first two, the plight of those two was worse, so that God knows not one of the whole four could have stirred from the place, but for the way they were all four loaded on Llamrei, Arthur's mare. And then Arthur seized the entrance to the cave, and from the entrance he took aim at the hag with Carnwennan his knife, and struck her across the middle until she was as two tubs. And Cadw of Prydein took the witch's blood and kept it with him.

And then Culhwch set forth, and Goreu son of Custennin with him, and every one that wished ill to Ysbaddaden Chief Giant, and those marvels with them to his court. And Cadw of Prydein came to shave his beard, flesh and skin to the bone, and his two ears outright. And Culhwch said, 'Hast thou had thy shave, man?' 'I have,' said he. 'And is thy daughter mine now?' 'Thine,' said he. 'And thou needst not thank me for that, but thank Arthur who has secured her for thee. Of my own free will thou shouldst never have had her. And it is high time to take away my life.' And then Goreu son of Custennin caught him by the hair of his head and dragged him behind him to the mound, and cut off his head, and set it on the bailey-stake. And he took possession of his fort and his dominions.

And that night Culhwch slept with Olwen, and she was his only wife so long as he lived. And the hosts of Arthur dispersed, every one to his country.

And in this wise did Culhwch win Olwen daughter of Ysbaddaden Chief Giant.

THE DREAM OF RHONABWY

Madawg son of Maredudd held Powys from end to end, that is, from Porffordd unto Gwafan in the uplands of Arwystli. And at that time he had a brother. He was not a man of rank equal with himself: he was Iorwoerth son of Maredudd. And he felt great heaviness and sorrow at seeing the honour and power that were his brother's, whereas he had naught. And he sought out his comrades and foster-brothers and took counsel of them what he should do about it. They decided by their counsel to send some from amongst them to demand provision for him. The offer Madawg made him was the captaincy of his war-band, and equal standing with himself, and steeds and arms and honour. And Iorwoerth rejected that, and went harrying into Lloegyr. And Iorwoerth made slaughter and burned houses and carried off prisoners.

And Madawg took counsel, and the men of Powys with him. They decided by their counsel to place a hundred men in every three commots in Powys, to seek him out. And they reckoned Rhychdir Powys, from Aber Ceirawg in Hallictwn as far as the Ford of Wilfre on Efyrnwy, as equal to the three best commots that were in Powys. And the man would not prosper with a war-band in Powys who would not prosper in that cultivated land. And as far as Didlystwn, a hamlet in that cultivated land, those men took their quarters.

And there was a man on that quest, his name was Rhonabwy. And Rhonabwy and Cynwrig Frychgoch, a man from Mawddwy, and Cadwgawn Fras, a man from Moelfre in Cynlleith, came to the house of Heilyn Goch son of Cadwgawn son of Iddon for lodgings. And as they came towards the house, they could see a black old hall with a straight gable end, and smoke a-plenty from it. And when they came inside, they could see a floor full of holes and uneven. Where there was a bump upon it, it was with difficulty a man might stand thereon, so exceeding slippery was the floor with cows' urine and their dung. Where there was a hole, a man would go over the ankle, what with the mixture of water and cow-dung; and branches of holly a-plenty on the floor after the cattle had eaten off their tips. And when they came to the main floor of the house they could see bare dusty dais boards, and a crone feeding a fire on the one dais, and when cold came upon her she would throw a lapful of husks on to the fire, so that it was not easy for any man alive to endure that smoke entering his nostrils. And on the other dais they could see a yellow ox skin. And good luck would it be for the one of them whose lot it would be to go on that skin.

And after they had sat down they asked the crone where were the people of the house. But the crone spoke nothing to them save incivility. And thereupon, lo, the people coming: a red-headed, exceeding bald and wizened man, with a bundle of sticks on his back, and a little skinny livid woman, and with her too a bundle under the arm. And a cold welcome they had for the men. And the woman lit a fire of sticks for them and went to cook, and brought them their food, barley-bread and cheese and watered milk.

And thereupon, lo, a storm of wind and rain, so that it was not easy for any to go to relieve himself. And so exceeding weary were they from their journey that they drowsed and went to sleep.

And when their resting-place was examined there was nothing on it save dusty flea-ridden straw-ends, and branch butts a-plenty throughout it, after the oxen had eaten all the straw that was on it above their heads and below their feet. A greyish-red, threadbare, flea-infested blanket was spread thereon, and over the blanket a coarse broken sheet in tatters, and a half-empty pillow and filthy pillow-case thereon, on top of the sheet. And they went to sleep. And sleep came heavily upon Rhonabwy's two companions after the fleas and the discomfort had fretted them. And Rhonabwy, since he could neither sleep nor rest, thought it would be less of a torture for him to go on the yellow ox skin on the dais, to sleep. And there he slept.

And the moment sleep came upon his eyes he was granted a vision, how he and his companions were traversing the plain of Argyngroeg; and his mind and purpose, it seemed to him, were towards Rhyd-y-Groes on the Severn. And as he journeyed he heard a commotion, and the like of that commotion he had never heard. And he looked behind him.

He could see a youth with yellow curly hair and his beard new trimmed, upon a yellow horse, and from the top of his two legs and the caps of his knees downwards green. And a tunic of yellow brocaded silk about the rider, sewn with green thread, and a gold-hilted sword on his thigh, and a scabbard of new cordwain for it, and a deerskin thong and a clasp of gold thereon. And over and above those a mantle of yellow brocaded silk sewn with green silk, and the fringes of the mantle green. And what was green of the rider's and his horse's apparel was green as the fronds of the fir trees, and what was yellow of it was yellow as the flowers of the broom. And so awe-inspiring did they see the rider that they were frightened and made to flee. And the rider pursued them, and when the horse breathed forth his breath the men grew distant from him, and when he drew it in they were drawn near to him, right to the horse's chest. And when he caught up with them they asked him for quarter. 'You shall have it gladly, and let there be no fear upon you.' 'Ah, chieftain, since thou hast granted us quarter, wilt thou tell us who thou art?' said Rhonabwy. 'I will not hide my identity from thee: Iddawg son of Mynio. But for the most part it is not by my name I am spoken of, but by my nickname.' 'Wilt thou tell us what thy nickname is?' 'I will. Iddawg the Embroiler of Britain am I called.' 'Chieftain,' said Rhonabwy, 'for what reason then art thou so called?' 'I will tell thee the reason. I was one of the envoys at the battle of Camlan, between Arthur and Medrawd his nephew. And a spirited young man was I then! And I so craved for battle that I kindled strife between them. This was the kind of strife I kindled: when the emperor Arthur would send me to remind Medrawd that he was his foster-father and uncle, and ask for peace lest the kings' sons of the Island of Britain and their noblemen should be slain, and when Arthur would speak to me the fairest words he could, I would speak those words the ugliest way I knew how to Medrawd. And because of that the name Iddawg the Embroiler of Britain was set on me. And because of that was woven the battle of Camlan.

But even so, three nights before the end of the battle of Camlan I parted from them, and I went to Y Llech Las[1] in Prydein to do penance. And I was there seven years doing penance, and I won pardon.'

Thereupon, lo, they could hear a commotion which was greater by far than the former commotion. And when they looked in the direction of the commotion, lo, a young man with yellow-red hair, without beard and without moustache, and a nobleman's bearing upon him, on a great charger. And from the top of his shoulders and the caps of his knees downwards the horse was yellow, and a garment about the man of red brocaded silk, sewn with yellow silk, and the fringes of the mantle yellow. And what was yellow of his and his horse's apparel was yellow as the flowers of the broom, and what of them was red was red as the reddest blood in the world. And then, lo, the rider overtaking them and asking Iddawg if he might have a share of those little fellows from him. 'The share it is proper for me to give, I will give: to be a comrade to them even as I myself have been.' And so the rider did, and went away. 'Iddawg,' said Rhonabwy, 'who was this horseman?' 'Rhwawn Bebyr son of Deorthach Wledig.'

And then they traversed the great plain of Argyngroeg as far as Rhyd-y-Groes on the Severn. And a mile from the ford, on either side the road, they could see the tents and the pavilions and the mustering of a great host. And they came to the bank of the ford. They could see Arthur seated on a flat island below the ford, and on one side of him Bedwin the bishop, and on the other side Gwarthegydd son of Caw, and a big auburn-haired youth standing before them, with his sword in its sheath in his hand, and a tunic and surcoat of pure black brocaded silk about him, and his face as white as ivory and his eyebrows black as jet; and where a man might see aught of his wrist between his gloves and his sleeves, it was whiter than the water-lily, and thicker it was than the small of a warrior's leg.

And then Iddawg and they too along with him came before Arthur and greeted him. 'God prosper thee,' said Arthur.

---

1 Y Llech Las: The Blue *or* Green *or* Grey Stone.

'Where, Iddawg, didst thou find those little fellows?' 'I found them, lord, away up on the road.' The emperor smiled wrily. 'Lord,' said Iddawg, 'at what art thou laughing?' 'Iddawg,' said Arthur, 'I am not laughing; but rather how sad I feel that men as mean as these keep this Island, after men as fine as those that kept it of yore.'

And then Iddawg said, 'Rhonabwy, dost see the ring with the stone in it on the emperor's hand?' 'I do,' said he. 'It is one of the virtues of the stone that thou shalt remember what thou hast seen here to-night. And hadst thou not seen the stone, thou shouldst remember not a whit of this adventure.'

And after that he saw a troop coming towards the ford. 'Iddawg,' said Rhonabwy, 'whose is the troop yonder?' 'The comrades of Rhwawn Bebyr son of Deorthach Wledig; and yonder men have mead and bragget in honour, and they have the wooing of the kings' daughters of the Island of Britain, without let; and they have a right thereto, for in every strait they come in his van and in his rear.' And no other colour could he see upon horse or man of that troop save that they were red as blood. And if one of the riders parted from that troop, like to a pillar of fire would he be, mounting into the sky. And that troop pitching its tents above the ford.

And thereupon they could see another troop coming towards the ford, and from the front saddlebows of the horses upwards as white as the water-lily, and thence downwards as black as jet. They could see a rider coming on ahead and spurring his horse into the ford till the water splashed over Arthur and the bishop and those who held counsel along with them, until they were as wet as if they had been dragged out of the river. And as he was turning his horse's head, the youth who was standing in front of Arthur struck the horse on its nostrils with the sword in its scabbard, so that it would be a marvel were it struck upon iron that it were not broken, let alone flesh or bone. And the rider drew his sword the length of half his scabbard and asked him, 'Why didst thou strike my horse, by way of insult, or by way of counsel to me?' 'Thou hadst need of counsel. What madness could make thee ride so recklessly that the water of the ford was splashed over Arthur and the holy bishop and their counsellors, till they were as wet as if they had been dragged out of the river?' 'Then I shall take it as counsel.' And he turned his horse's head back towards his troop.

'Iddawg,' said Rhonabwy, 'who was the rider just now?' 'He who is reckoned the most accomplished and wisest young man in this kingdom, Addaon son of Teliesin.' 'And who was the man who struck his horse?' 'A cross-grained froward youth, Elphin son of Gwyddno.'

And then a proud handsome man, with bold eloquent speech, said that it was a marvel how a host so big as this was contained within a place so exceeding strait as this; and that it was to him a greater marvel how there should be here at this very hour those who promised to be in the battle of Baddon by mid-day, fighting against Osla Big-knife. 'And choose thou, whether thou go or go not. I shall go.' 'Thou speakest true,' said Arthur, 'and let us go together.' 'Iddawg,' said Rhonabwy, 'who is the man who spoke so frowardly to Arthur as he spoke just now?' 'A man who had a right to speak to him as bluntly as he wished, Caradawg Stout-arm son of Llŷr Marini, chief counsellor and his first cousin.'

And after that Iddawg took Rhonabwy up behind him, and they set out, that great host, each troop in its place, in the direction of Cefyn Digoll. And when they had come to the middle of the ford on the Severn, Iddawg turned his horse's head around, and Rhonabwy looked upon the valley of the Severn. He could see two most leisurely troops coming towards the ford on the Severn; and a brilliant white troop coming, and a mantle of white brocaded silk about each man of them, and the fringes of each one pure black, and the knee-caps and the tops of the horses' two legs black, and the horses pale white all over save for that; and their standards pure white, and the tip of each one of them pure black.

'Iddawg,' said Rhonabwy, 'what is the pure white troop yonder?' 'Those are the men of Llychlyn,[2] and March son of Meirchawn at their head. A first cousin of Arthur is he.'

And then he could see a troop, and a pure black garment

2 Llychlyn: Scandinavia.

about each one of them, and the fringes of each mantle pure white, and from the top of the horses' two legs and the caps of their knees pure white; and their standards pure black, and the tip of each one of them pure white.

'Iddawg,' said Rhonabwy, 'what is the pure black troop yonder?' 'The men of Denmark, and Edern son of Nudd at their head.'

And when they overtook the host, Arthur and his host of the Mighty had descended below Caer Faddon, and the way that Arthur was going he could see that he and Iddawg were going too. And when they had descended, he could hear great and dreadful commotion amongst the host, and the man who would be now on the flank of the host would be back in their centre, and he who would be in their centre would be on the flank. And thereupon, lo, he could see a rider coming with mail upon him and his horse, and its rings as white as the whitest water-lily, and its rivets red as the reddest blood. And he riding in amongst the host.

'Iddawg,' said Rhonabwy, 'is the host fleeing before me?' 'The emperor Arthur never fled. And hadst thou been overheard making that remark thou wert a doomed man. But the rider thou seest yonder, that is Cei. The fairest man who rides in Arthur's court is Cei. And the man on the flank of the host is hurrying back to the centre to look on Cei riding, and the man in the centre is fleeing to the flank lest he be hurt by the horse. And that is the meaning of the commotion amongst the host.'

Thereupon they could hear Cadwr earl of Cornwall called for. Lo, he arising, and Arthur's sword in his hand, and the image of two serpents on the sword in gold; and when the sword was drawn from its sheath as it were two flames of fire might be seen from the mouths of the serpents, and so exceeding dreadful was it that it was not easy for any to look thereon. Thereupon, lo, the host settling down and the commotion ceasing. And the earl returned to the tent.

'Iddawg,' said Rhonabwy, 'who was the man who brought the sword to Arthur?' 'Cadwr earl of Cornwall, the man whose duty it is to array the king in arms on the day of battle and combat.'

And thereupon they could hear Arthur's servitor, Eiryn Wych

son of Peibyn, called for, a rough red-headed ugly man, with a red moustache, and bristling hair therein. Lo, he coming on a big red horse, with its mane parted on both sides of its neck, and with him a large handsome pack. And the big red servitor dismounted in Arthur's presence and drew forth a golden chair from the pack, and a mantle of ribbed brocaded silk. And he spread the mantle in front of Arthur, and an apple of red gold at each of its corners, and he set the chair on the mantle, and so big was the chair that three warriors armed might sit therein. Gwen[3] was the name of the mantle. And one of the properties of the mantle was that the man around whom it might be wrapped, no one would see him, whereas he would see every one. And no colour would ever abide on it save its own colour.

And Arthur seated himself upon the mantle, with Owein son of Urien standing before him. 'Owein,' said Arthur, 'wilt play gwyddbwyll?' 'I will, lord,' said Owein. And the red-headed servitor brought the gwyddbwyll to Arthur and Owein: gold pieces and a board of silver. And they began to play.

And when they were in this wise most engrossed in play over the gwyddbwyll, lo, they could see coming from a white red-topped pavilion, with the image of a pure black serpent on top of the pavilion, and bright red venomous eyes in the serpent's head, and its tongue flame-red, a young, curly-yellow-haired, blue-eyed squire, with a beard starting, and a tunic and surcoat of yellow brocaded silk about him, and a pair of hose of thin greenish-yellow cloth upon his feet, and over the hose two buskins of speckled cordwain, and buckles of gold across his insteps fastening them, and a heavy gold-hilted triple-grooved sword and a scabbard of black cordwain to it, and a tip of refined red gold to the scabbard, coming towards the place where the emperor and Owein were playing gwyddbwyll.

And the squire greeted Owein. And Owein marvelled that the squire greeted him and did not greet the emperor Arthur. And Arthur knew it was of that Owein was thinking, and he said to Owein, 'Marvel not that the squire greeted thee just now. He greeted me a while back. And it is to thee that his message

3 Gwen: White, fair.

is.' And then the squire said to Owein, 'Lord, is it with thy leave that the emperor's bachelors and his squires are contending with and harassing and molesting thy ravens? And if it is not with thy leave, have the emperor call them off.' 'Lord,' said Owein, 'thou hearest what the squire says? If it please thee, call them off my little ravens.' 'Play thy game,' said he. And then the squire returned towards his pavilion.

They finished that game and started another. And when they were towards the middle of the game, lo, a young ruddy curly-headed, auburn-haired, keen-eyed, well-built attendant, with his beard shaved, coming from a bright yellow pavilion, with the image of a bright red lion on top of the pavilion, and a tunic of yellow brocaded silk about him reaching to the small of his leg, sewn with threads of red silk, and a pair of hose on his feet of fine white buckram, and over and above the hose two buskins of black cordwain on his feet, and clasps of red gold upon them, and a huge heavy triple-grooved sword in his hand, and a sheath of red deerskin to it, and a gold tip to the scabbard, coming towards the place where Arthur and Owein were playing gwyddbwyll.

And he greeted him. And Owein was put out at being greeted, but Arthur was no more taken aback than before. The squire said to Owein, 'Is it against thy will that the emperor's squires are wounding thy ravens, killing some and molesting others? And if it is against thy will, beseech him to call them off.' 'Lord,' said Owein, 'call off thy men, if it please thee.' 'Play thy game,' said the emperor. And then the squire returned towards his pavilion.

That game was ended and another begun. And as they were beginning the first move in the game, they could see some distance away from them a spotted yellow pavilion, the largest that any one had seen, and the image of a golden eagle thereon, and a precious stone in the eagle's head. Coming from the pavilion they could see a squire with crisp yellow hair upon his head, fair and graceful, and a mantle of green brocaded silk about him, and a gold brooch in the mantle on his right shoulder as thick as a warrior's third finger, and a pair of hose upon his feet of fine totnes, and a pair of shoes of speckled cordwain upon his feet, and gold clasps thereto; the youth noble of countenance, with white face and ruddy cheeks, and great hawk-like eyes. In the squire's hand there was a thick speckled yellow spear, and a newly sharpened head on it, and upon the spear a conspicuous standard.

The squire came with rage and passion at a quick canter to the place where Arthur was playing with Owein over the gwyddbwyll. And they saw how he was in a rage. But even so he greeted Owein and told him how the most notable ravens among them had been slain. 'And those of them that are not slain have been wounded and hurt to that extent that not one of them can lift its wings one fathom from the ground.' 'Lord,' said Owein, 'call off thy men.' 'Play,' said he, 'if thou wilt.' And then Owein said to the squire, 'Away with thee, and in the place where thou seest the battle hardest raise on high the standard, and let it be as God will.'

And then the squire went on his way to the place where the battle was hardest on the ravens, and raised on high the standard. And even as it was raised, they too rose into the air in passion, rage and exultation, to let wind into their wings and to throw off their weariness. And having recovered their strength and their magic powers, in rage and exultation they straightway swooped down to earth upon the men who had earlier inflicted hurt and injury and loss upon them. Of some they were carrying off the heads, of others the eyes, of others the ears, and of others the arms; and they were raising them up into the air, and there was a great commotion in the air, what with the fluttering of the exultant ravens and their croaking, and another great commotion what with the cries of the men being gashed and wounded and others being slain. And Arthur's amazement was as great as Owein's over the gwyddbwyll, hearing that commotion.

And as they looked they could hear a rider coming towards them upon a dapple-grey horse. An exceeding strange colour was upon his horse, dapple-grey and his right leg bright red, and from the top of his legs to the middle of his hoof-horn bright yellow; the rider and his horse arrayed in heavy foreign armour. The housing of his horse from his front saddlebow upwards pure red sendal, and from the saddlebow downwards pure yellow sendal. A huge gold-hilted one-edged sword on the youth's thigh, and a new bright green scabbard to it, and a tip to the scabbard of laton of Spain; his sword belt of black fleecy cordwain, and gilt cross-bars upon it, and a clasp of ivory thereon. And a pure black tongue to the clasp. A gold helm upon the rider's head, and precious stones of great virtue therein, and on top of the helm the image of a yellow-red leopard with two bright red stones in its head, so that it was dreadful for a warrior, however stout his heart might be, to look on the face of the leopard, let alone on the face of the rider. A long heavy green-shafted spear in his hand, and from its hand-grip upwards bright red; the head of the spear red with the blood of the ravens and their plumage.

The rider came to the place where Arthur and Owein were over the gwyddbwyll, and they could see how he was weary and ill-tempered coming towards them. The squire greeted Arthur and said that Owein's ravens were slaying his bachelors and squires. And Arthur looked at Owein and said, 'Call off thy ravens.' 'Lord,' said Owein, 'play thy game.' And they played. The rider returned towards the battle, and the ravens were no more called off than before.

And when they had played awhile they could hear a great commotion, and the shrieking of men and the croaking of ravens in their strength bearing the men into the air and rending them betwixt them and letting them fall in pieces to the ground.

And out of the commotion they could see a horseman coming on a pale white horse, and the left leg of the horse pure black down to the middle of his hoof; the rider arrayed, he and his horse, in great heavy green armour, a surcoat about him of yellow ribbed brocaded silk, and the fringes of his cloak green. The housing of his horse pure black, and its fringes pure yellow. On the squire's thigh was a long heavy triple-grooved sword, and a sheath of red embossed leather to it, and the belt of fresh red deerskin, with many gold cross-bars thereon, and a clasp of walrus-ivory with a pure black tongue thereto. A gold helm on the rider's head, and magic sapphires in it, and on top of the helm the image of a yellow-red lion, and his tongue flame-red a foot-length out of his mouth, and bright red venomous eyes in his head. The rider coming with a stout ashen spear-shaft in his hand, and a new bloodstained head to it, and silver rivets therein. And the squire greeted the emperor. 'Lord,' said he, 'thy squires and thy bachelors have been slain, and the noblemen's sons of the Island of Britain, so that it will not be easy to defend this Island from this day forth for ever.' 'Owein,' said Arthur, 'call off thy ravens.' 'Lord,' said Owein, 'play this game.'

That game was ended and another begun. And when they were at the end of that game, lo, they could hear a great commotion and a shrieking of armed men and the croaking of ravens and their flapping their wings in the air and dropping the armour unshattered to the ground and dropping the men and the horses in pieces to the ground.

And then they could see a rider on a handsome black high-headed horse, and the top of the horse's left leg pure red, and his right leg to the middle of his hoof pure white; the rider and his horse arrayed in spotted yellow armour speckled with laton of Spain, and a cloak about him and about his horse, in two halves, white and pure black, and the fringes of his cloak of golden purple, and over his cloak a gold-hilted gleaming triple-grooved sword, the sword belt of yellow cloth of gold, and a clasp upon it of the eyelid of a pure black whale, and a tongue of yellow gold on the clasp. A gleaming helm of yellow laton on the rider's head, and gleaming crystal stones therein, and on top of the helm the image of a griffin, and a magic stone in his head; an ashen spear with rounded shaft in his hand, coloured with blue-azure; a new bloodstained point upon the shaft, riveted with refined silver. And the rider came in a rage to the place where Arthur was, and said how the ravens had slain his war-band and the noblemen's sons of this Island, and bade him have Owein call off his ravens. Then Arthur bade Owein call off his ravens. And then Arthur crushed the golden pieces that were on the board till they were all dust. And Owein bade Gwres son of Rheged lower his banner. And therewith it was lowered and all was peace.

Then Rhonabwy asked Iddawg who were the first three men who came to Owein to tell him how his ravens were being slain, and Iddawg said: 'Men who grieved that Owein should suffer loss, fellow chieftains and comrades of his, Selyf son of Cynan White-shank from Powys, and Gwgawn Red-sword, and Gwres son of Rheged, the man who bears his banner on the day of battle and combat.' 'Who,' asked Rhonabwy, 'are the last three men who came to Arthur to tell him how the ravens were slaying his men?' 'The best of men,' said Iddawg, 'and the bravest, and those to whom it is most hateful that Arthur should suffer loss in aught, Blathaon son of Mwrheth, and Rhwawn Bebyr son of Deorthach Wledig, and Hyfeidd One-cloak.'

And thereupon, lo, four-and-twenty horsemen coming from Osla Big-knife to ask a truce of Arthur till the end of a fortnight and a month. Arthur arose and went to take counsel. He went to the place where some way from him was a big curly-headed auburn man, and his counsellors were brought to him there: Bedwin the bishop, and Gwarthegydd son of Caw, and March son of Meirchawn, and Caradawg Stout-arm, and Gwalchmei son of Gwyar, and Edern son of Nudd, and Rhwawn Bebyr son of Deorthach Wledig, and Rhiogan son of the king of Ireland, and Gwenwynwyn son of Naf, Howel son of Emyr Llydaw, Gwilym son of the ruler of France, and Daned son of Oth, and Goreu son of Custennin, and Mabon son of Modron, and Peredur Longspear and Hyfeidd One-cloak, and Twrch son of Peryf, Nerth son of Cadarn, and Gobrw son of Echel Big-hip, Gweir son of Gwestel, and Cadwy son of Gereint, Dyrstan son of Tallwch, Morien Manawg, Granwen son of Llŷr, and Llacheu son of Arthur, and Llawfrodedd the Bearded, and Cadwr the earl of Cornwall, Morfran son of Tegid, and Rhyawdd son of Morgant, and Dyfyr son of Alun Dyfed, Gwyrhyr Interpreter of Tongues, Addaon son of Teliesin, and Llara son of Casnar Wledig, and Fflewdwr Fflam, and Greidiawl Gallddofydd, Gilbert son of Cadgyffro, Menw son of Teirgwaedd, Gyrthmwl Wledig, Cawrda son of Caradawg Stout-arm, Gildas son of Caw, Cadyrieith son of Saidi, and many a man of Norway and Denmark, and many a man of Greece along with them; and sufficient of a host came to that counsel.

'Iddawg,' said Rhonabwy, 'who is the auburn-haired man to whom they came just now?' 'Rhun son of Maelgwn Gwynedd, a man whose authority is such that all men shall come and take counsel of him.' 'For what reason was so young a youth as Cadyrieith son of Saidi brought into the counsel of men of such high rank as those yonder?' 'Because there was not in Britain a man more mighty in counsel than he.'

And thereupon, lo, bards coming to chant a song to Arthur. But never a man was there might understand that song save Cadyrieith himself, except that it was in praise of Arthur. And thereupon, lo, four-and-twenty asses coming with their burdens of gold and silver, and a weary worn man with each of them, bringing tribute to Arthur from the Isles of Greece. Then Cadyrieith son of Saidi asked that a truce be granted to Osla Big-knife till the end of a fortnight and a month, and that the asses which had brought the tribute be given to the bards, and what was upon them, as an earnest of reward, and that during the truce they should be given payment for their song. And they determined upon that. 'Rhonabwy,' said Iddawg, 'were it not wrong to forbid the young man who gave such munificent counsel as this from going to his lord's counsel?'

And then Cei arose and said, 'Whoever wishes to follow Arthur, let him be with him to-night in Cornwall; and as for him who does not wish that, let him come to meet with Arthur by the end of the truce.'

And with the magnitude of that commotion Rhonabwy awoke, and when he awoke he was on the yellow ox skin, having slept three nights and three days.

And this story is called the Dream of Rhonabwy. And here is the reason why no one, neither bard nor story-teller, knows the Dream without a book – by reason of the number of colours that were on the horses, and all that variety of rare colours both on the arms and their trappings, and on the precious mantles, and the magic stones.

THE THREE ROMANCES

THE LADY OF THE FOUNTAIN

The emperor Arthur was at Caer Llion on Usk. He was sitting one day in his chamber, and with him Owein son of Urien and Cynon son of Clydno and Cei son of Cynyr, and Gwenhwyfar and her handmaidens sewing at a window. And although it was said that there was a porter to Arthur's court, there was none. Glewlwyd Mighty-grasp was there, however, with the rank of porter, to receive guests and far-comers, and to begin to do them honour, and to make known to them the ways and usage of the court: whoever had right to go to the hall or chamber, to make it known to him; whoever had right to a lodging, to make it known to him. And in the middle of the chamber floor the emperor Arthur was seated on a couch of fresh rushes, with a coverlet of yellow-red brocaded silk under him, and a cushion and its cover of red brocaded silk under his elbow.

Thereupon Arthur said, 'Sirs, if you would not make game of me,' said he, 'I would sleep while I wait for my meat. And for your part you can tell tales and get a stoup of mead and chops from Cei.' And the emperor slept.

And Cynon son of Clydno asked of Cei that which Arthur had promised them. 'But I,' said Cei, 'would have the good tale that was promised me.' 'Why, man,' said Cynon, 'it were fairer for thee to fulfil Arthur's promise first; and afterwards, the best tale we know, we will tell it thee.'

Cei went to the kitchen and the mead-cellar and brought with him a stoup of mead and a gold goblet, and his fist full of spits with chops on them. And they took the chops and began drinking the mead. 'Now,' said Cei, 'it is for you to pay me my story.' 'Cynon,' said Owein, 'pay Cei his story.' 'Faith,' said Cynon, 'an older man and a better teller of tales art thou than I. More hast thou seen of wondrous things. Do thou pay Cei his tale.' 'Start thou,' said Owein, 'with the most wondrous thing thou knowest.' 'I will,' said Cynon.

'I was the only son of my father and mother, and I was high-spirited, and great was my presumption, nor did I believe that there was any one in the world who might get the better of me at any kind of feat. And after I had mastered every feat that was in the same country as myself, I made me ready and travelled the bounds of the world and its wilderness. And at long last I came upon the fairest vale in the world, and trees of an equal height in it, and there was a river flowing through the vale, and a path alongside the river. And I travelled along the path till mid-day; and on the other side. I travelled till the hour of nones. And then I came to a great plain, and at the far end of the plain I could see a great shining castle, and a sea close to the castle. And I came towards the castle. And lo, two curly-yellow-headed youths, with a frontlet of gold about the head of each of them, and a tunic of yellow brocaded silk upon each of them, and two buskins of new cordwain upon the feet of each, and buckles of gold on their insteps fastening them. And a bow of ivory in the hand of each of them, and strings of deer sinews thereto, and arrows with their shafts of walrus-ivory, winged with peacocks' feathers, and heads of gold on the shafts. And gold-bladed knives, and their hilts with walrus-ivory in each of the two bosses, and they shooting at their knives. And some way off from them I could see a curly-yellow-headed man in his prime, with his beard new trimmed, and a tunic and mantle of yellow brocaded silk about him, and a ribbon of gold threaded in the mantle, and two buskins of speckled cordwain upon his feet, and two gold bosses fastening them.

'And when I saw him I drew near to him and greeted him, and so courteous were his manners that or ever I greeted him he had greeted me. And he accompanied me to the castle. And there was no sign of habitation in the castle, save what was in the hall. But there there were four-and-twenty maidens sewing brocaded silk by a window, and I tell thee this, Cei, that to my mind the least fair of them was fairer than the fairest maiden thou didst ever see in the Island of Britain. The least lovely of them, lovelier was she than Gwenhwyfar, Arthur's wife, when she was ever loveliest, Christmas day or Easter day at Mass. And they rose up to meet me, and six of them took my horse and drew off my boots, and six others of them took my arms and cleansed them in a rocker till they were as bright as what is brightest. And the third six laid cloths on the tables and set out food; and the fourth six drew off me my travelling garb and placed another garb upon me, namely, a girdle and trousers of bliant, and a tunic and surcoat and mantle of yellow brocaded silk, with a wide orfray on the mantle, and drew under me and around me cushions a-plenty with covers of red bliant. And then I sat me down. And the six of them that took my horse made him faultless in all his harness, as well as the best grooms in Britain. And thereupon, lo, silver bowls, and in them water to wash, and towels of white bliant, and some green; and we washed. And the man just mentioned went to sit at table, and I next to him, and the ladies below me, save for those who were serving. And the table was of silver, and of bliant was the table napery. And there was no one vessel served at table save gold or silver or buffalo-horn. And our meat came before us. And thou canst be sure, Cei, that I never saw nor heard tell of meat or drink whose like I saw not there, save that the service of meat and drink I saw there was better than in any place ever.

'And we ate till the meal was half over, and till then neither the man nor any of the maidens spoke a single word to me. And when the man judged it likely that I had rather converse than eat, he asked me what journey I was on and what kind of man I was. And I made answer that it was high time I had some one who would converse with me, and that there was not a fault at court so great as their being men so poor at conversation. "Why, chieftain," said the man, "we would have conversed with thee long since, save that it would have hindered thee in thy eating. But now we will converse with thee."

'And then I told the man who I was and the journey I was on, and I declared that I was seeking some one who might get the better of me or I get the better of him. And then the man looked on me and smiled gently, and said to me, "Did I not believe that overmuch mischief should come upon thee for my telling it thee, I would tell thee of that thou art seeking." And I felt grief and sadness come over me, and the man could see that by me, and said to me, "Since thou hadst rather," said he, "that I tell thee of thy hurt than of thy good, tell it I will. Sleep here to-night,"

said he, "and rise early and take the road thou camest up through
the valley until thou enter the forest thou camest through, and
some distance into the forest a by-way will meet thee on thy
right, and journey along that until thou come to a great clearing
as of a level field, and a mound in the middle of the clearing,
and a big black man shalt thou see on the middle of the mound
who is not smaller than two of the men of this world. And one
foot has he, and one eye in his forehead's core; and he has a club
of iron, and thou canst be sure that there are no two men who
would not find their full load in the club. But his is not an ugly
disposition; yet he is an ugly man, and he is keeper of that forest.
And thou shalt see a thousand wild animals grazing about him.
And ask him the way to go from the clearing, and he will be
gruff with thee, but even so he will show thee a way whereby
thou mayest have that thou art seeking."

'And that night was long to me. And on the morrow early
I rose and arrayed me, and mounted my horse and went my way
through the valley and the forest, and I came to the by-way the
man spoke of, even to the clearing. And when I came there,
what wild animals I saw there were thrice as remarkable to me
as the man had said; and the black man was sitting on top of
the mound. Big the man told me he was: bigger by far was he
than that. And the iron club in which the man had said was the
full load of two men, I was sure, Cei, that there was therein
the full load of four warriors. It was in the black man's hand.
And I greeted the black man, but he spoke nothing to me save
incivility. And I asked him what power he had over the animals.
"I will show thee, little man," said he. And he took the club in
his hand, and with it struck a stag a mighty blow till it gave out
a mighty belling, and in answer to its belling wild animals came
till they were as numerous as the stars in the firmament, so that
there was scant room for me to stand in the clearing with them
and all those serpents and lions and vipers and all kinds of
animals. And he looked on them and bade them go graze. And
then they bowed down their heads and did him obeisance, even
as humble subjects would do to their lord.

'And he said to me, "Dost see then, little man, the power
I have over these animals?" And then I asked the way of him,

and he was rough with me, but even so he asked me where I wanted to go, and I told him what kind of a man I was and what I was seeking, and he then showed me. "Take," said he, "the path to the head of the clearing, and climb the slope up yonder till thou come to its summit. And from there thou shalt see a vale like a great waterway; and in the middle of the vale thou shalt see a great tree with the tips of its branches greener than the greenest fir trees. And under that tree is a fountain, and beside the fountain is a marble slab, and on the slab there is a silver bowl fastened to a silver chain, so that they cannot be separated. And take up the bowl and throw a bowlful of water over the slab, and then thou wilt hear a great peal of thunder; and thou wilt fancy that heaven and earth are quaking with the peal. And after the peal there shall come a cold shower, and it will be hard for thee to bear that and live. And hailstones will it be, and after the shower there will be clear weather, but there shall not be one leaf on the tree that the shower will not have carried away. And thereupon a flight of birds shall come to alight on the tree, and never hast thou heard in thine own country a song so delightful as that they shall sing. And even when thou shalt be most enraptured with the song, thou shalt hear a great panting and groaning coming towards thee along the valley. And thereupon thou shalt see a knight on a pure black horse, and a garment of pure black brocaded silk about him, and a pennon of pure black bliant upon his spear. And he will fall on thee as briskly as he can. If thou flee before him, he will overtake thee; if, on the other hand, thou abide his coming, and thou on a horse, he will leave thee on foot. And if thou find not trouble there, thou needst not look for trouble as long as thou live."

'And I took the path till I came to the top of the hill, and from there I could see even as the black man had told me. And I came to beside the tree, and I could see the fountain beneath the tree, and the marble slab beside it, and the silver bowl fastened to the chain. And I took up the bowl and threw a bowlful of water over the slab; and thereupon lo, a peal of thunder coming, far greater than the black man had said; and after the peal the shower. And I was sure, Cei, that neither man nor beast of those the shower overtook would escape with his life.

For never a hailstone of it would stop for skin nor flesh, till bone checked it. But I turned my horse's crupper to face the shower, and set the beak of my shield over my horse's head and mane, and the beaver over my own head, and in this wise I bore the shower. And as my life was at a point to depart my body, the shower came to an end. And when I looked at the tree there was not one leaf on it. And then the weather cleared. And thereupon, lo, the birds alighting on the tree and starting to sing; and I am sure, Cei, that never before nor since have I heard a song as delightful as that. And even when I was most enraptured, listening to the birds singing, lo, a panting coming along the valley towards me and saying to me, "Knight," it said, "what wouldst thou have of me? What harm have I done thee, that thou shouldst do to me and my dominion that which thou hast done to-day? Didst not know that to-day's shower has left alive in my dominions neither man nor beast of those it found out of doors?" And thereupon, lo, a knight on a pure black horse; and a pure black garment of brocaded silk about him, and an ensign of pure black bliant upon his lance. And I made an attack. And though that was a sharp encounter, it was not long before I was borne to the ground. And then the knight passed the shaft of his lance through my horse's bridle-rein, and away he went and the two horses with him, and left me there. As for me, the black man out of pride did not so much as fetter me, nor did he despoil me. And back I came, the way I had come before.

'And when I came to the clearing the black man was there, and I confess to thee, Cei, it is a wonder I did not melt into a liquid pool for shame at the mockery I got from the black man. And that night I came to the castle wherein we had been the night before. And I was made more welcome that night than the night before, and better was I fed, and I might have the conversation I desired from man and woman. But I found none to mention anything to me concerning my expedition to the fountain; nor did I mention it to any. And there I remained that night.

'And when I arose on the morrow, there was a tawny-black palfrey with a bright red mane on him, as red as lichen, all saddled ready. And after putting on my armour and leaving my blessing there, I came to my own court. And that horse I have still, in the stable yonder, and between me and God, Cei, I would still not exchange him for the best palfrey in the Island of Britain. And God knows, Cei, no man ever confessed against himself to a story of greater failure than this. And yet, how strange it seems to me that I have never heard tell, before or since, of any one who might know aught concerning this adventure, save as much as I have told, and how the root of this tale is in the dominions of the emperor Arthur without its being hit upon.'

'Why, sirs,' said Owein, 'were it not well to go and seek to hit upon that place?'

'By the hand of my friend,' said Cei, 'oft-times wouldst thou speak with thy tongue what thou wouldst not perform in deed.'

'God knows,' said Gwenhwyfar, 'it were better thou wert hanged, Cei, than that thou utter words as slanderous as those to a man like Owein.'

'By the hand of my friend, lady,' said Cei, 'thou hast uttered no greater praise of Owein than I myself.'

And with that Arthur awoke and asked whether he had slept at all. 'Aye, lord,' said Owein, 'a while.'

'Is it time for us to go to table?'

'It is, lord,' said Owein.

Then the horn was sounded to wash. And the emperor and all his household went to their meat. And when meat was ended, Owein slipped away and came to his lodging and made ready his horse and arms.

And when he saw day on the morrow he donned his armour and mounted his horse and he went his way to the bounds of the world and desolate mountains. And at last he hit upon the valley that Cynon had told him of, so that he knew for sure it was the one. And he travelled along the valley by the side of the river; and the other side of the river he travelled until he came to the waterway. And he travelled the waterway till he could see the castle. And he came towards the castle. He could see the youths shooting at their knives in the place where Cynon had seen them, and the yellow-haired man who owned the castle standing near them. And when Owein was at point to greet the yellow-haired man the yellow-haired man greeted Owein.

And he came forward to the castle, and he could see a chamber in the castle; and when he came to the chamber he could see the maidens sewing brocaded silk in golden chairs. And more remarkable by far to Owein was their exceeding fairness and beauty than Cynon had declared to him. And they arose to serve Owein as they had served Cynon. And more remarkable was his repast to Owein than to Cynon.

And midway through the meal the yellow-haired man asked Owein what journey he was on. And Owein told him the whole of his quest. 'And seeking the knight who guards the fountain would I wish to be.' And the yellow-haired man smiled gently, and it was hard for him to tell Owein of that adventure, even as it had been hard for him to tell it to Cynon. Even so, he told Owein everything concerning it; and they went to sleep.

And on the morrow early the maidens had Owein's horse made ready, and Owein went on his way till he came to the clearing wherein the black man was. And more remarkable was the size of the black man to Owein than to Cynon. And Owein asked the way of the black man, and he told it. And Owein, like Cynon, followed the path till he came to beside the green tree, and he could see the fountain and the slab beside the fountain, and the bowl upon it; and Owein took up the bowl and threw a bowlful of water upon the slab. And thereupon, lo, the peal of thunder, and after the peal the shower. Greater by far were these than Cynon had said. And after the shower the sky lightened; and when Owein looked on the tree there was not one leaf upon it. And thereupon, lo, the birds alighting on the tree and singing. And even when Owein was most enraptured with the birds' song he could see a knight coming along the vale, and Owein received him and encountered him with spirit. And they broke their two lances, and drew their swords and smote at each other, and thereupon Owein struck the knight a blow through his helm, both mail-cap and bourgoyne coif, and through skin, flesh and bone till it wounded the brain. And then the black knight knew that he had received a mortal blow, and turned his horse's head and fled. And Owein pursued him. But Owein could not get near enough to strike him with his sword, though he was not far off from him.

And thereupon Owein could see a great shining city. And they came to the gate of the city. And the black knight was let in, and the portcullis was let down upon Owein, and it struck him behind the hind-bow of the saddle, so that the horse was cut in two, right through him, and the rowels of the spurs close to Owein's heels, and so that the gate descended to the ground, and the rowels of the spurs and part of the horse outside, and Owein and the rest of the horse between the two gates. And the inner gate was closed, so that Owein might not get away; and Owein was in a quandary. And as Owein was thus, he could see through the join of the gate a road facing him and a row of houses either side of the road. And he could see a maiden with yellow curling hair, with a frontlet of gold on her head and a garment of yellow brocaded silk about her, and two buskins of speckled cordwain on her feet, and she coming towards the gate. And she bade open. 'God knows, lady,' said Owein, 'it can no more be opened to thee from here than thou canst deliver me from there.' 'God knows,' said the maiden, ''twere great pity thou mightst not be delivered. And it were only right for a woman to do thee a good turn. God knows I never saw a better young man for a woman than thou. Hadst thou a woman friend, best of woman's friends wouldst thou be; hadst thou a lady-love, best of lovers wouldst thou be. And so,' said she, 'what deliverance I can for thee, that will I do. Take this ring and put it on thy finger, and put this stone in thy hand, and close thy fist over the stone; and so long as thou conceal it, it will conceal thee too. And when they of the castle give heed, they will come to fetch thee, to put thee to death because of the man. And when they see thee not, that will vex them. And I shall be on the horse-block yonder, awaiting thee, and thou shalt see me even though I shall not see thee. And come thou and place thy hand upon my shoulder, and then I shall know thou hast come to me. And the way I go thence, come thou with me.'

And with that she went away thence from Owein. And Owein did everything the maiden bade him. And with that the men from the court came to look for Owein to put him to death. But when they came to look for him they saw nothing save half the horse. And that vexed them. And Owein slipped away from their midst, and came to the maiden and placed his hand on her shoulder, and she set off and Owein along with her until they came to the door of a large fair upper chamber. And the maiden opened the chamber, and they came inside and closed the chamber. And Owein looked around the chamber, and there was not in the chamber one nail not coloured with precious colour, and there was not one panel without its different kind of golden image thereon.

And the maiden kindled a charcoal fire, and took a silver bowl with water in it, and a towel of white bliant on her shoulder, and gave Owein water to wash. And she placed a silver table inlaid with gold before him, and yellow bliant as a cloth thereon, and she brought him his dinner. And Owein was certain that he had never seen any kind of food of which he did not there see plenty, save that the service of the food he saw there was better than in any other place ever. And he had never seen a place with so many rare dishes of meat and drink as there. And there was never a vessel from which he was served save vessels of silver or gold.

And Owein ate and drank till it was late afternoon. And thereupon, lo, they could hear a loud crying in the castle; and Owein asked the maiden, 'What outcry is this?' 'They are administering extreme unction to the nobleman who owns the castle,' said the maiden. And Owein went to sleep. And worthy of Arthur was the excellence of the bed that the maiden made for him, of scarlet and grey, and brocaded silk and sendal and bliant. And towards midnight they could hear a dreadful loud crying. 'What loud crying is this now?' asked Owein. 'The nobleman who owns the castle has but now died,' said the maiden. And after a while of day they could hear an immeasurable loud lamenting and outcry. And Owein asked the maiden, 'What means this outcry?' 'The body of the nobleman who owns the castle is being borne to the church.'

And Owein arose and dressed himself and opened a chamber window and looked towards the city, and he saw neither limit nor bound to the hosts filling the streets, and they fully armed, and many ladies with them horsed and a-foot, and all the clerics of the city chanting. And it seemed to Owein that the air rang, so great was the outcry and the trumpets and the clerics chanting. And in the middle of that host he could see the bier, and a pall of white bliant thereon, and wax tapers burning in great numbers around it, and there was not one man carrying the bier of lower rank than a mighty baron.

And Owein was certain that he had never beheld a train so beautiful as that with brocaded silk and satin and sendal. And following that host he could see a yellow-haired lady with her hair over her shoulders, and many a gout of blood on her tresses, and a torn garment of yellow brocaded silk about her, and two buskins of speckled cordwain upon her feet. And it was a marvel that the ends of her fingers were not maimed, so hard did she beat her two hands together. And Owein was certain that he had never beheld a lady as lovely as she, were she in her right guise. And louder was her shrieking than what there was of man and horn in the host. And when he beheld the lady he was fired with love of her, till each part of him was filled therewith. And Owein asked the maiden who the lady was. 'God knows,' said the maiden, 'a lady of whom it may be said that she is the fairest of women, and the most chaste, and the most generous, and the wisest and noblest. My mistress is she, and the Lady of the Fountain is she called, wife to the man thou slewest yesterday.' 'God knows of me,' said Owein, 'she is the lady I love best.' 'God knows,' said the maiden, 'she loves not thee, neither a little nor at all.'

And thereupon the maiden arose and kindled a charcoal fire, and filled a pot with water and set it to warm, and took a towel of white bliant and placed it round Owein's neck; and she took an ivory ewer and a silver bowl and filled it with warm water and washed Owein's head; and then she opened a wooden case and drew out a razor with its haft of ivory and two gold channellings on the razor. And she shaved his beard and dried his head and neck with the towel.

And then the maiden set up a table before Owein and brought him his dinner. And Owein was certain that never had he a dinner so choice as that, nor one more lavishly served. And when he had finished his dinner the maiden made ready the bed. 'Come hither,' said she, 'to sleep. And I will go a-wooing for thee.' And Owein went to sleep.

And the maiden closed the door of the upper chamber and went towards the castle. And when she came there, naught else was there save sadness and care, and the countess herself in the chamber, not bearing to see a soul for her sadness. And Luned came to her and greeted her; but the countess made her no answer. And the maiden was angered and said to her, 'What has come over thee that thou hast an answer for no one to-day?' 'Luned,' said the countess, 'what a face hast thou, not to come and show respect to the grief that was mine! And yet I made thee wealthy. And that was wrong of thee.' 'Faith,' said Luned, 'I did not think but that thy good sense might be better than it is. It were better for thee to seek and study to make good the loss of that nobleman than something else thou mayest never obtain.' 'Between me and God,' said the countess, 'I could never make good the loss of my lord in any other man in the world.' 'Thou couldst,' said Luned, 'take as husband a man who would be as good as, or better than he.' 'Between me and God,' said the countess, 'were it not repugnant to me to have put to death a creature I myself reared, I would have thee put to death for suggesting to me a thing so disloyal as that. But banished I will have thee!' 'I am glad,' said Luned, 'that thou hast no reason for this save that I have told thee thine own good, where thou couldst not thyself hit on it. And shame on whichever of us first sends to the other, whether it be I to seek invitation of thee, or thou to invite me.'

And thereupon Luned made off, and the countess arose and went to the chamber door after Luned, and coughed loudly, and Luned looked back. And the countess gave Luned a nod, and Luned came back to the countess. 'Between me and God,' said the countess to Luned, 'evil is thy nature. But since it was my own good thou wast telling me, show me what way that might be.' 'I will,' said she.

'Thou knowest that thy dominions cannot be defended save by main strength and arms; and for that reason seek quickly one who may defend them.' 'How can I do that?' asked the countess. 'I will show thee,' said Luned. 'Unless thou canst defend the fountain thou canst not defend thy dominions. There is none can defend the fountain save one of Arthur's household; and

I shall go,' said Luned, 'to Arthur's court. And shame on me,' said she, 'if I come away thence without a warrior who will keep the fountain as well or better than the man who kept it of yore.' 'That is not easy,' said the countess, 'but nonetheless go thou and put to the test that thou dost speak of.'

Luned set out under pretence of going to Arthur's court. And she came to the upper chamber to Owein; and there she remained along with Owein till it was time for her to have come from Arthur's court. And then she arrayed herself and came to see the countess. And the countess welcomed her. 'Thou hast news from Arthur's court?' asked the countess. 'The best news that I have, lady,' said she, 'is that I have prospered in my mission. And when wouldst thou have shown to thee the chieftain who has come with me?' 'Towards mid-day to-morrow,' said the countess, 'bring him to see me. And I shall have the town emptied against that time.'

And she came home. And towards mid-day on the morrow Owein put on a tunic and surcoat and a mantle of yellow brocaded silk, and a wide orfray of gold thread in the mantle, and two buskins of speckled cordwain on his feet, and the image of a golden lion fastening them. And they came to the countess's chamber; and the countess welcomed them. And the countess looked hard at Owein. 'Luned,' said she, 'this chieftain has not the look of a traveller.' 'What harm is there in that, lady?' asked Luned. 'Between me and God,' said the countess, 'that no man reft my lord's life from his body save this man.' 'All the better for thee, lady. Had he not been doughtier than he, he would not have taken his life. Nothing can be done in that affair,' said she, 'for it is over and done with.' 'Get you home,' said the countess, 'and as for me, I shall take counsel.'

And on the morrow the countess had the whole of her dominions summoned to one place, and she made known to them how her earldom was voided and might not be defended save by horse and arms and main strength. 'And I lay this choice before you: either do one of you take me, or let me take a husband from elsewhere who will defend it.'

They determined by their counsel to let her take a husband from elsewhere. And then she brought bishops and archbishops to her court to solemnize the marriage between her and Owein. And the men of the earldom did Owein homage. And Owein kept the fountain with spear and sword. This is how he kept it: whatever knight came there, Owein would overthrow them and hold them to ransom for their full worth; and that wealth Owein distributed amongst his barons and knights, so that his dominions had not love for a man in the whole world greater than their love for him. And three years was he thus.

And as Gwalchmei was one day walking with the emperor Arthur, he looked on Arthur and saw him sad and dejected. And Gwalchmei was much grieved to see Arthur in that state. And he asked him, 'Lord,' said he, 'what has befallen thee?' 'Between me and God, Gwalchmei,' said Arthur, 'there is longing upon me for Owein, who has been lost to me the space of three years, and if I be the fourth year without sight of him my life will not stay in my body. And I know for certain that it is because of Cynon's tale, son of Clydno, that Owein has been lost.' 'There is no need for thee, lord,' said Gwalchmei, 'to muster thy dominions to that end; but thou and the men of thy court may avenge Owein if he has been slain, or set him free if he is in prison. Or, if he be alive, bring him back with thee.' And what Gwalchmei said was determined on.

And Arthur went on his way, equipped with horses and arms, and the men of his household with him, to seek Owein. The number of his host was three thousand, not counting camp followers, and Cynon son of Clydno was guide to him. And Arthur came to the castle where Cynon had been. And when they came thither the youths were in the same place shooting, and the yellow-haired man standing near them. And when the yellow-haired man saw Arthur he greeted him and invited him, and Arthur accepted the invitation. And they proceeded to the castle. And although their host was a great one, their presence was not felt in the castle. And the maidens arose to serve them; and ever had they seen fault in every service save the service of the ladies. And no worse was the service for the grooms that night than would be for Arthur in his own court.

On the morrow early Arthur set out thence, with Cynon as

his guide. And they came to where the black man was, and more remarkable by far to Arthur was the size of the black man than had been told him. And they came to the top of the hill, and to the vale beside the green tree, and till they saw the fountain and the bowl and the slab. And then Cei came to Arthur and said, 'Lord,' said he, 'I know the meaning of all this adventure, and it is my plea that I be allowed to throw the water on the slab and to bear the first disadventure that may come.' And Arthur granted this.

And Cei threw a bowlful of the water upon the slab. And straight thereafter came the peal of thunder, and after the peal the shower; and they had never heard a peal of thunder and a shower like to those. And many camp followers who were in Arthur's train the shower slew. And after the shower had left off the sky lightened; and when they looked on the tree there was not one leaf thereon. And the birds alighted on the tree; and certain were they that they had never heard a song so delightful as the birds' singing. And thereupon they could see a knight on a pure black horse, and a garment of pure black brocaded silk about him, and coming briskly. And Cei encountered him and jousted with him. And not long was the jousting ere Cei was thrown. And then the knight pitched his tent, and Arthur and his host pitched their tents that night.

And next day when they arose in the morning there was the signal for combat upon the knight's lance. And Cei came to Arthur and said to him, 'Lord,' said he, 'unfairly was I over-thrown yesterday. And would it please thee that I go to-day to joust with the knight?' 'I give thee leave,' said Arthur. And Cei made for the knight, and straightway he threw Cei, and he looked on him and struck him on the forehead with the butt of his lance, so that his helm and the mail-cap were broken, and the skin and the flesh to the bone as wide as the head of the lance. And Cei came back to his comrades.

And thenceforward Arthur's retinue went each in his turn to joust with the knight, till there was none not thrown by the knight save Arthur and Gwalchmei.

And Arthur arrayed him to go and joust with the knight. 'Alas, lord,' said Gwalchmei, 'give me leave to go and joust with

the knight first.' And Arthur gave him leave. And he went to
joust with the knight, and a cloak of brocaded silk which the
earl of Anjou's daughter had sent him about him and his horse.
By reason of that, none from the host recognized him. And they
charged each other and jousted that day till eventide, and
neither of them was near throwing the other to the ground.

And on the morrow they went to joust, and keen lances with
them, but neither of them vanquished the other. And the third
day they went to joust, and strong stout keen lances with each
of them. And they were fired with rage, and on the very stroke
of noon they charged, and each of them gave the other such a
thrust that all the girths of their horses were broken, and so that
each of them was over his horse's crupper to the ground. And
they arose quickly and drew their swords and laid on; and the
host that beheld them thus felt certain that never had they seen
two men as valorous as those, or as strong. And were the night
dark, it would be light with the fire from their arms. And thereupon the knight gave Gwalchmei such a blow that the helm
turned from off his face, so that the knight knew he was
Gwalchmei. And then Owein said, 'Lord Gwalchmei, I knew
thee not by reason of thy cloak – and thou art my first cousin.
Take thou my sword, and my armour.' 'Thou, Owein, art master,' said Gwalchmei, 'and thine is the victory. Take thou my
armour.' And thereupon Arthur perceived them, and he came
to them. 'Lord,' said Gwalchmei, 'here is Owein hath vanquished me and will not take my armour from me.' 'Lord,' said
Owein, ''tis he that vanquished me and will not take my sword.'
'Give me your swords,' said Arthur, 'and then neither of you has
vanquished the other.' And Owein threw his arms around the
emperor Arthur's neck, and they embraced. And with that his
host came pressing and hurrying towards them to try and see
Owein and embrace him, and very nearly were there dead men
in that press.

And that night all went to their tents. And on the morrow
the emperor Arthur sought to depart. 'Lord,' said Owein, 'that
would not be right of thee. Three years ago I came away from
there, lord, and this place is mine, and from that day to this I
have been preparing a feast for thee, for I knew thou wouldst

come to look for me. And thou shalt come with me to rid thee of thy weariness, thou and thy men. And a bath you shall have.'

And they all came together to the castle of the Lady of the Fountain. And the feast that had been three years preparing was consumed in just three months. And never had they a feast more cheering than that, nor a better. And then Arthur sought to depart. And Arthur sent messengers to the countess, asking her to allow Owein to go with him to be shown to the noblemen of the Island of Britain and their good ladies for just three months. And the countess gave him her consent, but she found it hard.

And Owein came with Arthur to the Island of Britain. And after his coming amongst his kindred and his boon-companions, he remained three years instead of three months.

And as Owein was one day eating at table in the emperor Arthur's court at Caer Llion on Usk, lo, a maiden coming on a crisp-maned bay horse, and its mane reached to the ground, and a garment of yellow brocaded silk about her, and the bridle and what might be seen of the saddle was all of gold. And she came up to Owein and took away the ring that was upon his hand. 'Thus,' said she, 'does one do to a false treacherous deceiver, to bring shame on thy beard.' And she turned her horse's head and away.

And then remembrance of his adventure came to Owein, and he was sorrowful. And when he had finished eating he came to his lodging, and he was troubled greatly that night. And on the morrow early he arose, and it was not for Arthur's court that he made but the bounds of the world and desolate mountains. And he was wandering thus till his clothes perished, and till his body was nigh perished, and till long hair grew all over his body; and he would keep company with wild beasts and feed with them till they were used to him. And therewith he grew so weak that he might not keep up with them. And he came down from the mountains into the vale, and made for a park, the fairest in the world, and a widowed countess owned the park.

And one day the countess and her handmaidens went walking beside a lake that was in the park, until level with its centre. And they could see in the park the shape and likeness of a man.

And they became as it were terrified of him. But nevertheless they drew near him, and felt him, and regarded him closely. They could see the veins throbbing on him, and he himself moaning because of the sun. And the countess returned to the castle and took a jar of precious ointment and placed it in her maiden's hand. 'Go,' said she, 'and this with thee, and take yonder horse and the garments with thee, and set them near the man back there. And anoint him with this ointment, next his heart, and if there be life in him he will arise with this ointment. And watch what he will do.'

And the maiden came her way and applied all the ointment to him, and left the horse and the garments near at hand, and withdrew and went a little off from him, and hid and kept watch on him. And after a while she could see him scratching his arms and raising himself up and looking on his flesh, and he grew ashamed, so ugly did he see the appearance that was on him. And he perceived the horse and the garments a short way off from him, and he crawled until he reached the garments, and he drew them to him from the saddle and donned them, and with difficulty mounted the horse. And then the maiden revealed herself to him, and greeted him. And he welcomed the maiden, and he asked the maiden what land was that, and what place. 'Faith,' said the maiden, 'a widowed countess owns the castle yonder. And when her lord died he left her with two earldoms, but there is naught to her name this night save the one house yonder which the young earl who is her neighbour has not taken, because she would not go to him as wife.' 'That is pity,' said Owein; and Owein and the maiden went to the castle, and Owein alighted at the castle, and the maiden led him to a comfortable chamber and kindled a fire for him, and left him there.

And the maiden came to the countess, and placed the jar in her hand. 'Maiden,' said the countess, 'where is all the ointment?' 'It is gone, lady,' said she. 'Maiden,' said the countess, 'it is not easy for me to blame thee. But it was unfortunate for me that the sevenscore pounds' worth of precious ointment should be used up on a man without knowing who he is. But nonetheless, maiden, see to his needs so that he lacks for nothing.'

And that the maiden did, furnishing him with meat and drink

and fire and bed and bath till he was whole. And the hair fell away from Owein in scaly tufts. Three months was he undergoing this, and his flesh was then whiter than before.

And thereupon, one day, Owein could hear a commotion in the castle, and a great preparation, and arms being fetched in. And Owein asked the maiden, 'What commotion is this?' asked he. 'The earl of whom I told thee,' said she, 'is coming against the castle to try and ruin this lady, and a great host with him.' And then Owein asked the maiden, 'Has the countess a horse and arms?' 'Even so,' said the maiden, 'the best in the world.' 'Wilt thou go to the countess to request the loan of a horse and arms for me,' asked Owein, 'so that I might go to look on the host?' 'I will, gladly,' said the maiden.

And the maiden came to the countess and told her all that he had said. Then the countess laughed. 'Between me and God,' said she, 'I will give him a horse and arms for ever; and never has he had to his name a horse and arms better than they; and it pleases me that he should accept them, lest to-morrow they be taken by my enemies against my will. But I know not what he wants with them.'

And a handsome black gascon was brought, with a beechen saddle on him, and arms ample for man and horse. And he arrayed himself and mounted the horse and set off, and two squires with him, equipped with horses and arms. And as they came towards the earl's host they saw neither bound nor limit to it. And Owein asked the squires which troop the earl was in. 'In the troop,' said they, 'in which are those four yellow standards yonder. Two are in his van, and two in his rear.' 'Aye,' said Owein, 'get you back and wait for me in the castle gateway.' And they returned. And Owein proceeded through the two foremost troops, till he encountered the earl. And Owein dragged him from his saddle, so that he was between him and his saddlebow, and he turned his horse's head towards the castle. And whatever trouble he had, he brought the earl along with him till he came to the castle gate where the squires were waiting for him. And in they came, and Owein made over the earl as a gift to the countess, and spoke to her thus: 'See here a return for the blessed ointment I had of thee.'

And the host pitched its tents around the castle. And in return for life given to the earl he gave back to her the two earldoms; and in return for his liberty he gave up the half of his own dominions, and the whole of her silver and gold and her jewels, and sureties to that end.

And away went Owein, and the countess offered him a welcome, him and the whole of his dominions; but Owein desired nothing save to travel the bounds of the world and its wilderness.

And as he travelled in this wise he heard a loud roaring within a forest, and a second, and a third. And he came thither, and when he had come he could see a huge craggy hill in the middle of the forest, and a grey rock in the side of the hill; and there was a cleft in the rock, and in the cleft was a serpent, and beside the serpent was a pure white lion, and when the lion tried to get away thence the serpent would make a dart at him, and then he would give a roar. Then Owein unsheathed his sword and drew nigh to the rock; and as the serpent was coming from the rock Owein cut at it with the sword till it was in two halves on the ground. And he came to the road as before. He could see the lion following him and sporting about him like a greyhound he had himself reared.

And they travelled throughout the day till eventide. And when Owein thought it time to rest he dismounted and let his horse graze in a level wooded meadow. And Owein kindled a fire; and by the time Owein had the fire ready, the lion had enough firewood to last three nights. And the lion slipped away from him, and straightway, lo, the lion coming towards him with a fine big roebuck. And he dropped it in front of Owein and went to lie down between him and the fire.

And Owein took the roebuck and flayed it, and set chops on spits around the fire, and he gave the whole of the buck else to the lion to eat. And as Owein was about this he heard a loud moan, and a second and a third, and that nigh to him. And Owein asked whether it was any one of this world who made that. 'Aye, to be sure,' said the creature. 'Who art thou then?' asked Owein. 'Faith,' said she, 'I am Luned, the handmaiden of the Lady of the Fountain.' 'What dost thou there?' asked

Owein. 'I am being kept in durance,' said she, 'by reason of a young man who came from the emperor's court and was with her a while. And he went to visit Arthur's court and never came back. And such a friend was he to me, I loved him best of the whole world. Two of the countess's chamberlains made mock of him in my presence and called him false deceiver. I made answer that their two bodies might not contend against his body alone, and for that they imprisoned me in this vessel of stone, and declared that life should not stay in my body unless he came to defend me by a set day. And the day set was not later than the day after to-morrow. And I have none to seek for him. Owein was he, son of Urien.' 'And wouldst thou feel sure,' was his answer, 'that if that young man knew of this, he would come to defend thee?' 'Sure, between me and God,' said she.

And when the chops were cooked enough, Owein divided them into two halves between him and the maiden. And they ate, and after that they conversed till it was day on the morrow. And on the morrow Owein asked the maiden whether there was a place where he might get food and welcome that night. 'There is, lord,' said she. 'Go through there,' said she, 'to the ford, and take the road alongside the river, and after a while thou wilt see a great castle with many towers thereon; and the earl who owns that castle is the best man in the world for food, and there thou canst spend to-night.'

And no watchman ever watched over his lord as well as the lion watched over Owein the night before.

And then Owein accoutred his horse and journeyed forward through the ford till he saw the castle. And Owein came to the castle. And he was honourably received there, and his horse amply attended to, and plenty of fodder set before it. And the lion went to the horse's stall to lie down, so that none from the castle might dare go near the horse because of him. And Owein was certain that he had never seen a place whose service was as good as that; but each man there was as sad as if death were on each man of them. And they went to meat, and the earl sat on Owein's one hand, and an only daughter he had on Owein's other side. And Owein was certain that he had never beheld any maiden more lovely than she. And the lion came to between

Owein's two feet, under the table; and Owein fed it with every dish that was for himself. And Owein saw no fault there so great as the men's sadness.

And midway through the meal the earl bade Owein welcome. 'It was high time for thee to show cheer,' said Owein. 'God knows of us that it is not towards thee we are sad, but that a cause for sadness and care has befallen us.' 'What is that?' asked Owein. 'Two sons had I, and yesterday my two sons went to the mountain to hunt. There is a savage monster there, and he kills men and devours them. And he has caught my sons. And to-morrow is the day set between him and me, to hand over that maiden to him or that he kill my sons before my eyes. And there is the semblance of a man upon him, but he is not smaller than a giant.'

'Faith,' said Owein, 'that is pity. And which of those wilt thou do?' 'God knows,' said the earl, 'I judge it less shameful that my sons whom he got against my will should be slain than that my daughter be freely given him to be violated and slain.' And they talked of other matters. And Owein remained there that night.

And on the morrow early they heard a commotion great past telling. That was the big man coming, and the two boys with him. And the earl resolved to defend the castle against him and to abandon his two sons. Owein donned his armour and went out and pitted himself against the man, and the lion at his heels. And when the man saw Owein in arms he rushed at him and fought with him. And better by far did the lion fight against the big man than Owein. 'Between me and God,' said the man to Owein, 'I should not be hard put to it to fight with thee, were not the animal with thee.' And with that Owein drove the lion back into the castle, and fastened the gate upon him, and he came to fight as before against the big man. And the lion roared to realize Owein's plight. And he climbed till he was on the earl's hall, and from the hall on to the rampart, and from the rampart he leapt till he was with Owein. And the lion struck with his paw on the big man's shoulder till his paw was out through his fork, so that all his bowels might be seen slipping from him. And then the big man fell dead. And then Owein restored his two sons to the earl, and the earl offered Owein a welcome. But Owein would not have it, and came on to the meadow where Luned was.

And there he could see a great blaze of fire, and two handsome auburn curly-headed youths taking the maiden to throw her into the fire. And Owein asked what complaint they had against the maiden. And they told him their story, even as the maiden had told it the night before. 'And Owein has failed her, and therefore we will burn her.' 'Faith,' said Owein, 'that was a good knight, and I should marvel he had not come to defend her, had he known how it was with the maiden. And if you would have me go in his stead, why then I would for you.' 'That we will,' said the youths, 'by Him who made us!'

And they came to blows with Owein, and he was in sore straits with the two youths. And thereupon the lion came to Owein's assistance, and they got the better of the youths. And then they said, 'Ah, chieftain, it was not our compact to fight save with thee alone; and it is harder for us to fight with yonder animal than with thee.' And then Owein put the lion in the place where the maiden had been in durance, and made a wall of stones against the door, and went to fight with the men as before. And Owein had not yet come to his strength, and the two youths pressed him hard, and the lion roaring all the while because Owein was in sore straits. And the lion tore down the wall till he found a way out, and quickly he slew one of the youths, and straightway he slew the other. And in this wise they saved Luned from being burned.

And then Owein, and Luned with him, went to the dominions of the Lady of the Fountain. And when he came away thence he brought the lady with him to Arthur's court, and she was his wife so long as she lived.

And then he came his way to the court of the Black Oppressor, and fought with him; and the lion did not leave Owein till he had vanquished the Black Oppressor. And when he came his way to the Black Oppressor's court, he made for the hall, and there he beheld four-and-twenty of the fairest ladies that any one had ever seen. But the raiment upon them was not worth four-and-twenty silver pennies; and they were sad as death. And

Owein asked them the reason for their sadness. They said that they were the daughters of earls, and that they had not come thither save in company with him each one of them loved best. 'And when we came here we received joy and honour, and were made drunk. And when we were drunk the devil who owns this court came and slew all our husbands, and took away our horses and our raiment and our gold and our silver. And the bodies of the men are in this very house, and many corpses along with them. And there for thee, chieftain, the reason for our sadness. And we are grieved, chieftain, that thou too art come hither, lest ill befall thee.'

And Owein was grieved thereat, and he went to go walking outside. And he saw a knight coming towards him and receiving him with joy and affection, as though he were his brother. That was the Black Oppressor. 'God knows,' said Owein, ''twas not to win thy favour I came hither.' 'God knows,' replied he, 'thou wilt not get it then.'

And straightway they made for each other and encountered furiously. And Owein put forth his strength against him, and bound him with his hands behind his back. And the Black Oppressor asked Owein for quarter, and said to him, 'Lord Owein,' said he, 'there was a prophecy that thou shouldst come hither to subdue me; and come thou hast, and that thou hast done. And a despoiler was I here, and a house of spoil was my house; but grant me my life and I will become a hospitaller, and I will maintain this house as a hospice for weak and for strong so long as I live, for thy soul's sake.' And Owein accepted that of him. And Owein remained there that night.

And on the morrow he took the four-and-twenty ladies and their horses and raiment and what wealth and jewels had come with them, and he journeyed, and they with him, to Arthur's court. And a welcome had Arthur given him before when he lost him, and a greater welcome now. And of those ladies, she who desired to remain in Arthur's court might have her wish, and she who wished to depart might take her leave.

And Owein remained in Arthur's court from that time forth, as captain of the war-band, and beloved of him, until he went to his own possessions. Those were the Three Hundred Swords of Cenferchyn and the Flight of Ravens. And wherever Owein went, and they with him, he would be victorious.

And this tale is called the Tale of the Lady of the Fountain.

PEREDUR SON OF EFRAWG

Earl Efrawg held an earldom in the North, and seven sons had he. But it was not by his dominion chiefly that Efrawg maintained himself, but by tournament and combats and wars. And as often befalls him who follows the wars, he was slain, both he and his six sons. And his seventh son was called Peredur. And he was youngest of his seven sons. He was not of an age to go to war or combat. Had he been of age he would have been slain as his father and his brothers were slain.

He had a wise, sagacious woman for mother. She gave thought to her son and his dominion. She took counsel with herself to flee with her son into a desert and a wilderness, and to quit inhabited parts. Never a one took she in her company save women and boys, and meek contented folk who were incapable of combats or wars, and for whom such would be unseemly. Never a one would dare mention steeds or arms in a place where her son might overhear, lest he set his heart upon them. And every day the boy would go to the long forest to play and to throw holly darts.

And one day he saw a flock of goats that was his mother's and two hinds nearby the goats. The boy stood and marvelled to see those two without horns, and horns on each one of the others. And he supposed they had been long lost, and that thereby they had lost their horns. And by strength and fleetness of foot he drove the hinds along with the goats into a house that was for the goats at the far end of the forest. He came back home. 'Mother,' said he, 'a strange thing have I seen nearby: two of thy goats run wild, and having lost their horns for being so long wild in the woods. And never had mortal more trouble than I had, driving them in.' Thereupon every one arose and came to look. And when they saw the hinds they marvelled greatly that any one had strength enough and fleetness of foot as to be able to overtake them.

And one day they saw three knights coming along a bridle-path beside the forest. They were Gwalchmei son of Gwyar, and

164

Gweir son of Gwestyl, and Owein son of Urien, and Owein bringing up the rear, following after the knight who had distributed the apples in Arthur's court. 'Mother,' said he, 'what are those yonder?' 'Angels, my son,' said she. 'I will go as an angel along with them,' said Peredur; and he came to the path to meet the knights. 'Say, friend,' said Owein, 'hast seen a knight go hereby to-day or yesterday?' 'I know not,' he replied, 'what a knight is.' 'Such a thing as I am,' said Owein. 'Wert thou to tell me that which I would ask of thee, I in turn would tell thee that which thou dost ask.' 'I will, gladly,' said Owein. 'What is that?' he asked, of the saddle. 'A saddle,' said Owein. Peredur inquired what everything was, and what might be intended and what done therewith. Owein told him in full what everything was, and what might be done therewith. 'Keep on thy way,' said Peredur. 'I have seen such a man as thou dost ask after. And I too will follow thee as a knight this very hour.'

Then Peredur returned to where were his mother and the retinue. 'Mother,' said he, 'those yonder are not angels, but knights.' Then she fell into a dead faint. And Peredur then went off to where the horses were which carried firewood for them and brought meat and drink from inhabited parts to the desert. And he took a wan, piebald, bony nag, the strongest as he thought, and he pressed a pannier on it, as a saddle, and in everything he imitated with withes the trappings he had seen. And back he came to where his mother was.

Thereupon, lo, the countess coming out of her faint. 'Aye,' said she, 'is it depart thou wilt?' 'Aye,' said he. 'Stay for counsel from me ere thou set out.' 'Speak,' said he, 'quickly. I will stay for it.' 'Go thy way,' said she, 'to Arthur's court, where are the best of men and the most generous and bravest. Wherever thou seest a church, recite thy pater thereto. If thou see meat and drink, shouldst thou be in need thereof and it be not given thee of courtesy and good will, take it thyself. If thou hear an outcry, make towards it, and a woman's outcry above any cry in the world. If thou see a fair jewel, take it and give it to another, and thou shalt have fame thereby. If thou see a fair lady, make love to her, even though she desire thee not. A better man and a nobler than before will it make thee.'

And he set out on his way, with a handful of sharp-pointed darts in his hand. And two nights and two days was he travelling desert and wilderness, without meat, without drink. And then he came to a great desolate forest; and far into the forest he saw a clearing as of a field, and in the clearing he could see a pavilion, and taking it to be a church he recited his pater to the pavilion. And he came towards the pavilion. And the doorway of the pavilion was open, and a chair of gold near the doorway, and a handsome auburn-haired maiden sitting in the chair, and a frontlet of gold about her forehead, and sparkling stones in the frontlet, and a thick gold ring on her hand.

And Peredur dismounted and came inside. The maiden made him welcome and greeted him, and at the end of the pavilion he could see a table and two flagons full of wine, and two loaves of white bread, and chops of the flesh of sucking pigs. 'My mother,' said Peredur, 'bade me wherever I saw meat and drink, to take it.' 'Go then, chieftain,' said she, 'to the table. And God's welcome to thee.' Peredur went to the table, and Peredur took one half of the meat and drink for himself, and the other half he left for the maiden. And when he had finished eating, he arose and came to where the maiden was. 'My mother,' said he, 'bade me take a fair jewel wherever I might see it.' 'Take it then, friend,' said she. '''Tis not I will begrudge it thee.' Peredur took the ring, and he went down on his knee and gave the maiden a kiss, and took his steed and departed thence.

Thereafter, lo, the knight that owned the pavilion coming: he was the Proud One of the Clearing. And he could see the horse's tracks. 'Say,' said he to the maiden, 'who has been here since myself?' 'A man of odd appearance, lord,' said she, and she described Peredur's appearance and manner. 'Say,' said he, 'has he had to do with thee?' 'He has not, by my faith,' said she. 'By my faith, I do not believe thee. And till I meet with him, to wreak my wrath and my shame on him, thou shalt not be two nights together in one and the same place.' And the knight arose to set out and seek for Peredur.

But Peredur proceeded in the direction of Arthur's court. And before he came to Arthur's court, another knight came to the court and gave a thick gold ring to a man at the entrance to hold his horse. And he himself came forward to the hall where were Arthur and his retinue, and Gwenhwyfar and her maidens, and a chamberlain serving Gwenhwyfar from a goblet. And the knight took the goblet from Gwenhwyfar's hand and emptied the liquor that was therein over her face and breast, and gave Gwenhwyfar a great box on the ear. 'If there be,' said he, 'any one who would contend with me for this goblet, and avenge this injury to Gwenhwyfar, let him follow me to the meadow and I will await him there.' And the knight took his horse and made for the meadow. Then every one hung his head lest he be asked to go and avenge the injury to Gwenhwyfar, and they thinking it likely that none would commit such an outrage as that unless he had with him might and prowess or magic and enchantment, so that none might wreak vengeance on him.

Thereupon, lo, Peredur coming into the hall on a wan, pie-bald, bony nag, with uncouth slovenly trappings thereon, and a sorry figure in a court so distinguished as that. And Cei was standing in the middle of the hall floor. 'Say,' said Peredur, 'thou tall man yonder, where is Arthur?' 'What wouldst thou,' said Cei, 'with Arthur?' 'My mother bade me come to Arthur to be ordained an ordained knight.' 'By my faith,' said Cei, 'too slovenly hast thou come, in horse and arms.' And thereupon the household caught sight of him, and they began to make fun of him and throw sticks at him, and they feeling pleased that such a one as he should have come, for the other matter to be forgotten.

And thereupon, lo, the dwarf coming in, who had come a year's space before that to Arthur's court, he and his she-dwarf, to seek hospitality of Arthur. And that they received of Arthur, but save for that for the space of a year they spoke not one word to any one. When the dwarf perceived Peredur, 'Ah, ha,' said he, 'God's welcome to thee, fair Peredur son of Efrawg, chief of warriors and flower of knights.' 'Faith, fellow,' said Cei, 'a sorry stroke that, to be a year dumb in Arthur's court, at liberty to choose thy fellow-talker and to choose thy fellow-drinker, and to call such a man as this, in the presence of the emperor and his household, chief of warriors and flower of knights!' And he gave him a box on the ear till he was headlong to the floor in a dead faint.

Thereupon, lo, the she-dwarf coming. 'Ah, ha,' said she, 'God's welcome to thee, fair Peredur son of Efrawg, flower of warriors and candle of knights.' 'Aye, wench,' said Cei, 'a sorry stroke that, to be a year dumb in Arthur's court, without saying one word to any one, and to call such a man as this to-day, in the presence of Arthur and his warriors, flower of warriors and candle of knights!' And he fetched her a kick till she was in a dead faint. 'Tall man,' said Peredur then, 'tell me, where is Arthur?' 'Cease thy babble,' said Cei. 'Go after the knight who went hence to the meadow, and take the goblet from him, and overthrow him and take his horse and arms, and after that thou shalt be ordained an ordained knight.' 'Tall man,' said he, 'I will do that.' And he turned his horse's head, and out and to the meadow.

And when he came, the knight was riding his horse in the meadow, greatly presumptuous in his might and prowess. 'Say,' said the knight, 'didst see any one from the court coming after me?' 'The tall man who was there,' said he, 'bade me overthrow thee, and take the goblet and the horse and arms for myself.' 'Hold thy tongue,' said the knight. 'Go back to the court and in my name bid Arthur come, either he or another, to joust with me. And unless he come quickly, I will not wait for him.' 'By my faith,' said Peredur, 'take thy choice: with or without thy leave I will have the horse and arms and the goblet.' And then the knight bore down upon him angrily, and with the butt of his spear dealt him a mighty painful blow between shoulder and neck. 'Fellow,' said Peredur, 'not thus would my mother's servants play with me. I will play with thee even thus!' And he took aim at him with a sharp-pointed spear and hit him in the eye, so that it went out through the nape of the neck, and he stone-dead to the ground.

'Faith,' said Owein son of Urien to Cei, 'that was an ill stroke of thine over a fool thou didst send after the knight. And one of two things has come to pass: either he has been overthrown or he has been slain. If he has been overthrown, he will be reckoned a man of rank by the knight, and eternal disgrace to Arthur and his warriors. If he has been slain, the disgrace will betide even so, and more than that, the sin of it upon thee. And may I lose all face unless I go and learn how his adventure has befallen.' And then Owein came his way to the meadow, and when he came, Peredur was dragging the man behind him the length of the meadow. 'Stay, chieftain,' said Owein, 'I will take off the armour.' 'Never,' said Peredur, 'will this iron tunic come away from him. It is part and parcel of him.' Then Owein drew off the armour and the raiment. 'Here at last, friend,' said he, 'are a horse and arms for thee, better than the others. And take them gladly and come along with me to Arthur, and thou shalt be ordained an ordained knight.' 'May I lose all face,' said Peredur, 'if I go. But take the goblet from me to Gwenhwyfar, and tell Arthur that wherever I may be, I will be his man. And if I can do him good and service, I will do it. And tell him I will never go to his court until I meet the tall man who is there, to avenge the injury to the dwarf and she-dwarf.' Then Owein came his way to the court and told his adventure to Arthur and Gwenhwyfar and each one of the household, and the threat to Cei. And Peredur too went his way.

And as he was going his way, lo, a knight encountering him. 'Whence comest thou?' asked the knight. 'I come from Arthur's court,' said he. 'Art thou Arthur's man?' 'Aye, by my faith,' said he. 'A proper place to acknowledge Arthur!' 'Why?' asked Peredur. 'I will tell thee,' said he. 'A robber and riever on Arthur have I been ever, and what of his men have met with me, I have slain.' It was without more delay they encountered, and not long were they ere Peredur threw him so that he was over his horse's crupper to the ground. The knight asked for quarter. 'Quarter thou shalt have,' said Peredur, 'on thy swearing to go to Arthur's court and tell Arthur that it was I who overthrew thee, in service and honour to him. And tell him that never will I set foot in his court till I encounter the tall man who is there, to avenge the injury to the dwarf and she-dwarf.' And the knight, with his oath pledged thereto, set out on his way to Arthur's court and told his adventure in full, and the threat to Cei.

But Peredur went his way. And that same week there met him sixteen knights, and he overthrew them every one, and they made their way to Arthur's court, bearing with them the same tale as the first he overthrew, and the same threat to Cei. And

Cei won a rebuke from Arthur and the household, and he was worried then by reason of that.

But Peredur set out on his way. And at last he came to a great desolate forest, and at the forest's edge there was a lake, and the other side of the lake there was a great court, and a brave rampart round about it. And on the shore of the lake there was a hoary-headed man seated on a cushion of brocaded silk, and a garment of brocaded silk about him, and youths fishing in a boat on the lake. When the hoary-headed man saw Peredur coming, he arose and made for the court, and the man was lame. Peredur too came his way to the court, and the gate was open, and he came into the hall. And when he came, the hoary-headed man was seated on a cushion of brocaded silk, and a big blazing fire starting to burn. And a number of the household arose to meet Peredur, and they helped him to alight and drew off his armour. And the man brought down his hand on the end of the cushion, and asked the squire to come and sit on the cushion. And they sat down together and conversed. And when it was time, the tables were set up and they went to meat. And he was placed to sit and eat on the man's one hand. When meat was ended, the man asked Peredur if he knew well how to smite with a sword. 'I know not,' said Peredur, 'but that, were I to receive instruction, I should know.' 'Whoever might know,' said he, 'how to play with a stick and shield, would know how to smite with a sword.' Two sons had the hoary-headed man, a yellow-haired youth and an auburn-haired youth. 'Rise up, lads,' said he, 'to play with the sticks and shields.' The youths went to play. 'Say, friend,' said the man, 'which of the youths plays the better?' 'It is my opinion,' said Peredur, 'that the yellow-haired youth could long since have drawn blood from the auburn-haired youth, had he wished it.' 'Take, friend, the stick and shield from the auburn-haired youth's hand, and draw blood from the yellow-haired youth, if thou canst.' Peredur arose and took the stick and shield and raised his hand against the yellow-haired youth until his eyebrow was down over his eye, and the blood running in streams. 'Aye, friend,' said the man, 'come now and sit down – and thou wilt be the best man that smites with a sword in this Island. And thy uncle, thy mother's brother, am I. And thou shalt be with me this while, learning manners and etiquette. Leave be now thy mother's words, and I will be thy teacher and will ordain thee an ordained knight. Henceforth this is what thou must do: even though thou see what is strange to thee, ask not after it, unless there be such courtesy that thou be told of it. Not upon thee will the fault be, but upon me, for I am thy teacher.' And they had every kind of honour and service, and when it was time they went to sleep.

As soon as day came Peredur arose and took his horse, and with his uncle's leave he set out on his way, and he came to a great forest, and at the far end of the forest he came to a level meadow, and the other side of the meadow he could see a great rampart and a brave court. And Peredur made towards the court, and he found the door open and made for the hall. And when he came, there was a handsome hoary-headed man seated at the side of the hall, and squires in great numbers about him, and every one arose to meet the squire, and excellent were they in courtesy and service to him. And he was placed to sit one side of the nobleman who owned the court, and they conversed. And when time came to go to meat, he was placed to sit and eat one side of the nobleman. When they had made an end of eating and drinking as long as was pleasing to them, the nobleman asked him if he knew how to smite with a sword. 'Were I to receive instruction,' said Peredur, 'I think I should know.'

There was a great iron column in the hall floor, a warrior's grasp round about. 'Take yonder sword,' said the man to Peredur, 'and smite the iron column.' Peredur arose and smote the column so that it was in two pieces, and the sword in two pieces. 'Place the pieces together and join them.' Peredur placed the pieces together and they were joined as before. And a second time he smote it so that the column broke in two pieces, and the sword in two pieces. And as before they were joined together. And the third time he smote it so that the column broke in two pieces, and the sword in two pieces. 'Place them together again and join them.' Peredur placed them together the third time, but neither the column nor the sword would be joined. 'Aye, lad,' said he, 'come and sit down, and God's blessing be with thee. Thou art the best man that smites with a

sword in the kingdom. Two thirds of thy strength hast thou
come by, and the third is still to come. And when thou hast
come by it all, thou wilt yield to none. And an uncle of thine,
thy mother's brother, am I, brother to the man in whose court
thou wast last night.' And Peredur sat one side of his uncle, and
they conversed.

Thereupon he could see two youths coming into the hall, and
from the hall proceeding to a chamber, and with them a spear
of exceeding great size, and three streams of blood along it,
running from the socket to the floor. And when they all saw the
youths coming after that fashion, every one set up a crying and
a lamentation, so that it was not easy for any to bear with them.
The man did not, for all that, interrupt his conversation with
Peredur. The man did not tell Peredur what that was, nor did
he ask it of him. After silence for a short while, thereupon, lo,
two maidens coming in, and a great salver between them, and a
man's head on the salver, and blood in profusion around the
head. And then all shrieked and cried out, so that it was hard
for any to be in the same house as they. At last they desisted
therefrom, and sat as long as they pleased, and drank. Thereafter
a room was made ready for Peredur, and they went to sleep.

On the morrow early Peredur arose and with his uncle's leave
went on his way. From there he came to a forest, and far into
the forest he could hear a shrieking. He came towards the place
where the shrieking was. And when he came he could see a
handsome auburn-haired woman and a horse with its saddle on
it standing beside her, and a man's corpse between the woman's
hands, and as she sought to place the corpse in the saddle the
corpse would fall to the ground. And then she would utter a
shriek. 'Say, sister,' said he, 'what shrieking is this of thine?'
'Alas, thou accursed Peredur,' said she, 'small relief from my
affliction did I ever get from thee.' 'Why,' said he, 'should I be
accursed?' 'Because thou art the cause of thy mother's death. For
when thou didst set out against her will, pain leapt within her,
and of that she died. And inasmuch as thou art cause of her
death, thou art accursed. And the dwarf and the she-dwarf thou
sawest in Arthur's court, that was the dwarf of thy father and
thy mother. And I am a foster-sister of thine, and this is my

husband whom the knight that is in the clearing in the forest has slain. And go not near him lest thou be slain.' 'Wrongly, sister mine,' said he, 'dost thou blame me. Because I have been with you as long as I have, scarcely will I overcome him; and were I to be longer, never would I overcome him. And as for thee, cease now thy lamentation, for deliverance is nearer to thee than before. And I will bury the man and will go along with thee to where the knight is, and if I can exact vengeance, I will.'

After burying the man, they came to where the knight was in the clearing, riding his horse. Straightway the knight asked Peredur whence he came. 'I come from Arthur's court.' 'Art thou Arthur's man?' 'Aye, by my faith.' 'A proper place for thee to acknowledge fealty to Arthur.' It was without more delay they made for each other, and there and then Peredur overthrew the knight. The knight asked for quarter. 'Quarter thou shalt have, on condition that thou take this woman to wife; and whatever good thou mayst do to woman, that thou do it to her for having slain her husband without cause; and that thou go thy way to Arthur's court and tell him it was I who overthrew thee, in service and honour to Arthur; and that thou tell him I will not go to his court till I encounter the tall man who is there, to avenge the injury to the dwarf and the maiden.' And Peredur took surety of him to that end. And he set the woman on a horse, in array along with himself, and came his way to Arthur's court and told Arthur his adventure, and the threat to Cei. And Cei won a rebuke from Arthur and the household for driving away from Arthur's court a lad as excellent as Peredur. 'That squire will never come to the court,' said Owein, 'nor will Cei go from the court.' 'By my faith,' said Arthur, 'I will search the wilderness of the Island of Britain for him till I find him. And then let each of them do his worst to the other.'

But Peredur went on his way and came to a great desolate forest. In the forest he saw the tracks of neither man nor herd, but thick growth and vegetation. And when he came to the far end of the forest he could see a great ivy-clad rampart, and numerous strong towers thereon. And near to the gate the vegetation was taller than elsewhere. With the butt of his spear he struck on the gate. Thereupon, lo, a lean tawny-haired youth in the embrasure above him. 'Take thy choice, chieftain,' said he, 'whether I open the gate to thee or make known to whoever is master that thou art in the gateway.' 'Make known that I am here. And if it is desired that I come inside, come I will.' The squire came back quickly and opened the gate to Peredur, and he came into the hall. And when he came into the hall he could see eighteen lean red-headed youths of the same growth and the same mien and the same age and the same garb as the youth that opened the gate to him. And excellent was their courtesy and their service. They helped him to alight and drew off his armour. And they sat and conversed.

Thereupon, lo, five maidens coming from a chamber into the hall. And the chiefest maiden of them, certain was he that he had never seen in any other a sight as fair as she. An old garment of torn brocaded silk about her that had once been good. Where her flesh might be seen through it, whiter was it than flowers of the whitest crystal; but her hair and her eyebrows, blacker were they than jet. Two small red spots on her cheeks, redder were they than aught reddest. The maiden greeted Peredur and embraced him, and sat down one side of him. It was not long thereafter that he could see two nuns coming in, and a flagon full of wine with the one and six loaves of wheaten bread with the other. 'Lady,' said they, 'God knows that there was not save as much again of meat and drink for the convent yonder to-night.' Then they went to meat. And Peredur saw by the maiden that she was wishing to give him more than another of the meat and drink. 'Sister mine,' said he, 'I will share out the meat and drink.' 'Not so, friend,' said she. 'If not, shame on my beard,' said he. Peredur took the bread and gave to each as good as his fellow, and so likewise with the drink to the measure of a cupful.

When meat was ended, 'It would please me,' said Peredur, 'were I to have a comfortable place to sleep.' A chamber was made ready for him, and Peredur went to sleep. 'Sister,' said the youths to the maiden, 'this is our counsel to thee.' 'What is that?' she asked. 'That thou go to the squire, to the chamber close by thee, to offer thyself to him in the way that may seem good to him, either as his wife or as his paramour.' 'That,' said she, 'is a thing which is unseemly. I have never had to do with a man, and to offer myself to him before being wooed by him, that I cannot do for any thing.' 'By our confession to God,' said they, 'unless thou do that, we will leave thee here to thy enemies.' Thereupon the maiden arose, shedding tears, and came straight to the chamber. And with the noise of the door opening, Peredur awoke. And the maiden had tears running down her cheeks. 'Say, sister,' said Peredur, 'what weeping is this of thine?' 'I will tell thee, lord,' said she. 'My father owned this court, and the best earldom in the world under it. Now there was a son of another earl asking me of my father. I would not go to him of my own free will, nor would my father give me against my will to him or any one else. And my father had no children save me. And after my father's death the dominion fell into my hand. Still less eager was I then to have him than before. So he made war on me and conquered my dominion save for this one house. And so exceeding doughty the men thou hast seen, they my foster-brothers, and so exceeding strong the house, it would never be taken, and we in it, so long as meat and drink remained. But those have come to an end, save for the way the nuns thou didst see were succouring us, because the country and the dominion are open to them. But now they too have neither meat nor drink. And there is no respite beyond to-morrow before the earl comes with all his power against this place. And if he take me, my fate will be no better than to be given to the grooms of his horses. And I am come to offer myself to thee, lord, in the way that may seem good to thee, in return for thy being a help to us to carry us hence or to defend us here.' 'Go, my sister, and sleep,' said he, 'and I shall not leave thee without doing one or the other.'

Back came the maiden, and she went to sleep. On the morrow early the maiden arose and came to where Peredur was and greeted him. 'God prosper thee, friend. And hast thou news?' 'There is nothing save good, lord, so long as thou art well – and that the earl and all his power have beset the house. And no one has seen a place with more tents or knights calling on another to joust.' 'Aye,' said Peredur, 'let my horse be made ready for me too, and I will arise.' His horse was accoutred for him, and he too arose and made for the meadow. And when he came, there was a knight riding his horse, having raised the signal for combat. Peredur threw him over his horse's crupper to the ground. And many did he overthrow that day, and in the afternoon towards the close of day there came a knight in special to encounter him, and him he overthrew. He asked for quarter. 'Who art thou then?' asked Peredur. 'Faith,' said he, 'captain of the earl's war-band.' 'What of the countess's dominion is there in thy power?' 'Faith,' said he, 'a third.' 'Aye,' said he, 'restore to her the third of her dominion in full, and what profit thou hast had of it in full, and meat for a hundred men, and their drink, and their horses and their arms to-night to her in her court, and thou thyself her prisoner, save that thou forfeit not thy life.' That was had forthwith. The maiden was joyously happy that night, a third of her dominion hers, and abundance of horses and arms and meat and drink in her court. They took their ease so long as it pleased them, and they went to sleep.

On the morrow early Peredur made for the meadow, and he overthrew hosts that day. And at the close of day there came an arrogant knight in special, and him he overthrew, and he asked for quarter. 'Who art thou then?' asked Peredur. 'Court steward,' said he. 'What is there in thy hand of the maiden's dominion?' 'The third,' said he. 'The third of her dominion to the maiden, and what profit thou hast had of it in full, and meat for two hundred men, and their drink, and their horses and their arms, and thou thyself her prisoner.' That was had forthwith.

And the third day Peredur came to the meadow, and he overthrew more that day than any day else. And at last the earl came to encounter him, and he threw him to the ground, and the earl asked for quarter. 'Who art thou then?' asked Peredur. 'I will not conceal myself,' said he, 'I am the earl.' 'Aye,' said he, 'the whole of her earldom to the maiden, and further, thine own earldom too, and meat for three hundred men, and their drink, and their horses and their arms, and thou thyself in her power.'

And Peredur was thus enforcing tribute and submission to the maiden three weeks. And after establishing and settling her into her dominion, 'With thy leave,' said Peredur,' 'I will set out on my way.' 'Is that, my brother, what thou desirest?' 'Aye, by my faith, and had it not been for love of thee I had not been here long since.' 'Friend,' said she, 'who art thou then?' 'Peredur son of Efrawg, out of the North. And if either affliction or peril come upon thee, send to let me know, and I will defend thee if I can.'

Then Peredur set out, and far from thence there met him a lady riding, and a lean sweaty horse under her; and she greeted the knight. 'Whence comest thou, my sister?' asked Peredur. She told him of the plight she was in and that journey. She was the wife of the Proud One of the Clearing. 'Aye,' said Peredur, 'I am the knight because of whom thou hast had that affliction. And he that brought it upon thee shall repent it.' And thereupon, lo, a knight coming and asking Peredur if he had seen such a knight as he was after. 'Cease thy prattle,' said Peredur. 'I am he thou dost seek, and by my faith the maiden is innocent for me.' Nevertheless they encountered, and Peredur overthrew the knight. He asked for quarter. 'Quarter thou shalt have, on condition thou return the way thou hast been, to make it known that the maiden has been found innocent, and that in her redress I overthrew thee.' The knight pledged his word thereto.

And Peredur went on his way. And on a mountain ahead of him he could see a castle. And he came towards the castle and hammered the door of the gateway with the butt of his spear. Thereupon, lo, a handsome auburn-haired youth opening the gate, in stature and girth a warrior, but in age a lad. When Peredur came into the hall, there was a big handsome woman seated in a chair, and numerous handmaidens about her. And the good lady made him welcome. And when it was time to go to meat they went. And after meat, ' 'Twere well for thee, chieftain,' said the woman, 'to go elsewhere to sleep.' 'May I not sleep here?' 'Nine witches, friend,' said she, 'are there here, and their father and mother with them. They are the witches of Caer Loyw. And by daybreak we shall be no nearer to escaping than to being slain. And they have overrun and laid waste the dominion save for this one house.' 'Aye,' said Peredur, 'here would I be to-night. And if trouble comes, if I can do good, that I will. Harm, however, I will not do.' They went to sleep.

And at daybreak Peredur could hear a shrieking, and quickly

Peredur arose in his shirt and trousers, and his sword about his neck, and out he came. And when he came, there was a witch overtaking the watchman, and he shrieking. Peredur fell upon the witch and struck her on the head with his sword until her helm and headpiece spread like a salver on her head. 'Thy mercy, fair Peredur son of Efrawg, and the mercy of God!' 'How knowest thou, hag, that I am Peredur?' 'It was fated and foreseen that I should suffer affliction from thee, and that thou shouldst take horse and arms from me. And thou shalt be with me awhile, being taught to ride thy horse and handle thy weapons.' 'On these terms,' he replied, 'shalt thou have mercy: thy pledge that thou never do hurt to this countess's dominion.' Peredur took assurance thereof, and by leave of the countess he set off with the witch to the Witches' Court. And he was there three weeks on end. And then Peredur took his choice of horse and arms, and set out on his way.

And at the close of day he came to a valley, and at the far end of the valley he came to a hermit's cell. And the hermit made him welcome, and he was there that night. On the morrow early he arose, and when he came outside, a fall of snow had come down the night before. And a wild she-hawk had killed a duck alongside the cell, and what with the horse's clatter the she-hawk rose up, and a raven alighted on the bird's flesh. Peredur stood and likened the exceeding blackness of the raven, and the whiteness of the snow, and the redness of the blood, to the hair of the woman he loved best, which was black as jet, and her flesh to the whiteness of snow, and the redness of the blood in the white snow to the two red spots in the cheeks of the woman he loved best.

Meantime Arthur and his retinue were searching for Peredur. 'Know ye,' asked Arthur, 'who is the knight with the long spear who is standing in the valley above?' 'Lord,' said one, 'I will go to discover who he is.' Then the squire came to where Peredur was and asked him what he was doing there and who he was. And so fixed were Peredur's thoughts on the woman he loved best, he gave him no answer. He then struck at Peredur with a spear, but Peredur turned on the squire and hurled him over his horse's crupper to the ground. And one after another there came four-and-twenty knights, but he would make answer to one no more than to his fellow, save the same play with each one, to hurl him with one thrust over his horse to the ground. Then Cei came to him, and spoke to Peredur rudely and harshly. And Peredur took him with a spear under his jaws and threw him a great fall away from him, so that his arm and his shoulder-blade were broken, and he rode over him one-and-twenty times. And while he was in a dead faint, so exceeding great was the hurt he had received, his horse returned, careering wildly. And when each of the retinue saw the horse coming without the man upon him, they came in haste to where the encounter had been. And when they came thither they thought that Cei had been slain. Yet they saw that were he to have a physician who might join the bone, and bandage his joints well, he would be none the worse. Peredur moved not from his meditation more than before, despite seeing the press around Cei. And Cei was brought to Arthur's pavilion, and Arthur had skilful physicians brought to him. Arthur was grieved that Cei had met with that hurt, for he had great love for him.

And then Gwalchmei said, 'No one ought unmannerly to disturb an ordained knight from the meditation he might be in; for it may be either that loss has come upon him or that he is thinking of the woman he loved best. And that unmannerliness, it may be, was shown by the man who met him last. And if it please thee, lord, I will go and see whether the knight has moved from that meditation. And if he has so, I will ask him lovingly to come and see thee.' And then Cei sulked and spoke bitter, jealous words. 'Gwalchmei,' said he, 'well do I know thou wilt lead him by the reins. Yet small renown and honour is it for thee to overcome the tired knight, fatigued with battle. Even so, however, hast thou overcome many of them. And so long as thy tongue and thy fair words last thee, a tunic of thin bliant around thee will be armour enough for thee. And thou wilt not need to break spear or sword fighting with the knight thou mayest find in that condition.' And then Gwalchmei said to Cei, 'Thou couldst have spoken what would be more pleasing, hadst thou wished it. And it is not on me it befits thee to vent thy wrath and indignation. I think it likely, even so, that I shall bring the knight along with me without breaking arm or shoulder of mine.' Then Arthur said to Gwalchmei, 'Thou speakest like a wise and prudent man. And go thou on, and take arms enough about thee, and choose thy horse.'

Gwalchmei arrayed himself, and went forward quickly at his horse's pace to where Peredur was. And he was resting upon his spear shaft and thinking the same thoughts. Gwalchmei came to him with no sign of hostility about him, and said to him, 'If I knew it would please thee as it pleases me, I would converse with thee. Yet am I a messenger to thee from Arthur, to beg thee come and see him. And two men have come before me on that same errand.' 'That is true,' said Peredur, 'and ungraciously they came. They fought with me, and I disliked that in so far as I disliked being disturbed in the meditation I was in. Thinking was I of the woman I loved best. This is the reason why remembrance thereof came to me: I was looking on the snow and the raven, and the blood-drops of the duck which the she-hawk had killed in the snow. And I was thinking that similar was the exceeding whiteness of her flesh to the snow, and the exceeding blackness of her hair and her brows to the raven, and the two red spots that were in her cheeks to the two drops of blood.' Said Gwalchmei, 'Those were not ungentle thoughts, nor was it strange though thou disliked to be drawn from them.' Said Peredur, 'Wilt thou tell me if Cei is in Arthur's court?' 'He is,' he replied. 'He was the last knight that encountered thee. And no good came to him from the encounter: he broke his right arm and shoulder-blade with the fall he got from the thrust of thy spear.' 'Aye,' said Peredur, 'I mind not beginning thus to avenge the injury to the dwarf and she-dwarf.' Gwalchmei marvelled to hear him speak of the dwarf and she-dwarf. And he drew near him and embraced him and asked what was his name. 'Peredur son of Efrawg am I called,' said he, 'and thou, who art thou?' 'Gwalchmei am I called,' he replied. 'Glad am I to see thee,' said Peredur. 'In every land I have been in I have heard of thy fame for prowess and good faith. And I request thy fellowship.' 'Thou shalt have it, by my faith, and do thou grant me thine.' 'Thou shalt have it, gladly,' said Peredur.

They set off together in joy and amity towards the place

where Arthur was. And when Cei heard that they were coming, he said, 'I knew Gwalchmei would not need to fight with the knight. Nor is it to be wondered at that he has won renown. He does more with his fair words than we by dint of our arms.' And Peredur and Gwalchmei went to Gwalchmei's tent to take off their armour. And Peredur took just such a garment as was on Gwalchmei, and they went hand in hand to where Arthur was, and greeted him. 'See, lord,' said Gwalchmei, 'the man thou hast been a long while seeking.' 'Welcome to thee, chieftain,' said Arthur, 'and thou shalt stay with me. And had I known that thy progress would be as it has been, thou hadst not left me when thou didst. Yet the dwarf and she-dwarf, to whom Cei did hurt, foretold it of thee – and them thou hast avenged.' And thereupon the queen and her handmaidens coming, and Peredur greeted them, and they too saluted him and made him welcome. Great respect and honour did Arthur show Peredur, and they returned to Caer Llion.

And the first night Peredur came to Caer Llion to Arthur's court, he happened to be walking to and fro within the castle after meat. Lo, Angharad Golden-hand meeting him. 'By my faith, sister,' said Peredur, 'a gracious, lovable maiden art thou, and I could bring myself to love thee best of women, would it please thee.' 'I pledge my faith thus,' said she, 'that I will neither love thee, nor have thee, to all eternity.' 'I too pledge my faith,' said Peredur, 'that I will never speak word to a Christian till thou confess to loving me most of men.'

On the morrow Peredur departed, and he followed the high road along the ridge of a great mountain. And at the far end of the mountain he could see a round valley, and the bounds of the valley wooded and craggy, and the floor of the valley was meadows, and ploughed lands between the meadows and the forest. And in the heart of the forest he could see big black houses, of uncouth workmanship. And he dismounted and led his horse towards the forest, and a distance into the forest he could see the side of a sharp rock, and the path leading towards the side of the rock, and a lion tied to a chain and sleeping at the side of the rock. And he could see a deep pit of dreadful size below the lion, and within it its fill of the bones of men and beasts. And Peredur drew his sword and smote the lion so that it fell hanging by the chain over the pit. And with a second blow he smote the chain so that it was broken and the lion fell into the pit. And Peredur led his horse across the side of the rock till he came to the valley. And about the centre of the valley he could see a fair castle, and he came towards the castle. And in a meadow by the castle he could see a big grey-headed man (bigger was he than any man he had ever seen), and two young lads shooting at the walrus-ivory hafts of their knives; the one of them an auburn-haired youth, the other a yellow-haired youth. And he came on to where the grey-headed man was, and Peredur greeted him. And the grey-headed man said, 'Shame on my porter's beard!' And then Peredur understood that the lion was the porter. And then the grey-headed man and the youths along with him went to the castle, and Peredur went with them; and a fair noble place could he see there. And they made for the hall, and the tables had been set up, and meat and drink in abundance upon them.

And thereupon he could see coming from the chamber an aged woman and a young woman. And they were the biggest women of all he had ever seen. And they washed and went to eat. And the grey-headed man went to the highest place at the head of the table, and the aged woman next to him. And Peredur and the maiden were placed together, and the two young lads waiting upon them. And the maiden looked on Peredur and was sad. And Peredur asked the maiden why she was sad. 'Friend, since first I saw thee, 'tis thou I have loved best of men. And it grieves me to see for a youth as noble as thou the doom that will be thine to-morrow. Didst thou see the many black houses in the heart of the forest? All those are vassals of my father's, the grey-headed man yonder, and giants are they all. And to-morrow they will rise up against thee and slay thee. And the Round Valley is this valley called.' 'Alas, fair maiden, wilt thou see that my horse and arms are in the same lodging as myself to-night?' 'I will, between me and God, if I can gladly.'

When they thought it more timely to take sleep than to carouse, to sleep they went. And the maiden saw to it that Peredur's horse and arms were in the same lodging as himself.

And on the morrow Peredur could hear the clamour of men and horses around the castle. And Peredur arose, and armed himself and his horse, and he came to the meadow. And the aged woman and the maiden came to the grey-headed man. 'Lord,' said they, 'take a pledge of the squire that he will say nothing of what he has seen here, and we will vouch for him that he keep to it.' 'I will not, by my faith,' said the grey-headed man. And Peredur fought against the host, and by evening he had slain a third of the host without any doing him hurt. And then the aged woman said, 'Now, the squire has slain many of thy host. And show him mercy.' 'I will not, by my faith,' he replied. And the aged woman and the fair maiden were watching from the castle embrasure. And with that Peredur encountered the yellow-haired youth and slew him. 'Lord,' said the maiden, 'show mercy to the squire.' 'I will not, between me and God,' said the grey-headed man. And thereupon Peredur encountered the auburn-haired youth and slew him. 'It were better for thee hadst thou shown mercy to the squire before thy two sons were slain. And hard will it be for thee thyself to escape – if escape thou dost.' 'Go then, maiden, and request the squire to show us mercy, though we have not shown it to him.' And the maiden came to where Peredur was, and she asked for mercy for her father and for all who had escaped alive of his men. 'Thou shalt have it, on condition that thy father and each one of those who are under him go to do homage to the emperor Arthur, and to tell him that it was Peredur his man did this service.' 'We will, between me and God, gladly.' 'And that you receive baptism, and I will send to Arthur to ask him to bestow this valley upon thee and thy heirs after thee for ever.' And then they came inside, and the grey-headed man and the big woman greeted Peredur. And then the grey-headed man said, 'Since I have had authority over this valley, I have not seen a Christian who might depart with his life, save for thyself. And we will go to do homage to Arthur, and to receive faith and baptism.' And then Peredur said, 'For me, I thank God that I have not broken my oath to the woman I love best, that I would not speak one word to a Christian.' They tarried there that night.

On the morrow early the grey-headed man and his followers

with him went to Arthur's court. And they did homage to Arthur, and Arthur had them baptized. And the grey-headed man told Arthur that it was Peredur who had overcome him. And Arthur bestowed the valley on the grey-headed man and his followers, to hold it subject to him, as Peredur bade. And with leave of Arthur the grey-headed man departed for the Round Valley.

But Peredur went his way on the morrow early, through a long tract of wilderness, without meeting a dwelling. But at last he came to a small mean dwelling, and there he heard how there was a serpent lying upon a ring of gold, without leaving a dwelling seven miles any side thereof. And Peredur went to where he heard the serpent was, and he fought against the serpent with passion, valour and desperation, and at last he slew it and took the ring for himself. And he was wandering thus for a long time, without speaking one word to any Christian, and till he was losing his colour and his mien by reason of an exceeding longing for Arthur's court and the woman he loved best and his companions.

Then he went his way to Arthur's court, and on the way there met him Arthur's retinue, and Cei ahead of it going an errand for them. Peredur knew each one of them, but not one of the retinue knew him. 'Whence comest thou, chieftain?' asked Cei, and a second time, and a third; but no answer would he give. Cei pierced him with a spear through his thigh-bone, and lest he be compelled to speak and break his vow he passed on without taking vengeance on him. And then Gwalchmei said, 'Between me and God, Cei, that was a sorry stroke of thine, to assault a squire such as this for that he was unable to speak.' And he returned to Arthur's court. 'Lady,' said he to Gwenhwyfar, 'see how grievous an assault Cei made upon this squire for that he was unable to speak. And for God's sake, and for mine, have him made whole against my return, and I will repay it thee.'

And before the men came from their errand, there came a knight to the meadow beside Arthur's court, to seek a man to do battle. And that he got. And he overthrew him, and for a week he was overthrowing a man daily. And one day Arthur and his retinue were coming to the church. They could see the knight, with the signal raised for combat. 'Men,' said Arthur, 'by the valour of men I shall not go hence till I have my horse and arms, to overthrow yonder springald.' Then attendants went to fetch Arthur his horse and arms. And Peredur met the attendants going by, and he took the horse and arms, and made for the meadow. Seeing him arise and go to encounter the knight, every one went upon the tops of the houses and the hills and the high places to watch the encounter. Peredur beckoned with his hand to the knight, to bid him start against him. And the knight charged against him, but for all that he did not budge from the spot. And then Peredur spurred on his horse and bore down on him with passion and wrath, terrible-bitter, proudly eager, and struck him a blow venomous-keen, bitter-sharp, and valorous-strong, under his jaws, and lifted him out of his saddle and hurled him a great distance away from him. And he returned and left the horse and arms with the attendants even as before. And himself on foot he made for the court. And the Dumb Knight was Peredur called then.

Lo, Angharad Golden-hand meeting him. 'Between me and God, chieftain, 'twere pity thou couldst not speak. And couldst thou speak, I would love thee most of men. And by my faith, even though thou canst not, I will love thee most.' 'God repay thee, sister. By my faith, I too will love thee.' And then it was known that he was Peredur. And then he held fellowship with Gwalchmei and Owein son of Urien and all the household, and he tarried in Arthur's court.

Arthur was at Caer Llion on Usk, and he went to hunt, and Peredur along with him. And Peredur loosed his dog upon a stag and the dog killed the stag in a wilderness. And some way off from him he could see signs of habitation, and he came towards the habitation. And he could see a hall, and at the hall door he could see three bald-headed swarthy youths playing gwyddbwyll. And when he came inside he could see three maidens seated on a couch, and royal apparel about them as was meet for folk of noble birth. And he went to sit with them on the couch, and one of the maidens looked closely at Peredur, and she wept. And Peredur asked her why she was weeping. 'Because it is so grievous to me to see slain a youth as fair as thou.' 'Who would slay me?' 'Were it not perilous for thee to stay in this place, I would tell thee.' 'However great my danger be, staying, I will hear it.' 'He who is our father owns this court, and he slays every one that comes to this court without his leave.' 'What kind of man is your father, that he can so slay every one?' 'A man who does treachery and malice to his neighbours, and he makes no redress to any for it.'

And then he could see the young men arising and clearing the board of the pieces. And he could hear a great clatter, and after the clatter he could see a big black one-eyed man coming in. And the maidens arose to meet him, and they drew off his garb from about him. And he went to sit down. After he had recovered himself and was at his ease, he looked upon Peredur and asked, 'Who is the knight?' 'Lord,' she replied, 'the fairest and noblest young man thou hast ever seen, and for God's sake, and the sake of thine own pride, deal gently with him.' 'For thy sake I will deal gently with him, and will grant him his life for to-night.' And then Peredur came to them near the fire, and took meat and drink, and conversed with the maidens. And then Peredur, having grown tipsy, said to the black man, 'I marvel how exceeding mighty thou reckonest thou art. Who put out thine eye?' 'It has been one of my peculiarities that whoever should ask me what thou dost ask should not have his life at my hand, neither for gift nor for fee.' 'Lord,' said the maiden, 'even though he speak foolish things regarding thee, in drunkenness and elation, make good the word thou didst speak just now and promised me.' 'And I will do that gladly, for thy sake. I will grant him his life gladly, for to-night.' And they left it at that that night.

And on the morrow the black man arose and donned his armour, and bade Peredur, 'Get up, man, to suffer death,' said the black man. Peredur said to the black man, 'Do one of two things, black man, if thou art thinking to fight with me: either put off thine armour from about thee, or give me other armour to fight with thee.' 'Why, man,' said he, 'couldst fight, wert thou to have arms? Take what arms thou wilt.' And thereupon the maiden came to Peredur with arms which he approved. And he did battle with the black man until the black man must needs ask quarter of Peredur. 'Black man, thou shalt have quarter for as long as thou art telling me who thou art and who plucked out thine eye.' 'Lord, I will tell: fighting against the Black Worm of the Barrow. There is a mound that is called the Dolorous Mound, and in the mound there is a barrow, and in the barrow there is a Worm, and in the Worm's tail there is a stone, and the virtues of the stone are that whosoever should have it in the one hand, what he would desire of gold he should have in his other hand; and it was fighting against that Worm I lost my eye. And my name is the Black Oppressor. The reason why I was called the Black Oppressor is that I would not leave one man around me to whom I would not do violence; and I would make redress to none.' 'Aye,' said Peredur, 'how far from here is the mound thou tellest of?' 'I will recount for thee the stages of thy journey thither, and I will tell thee how far it is. The day thou settest out hence thou wilt come to the court of the Sons of the King of Suffering.' 'Why are they so called?' 'An Addanc of the Lake kills them once each day. When thou goest thence thou wilt come to the court of the Lady of the Feats.' 'What feats are hers?' 'A war-band of three hundred men has she. Every stranger who comes to the court, the feats of her war-band are told him. The reason for this is that the three hundred of the war-band sit next to the lady, and not out of disrespect to the guests, but in order to tell the feats of her war-band. The day thou settest out thence thou wilt go as far as the Dolorous Mound, and there are the owners of three hundred pavilions around the Mound, guarding the Worm.' 'Since thou hast been a plague so long, I shall bring it about that thou wilt never be such henceforth.' And Peredur slew him.

And then the maiden who had started to converse with him said, 'Hadst thou been poor coming here, henceforth thou wouldst be rich, by reason of the treasure of the black man thou hast slain. And thou seest the many pleasant maidens who are in this court: thou couldst woo whichever of them thou wouldst desire.' 'I came not from my country hither, lady, to take a wife. But pleasant young men do I see there. Let each one of you match with the other, according to his desire. And I want nothing of your goods. I have no need thereof.'

Peredur set out on his way thence, and he came to the court of the Sons of the King of Suffering. And when he came to the court, he could see none but women. And the women rose before him and made him welcome. And at the beginning of their converse he could see a horse coming, and a saddle on him, and a corpse in the saddle. And one of the women rose up and took the corpse from the saddle, and bathed it in a tub that was below the door with warm water therein, and applied precious ointment to it. And the man rose up alive, and came to where Peredur was and saluted him and made him welcome. And two other men came inside in their saddles, and the woman gave those two the same treatment as the one before. Then Peredur asked the chieftain why they were thus. And they said that there was an Addanc in a cave, and it slew them each day. And they left it at that that night.

And on the morrow the squires set off, and Peredur asked them for the sake of their lady-loves to be allowed along with them. They refused him. 'Wert thou to be slain there, thou wouldst have none who might make thee alive again.' And then they journeyed on, and Peredur journeyed after them. And when they had disappeared, so that he might not see them, there then met him, seated on top of a mound, the fairest woman he had ever seen. 'I know thy journey,' said she. 'Thou art going to fight with the Addanc, and he will slay thee, yet not through his might but through guile. He has a cave, and there is a stone pillar in the entrance of the cave, and he sees all those who come inside, but never a one sees him. And with a poisoned stone-spear from the shelter of the pillar he kills every one. And wert thou to pledge thy word to love me best of women, I would give thee a stone so that thou shouldst see him when thou went inside, but he not see thee.' 'I will, by my faith,' said Peredur. 'Since first I saw thee I have loved thee, and where should I seek for thee?' 'When thou seekest for me, seek in the direction of India.' And then the maiden disappeared, after placing the stone in Peredur's hand.

And he came his way towards a river valley, and the bounds

of the valley were forest, and on either side of the river, level
meadows. And one side of the river he could see a flock of white
sheep, and on the other side he could see a flock of black sheep.
And as one of the white sheep bleated, one of the black sheep
would come across, and would be white; and as one of the black
sheep bleated, one of the white sheep would come across, and
would be black.

And he could see a tall tree on the river bank, and the one
half of it was burning from its roots to its tip, and the other half
with green leaves on it. And beyond that he could see a squire
seated on top of a mound, and two greyhounds, white-breasted,
brindled, on a leash, lying beside him. And he felt certain that
he had never seen a squire of such princely mien as he. And in
the forest fronting him he could hear staghounds raising a herd
of stags. And he greeted the squire. And the squire greeted
Peredur. And Peredur could see three paths leading away from
the mound, two paths wide, and the third narrower. And
Peredur asked where the three paths went. 'One of these paths
goes to my court, and I advise thee one of two things: either to
go on ahead to the court, to my wife who is there, or that thou
wait here and thou shalt see the staghounds driving the tired
stags from the forest into the open. And thou shalt see the best
greyhounds thou hast ever seen, and the strongest for stags,
killing them by the water near at hand. And when it is time for
us to go to our meat, my groom will bring my horse to meet me,
and thou shalt be made welcome there to-night.' 'God repay
thee. I will not bide, but will go on my way.' 'The second path
goes to the town that is there nearby, and therein meat and
drink will be found for sale. And the path that is narrower than
the others goes towards the Addanc's cave.' 'By thy leave, squire,
towards that place will I go.'

And Peredur came towards the cave, and took the stone in
his left hand and his spear in his right hand. And as he came
inside, he caught sight of the Addanc and thrust him through
with a spear, and cut off his head. And when he came out of the
cave, lo, in the entrance of the cave his three companions. And
they greeted Peredur and said it was of him there was a prophecy
that he should slay that plague. And Peredur gave the head to

the squires, and they in return offered him the one he might choose to wife of their three sisters, and half their kingdom along with her. 'I came not hither to take a wife,' said Peredur, 'but if I desired any woman, maybe it is your sister whom I would desire the first.'

And Peredur went on his way. And he could hear a commotion behind him, and he looked behind him and could see a man on a red horse, and red armour upon him. And the man came level with him and greeted Peredur in the name of God and man. And Peredur too greeted the squire kindly. 'Lord, 'tis to make a request of thee that I am come.' 'What is thy request?' asked Peredur. 'That thou take me for thy man.' 'And whom would I take for my man, were I to take thee?' 'I will hide not my identity from thee. Edlym Red-sword am I called, an earl from Eastern parts.' 'I marvel thou dost offer thyself as man to a man whose dominion is no greater than thine own. For I too have but an earldom. But since thou seest fit to come as my man I will take thee, gladly.'

And they came towards the countess's court. And they were made welcome in the court, and were told how it was not out of disrespect to them that they were placed below the war-band, but such was the custom of the court. For whoever overthrew the three hundred of her war-band would be allowed to eat next to her, and she would love him best of men. And after Peredur had thrown the three hundred of her war-band to the ground and sat at her one hand, the countess said, 'I thank God I have had a youth so fair and brave as thou, since I have not had the man I loved best.' 'Who was the man thou didst love best?' 'By my faith, Edlym Red-sword was the man I loved best, but I have never seen him.' 'Faith,' said he, 'Edlym is my comrade, and here he is. And for his sake I came to play with thy war-band. And he could have done it better than I, had he so wished. And I will bestow thee upon him.' 'God thank thee, fair squire, and I will take the man I love best.' And that night Edlym and the countess slept together.

And on the morrow Peredur set out towards the Dolorous Mound. 'By thy hand, lord, I will go along with thee,' said Edlym. They came their way to where they might see the

Mound and the pavilions. 'Go,' said Peredur to Edlym, 'to yonder men, and bid them come to do me homage.' Edlym came to them, and said to them thus, 'Come ye to do homage to my lord.' 'Who is thy lord?' they asked. 'Peredur Longspear is my lord,' said Edlym. 'Were it permitted to put an envoy to death, thou shouldst not return alive to thy lord, for making so arrogant a request to kings and earls and barons as to come to do homage to thy lord.' Edlym came back to Peredur. Peredur bade him go back to them and give them the choice: either to do him homage or to fight with him. They chose to fight with him. And Peredur threw the owners of a hundred pavilions that day to the ground. And on the morrow he threw the owners of another hundred to the ground. And the third hundred resolved in council to do homage to Peredur. And Peredur asked them what they were doing there. And they said that they were guarding the Worm until it were dead. 'And then we would fight for the stone, and whoever would be uppermost of us should have the stone.' 'Wait for me here,' said Peredur, 'I will go to encounter the Worm.' 'Not so, lord,' said they, 'let us go together to fight with the Worm.' 'Why,' said Peredur, 'I will not have that. Should the Worm be slain, I would have no more fame than any one of you.' And he went to where the Worm was and slew it, and came to them. 'Count your charges since you came here, and I will repay it thee in gold,' said Peredur. He paid them as much as each one said was owing him. And he asked nothing of them save to acknowledge that they were his men. And he said to Edlym, 'To the woman thou lovest best shalt thou go, and I will go on my way, and will requite thee for becoming my man.' And then he gave the stone to Edlym. 'God repay thee, and may God speed thee.' And away went Peredur.

And he came to a river valley, the fairest he had ever seen, and many pavilions of divers colours could he see there. And more wondrous to him than that was to see as many as he saw of watermills and windmills. There met him a big auburn-haired man, and the look of a craftsman about him. And Peredur asked who he was. 'Head miller am I over all the mills yonder.' 'Shall I have lodging of thee?' asked Peredur. 'Thou shalt,' he replied, 'gladly.' He came to the miller's house, and he saw that the miller's was a pleasant, fair dwelling. And Peredur asked the miller for money on loan, to buy meat and drink for himself and the people of the house; and he would pay it him before he went away thence. He asked the miller what was the reason for that muster. The miller said to Peredur, 'It is one of two things: either thou art a man from afar or thou art a fool. The empress of great Constantinople is there, and she has no desire save for the bravest man, for she has no need of wealth. And food might not be brought to all the thousands that are here, and it is for that reason there are all these mills.' And that night they took their ease.

And on the morrow Peredur arose and equipped himself and his horse to go to the tournament. And he could see a pavilion amongst the other pavilions, the fairest he had ever seen. And he could see a fair maiden craning her head through a window of the pavilion. And he had never seen a fairer maiden, and a robe of gold brocaded silk about her. And he looked hard at the maiden, and great love of her entered into him. And he was thus gazing at the maiden from the morning till mid-day, and from mid-day till it was afternoon. And the tournament had then come to an end, and he came to his lodging. And he put off his armour from about him, and asked the miller for money on loan. And the miller's wife was indignant with Peredur, but nevertheless the miller gave him money on loan. And on the morrow he did even as he had done the day before. And that night he came to his lodging and took money on loan from the miller. And the third day, when he was in the same place gazing at the maiden, he felt a mighty blow between his shoulder and neck, from an axe-haft. And when he looked behind him upon the miller, the miller said to him, 'Do one of two things,' said the miller, 'either turn away thy head or go to the tournament.' And Peredur smiled at the miller and went to the tournament. And those who encountered him that day, he threw them all to the ground. And as many as he threw, he sent the man as a gift to the empress, and the horses and suits of armour as a gift to the miller's wife, in earnest of her money lent. Peredur followed the tournament until he threw every one to the ground, and those whom he threw to the ground, he sent the men to the empress's prison and the horses and suits of armour to the miller's wife, in earnest of the money lent.

The empress sent to the Knight of the Mill to bid him come and see her. And he denied the first messenger, and the second went to him. And the third time she sent a hundred knights to bid him come and see her. And if he came not of his own free will, she bade them bring him against his will. And they came to him and declared their message from the empress. He played with them well. He had them tied as one ties a roebuck and thrown into the mill-dyke. And the empress sought counsel of a wise man who was in her council. And he told her, 'I will go to him on thy errand.' And he came to Peredur and greeted him, and bade him for the sake of his lady-love come and see the empress. And he came, he and the miller. And the first place he came to in the pavilion, there he sat; and she came one side of him, and there was brief converse between them. And Peredur took leave and went to his lodging.

On the morrow he went to see her, and when he came to the pavilion there was no part of the pavilion which was in poorer state than the rest, for they knew not where he would sit. Peredur sat one side of the empress, and he conversed graciously. When they were thus, they could see coming inside a black man, and a goblet of gold in his hand, full of wine, and he went down on his knee before the empress and bade her give it not save to one who would come to fight with him for her. And she looked at Peredur. 'Lady,' said he, 'give me the goblet.' And he drank the wine and gave the goblet to the miller's wife. And when they were thus, lo, a black man who was bigger than the other, and a beast's claw in his hand, in the shape of a goblet, with its fill of wine. And he gave it to the empress and bade her give it not save to one who would fight with him. 'Lady,' said Peredur, 'give it me.' And she gave it to Peredur. And Peredur drank the wine and gave the goblet to the miller's wife. When they were thus, lo, a red curly-headed man who was bigger than either of the other men, and a goblet of crystal stone in his hand, with its fill of wine therein. And he sank down on his knee and gave it into the empress's hand, and bade her give it not save to one who would fight with him for her. And she gave it to Peredur, and he then sent it to the miller's wife. That night Peredur went to his lodging. And on the morrow he equipped himself and his horse and came to the meadow; and Peredur killed the three men, and then he came to the pavilion. And she said to him, 'Fair Peredur, remember the pledge thou gavest me when I gave thee the stone, when thou didst slay the Addanc.' 'Lady,' he replied, 'thou sayest truth, and I will remember it.' And Peredur ruled with the empress fourteen years, as the story tells.

Arthur was at Caer Llion on Usk, a main court of his. And in the middle of the hall floor there were four men seated upon a mantle of brocaded silk: Owein son of Urien, and Gwalchmei son of Gwyar, and Hywel son of Emyr Llydaw, and Peredur Longspear. And thereupon they could see coming in a black curly-headed maiden on a yellow mule, and rough thongs in her hand, urging on the mule; and a rough unlovely look about her. Blacker were her face and her hands than the blackest iron that had been steeped in pitch; and it was not her colour that was ugliest, but her shape: high cheeks and hanging, baggy-fleshed face, and a stub wide-nostrilled nose, and the one eye mottled green, most piercing, and the other black, like jet, deep sunk in her head. Long yellow teeth, yellower than the flowers of the broom, and her belly swelling from her breast-bone higher than her chin. Her backbone was shaped like a crutch; her two hips were broad in the bone, but everything narrow thence down-wards, save that her feet and knees were clumped. She greeted Arthur and all his household save Peredur. And to Peredur she spoke wrothful ugly words. 'Peredur, I greet thee not, for thou dost not merit it. Blind was fate when she bestowed favour and fame upon thee. When thou camest to the court of the Lame King, and when thou sawest there the squire bearing the sharpened spear, and from the tip of the spear a drop of blood, and that running as it were a torrent as far as the squire's grip – and other marvels besides thou sawest there, but thou didst not ask after their meaning nor the cause of them. And hadst thou so asked, the king would have had health and his kingdom in peace. But henceforth strife and battle, and the loss of knights, and women left widowed, and maidens without succour, and that all because of thee.' And then she said to Arthur, 'With thy leave, lord, far off is my lodging from hence, not other than in Proud Castle. I know not whether thou hast heard tell of it. And therein there are five hundred and sixty-six ordained knights, and the woman each one loves best along with him; and whoever desires to win fame at arms and in jousting and fighting, he will get it there if he deserve it. And yet he who would have pre-eminence in fame and renown, I know where he would get it. There is a castle on a prominent mountain, and therein is a maiden, and it is being besieged, and whoever might relieve it would win the highest renown in the world.' And thereupon she departed on her way.

Said Gwalchmei, 'By my faith, I will not sleep in peace till I know whether I can set the maiden free.' And many of Arthur's household were of one mind with him. Yet Peredur spoke otherwise. 'By my faith, I will not sleep in peace till I know the story and the meaning of the spear the black maiden told of.' And as everyone was making ready, lo, a knight coming to the gate, and the size and strength of a warrior in him, equipped with horse and arms, and he came on and greeted Arthur and all his household save Gwalchmei. And on the knight's shoulder there was a gold-chased shield, and a bar of blue-azure thereon, and all his armour was of that same colour. And he said to Gwalchmei, 'Thou slewest my lord through thy deceit and treachery, and that will I prove upon thee.' Gwalchmei arose. 'This,' said he, 'my gage against thee, either here or where thou wilt, that I am neither deceiver nor traitor.' 'In the presence of the king who is over me I would have the combat between thee and me.' 'Gladly,' said Gwalchmei, 'go thy way. I will follow thee.' The knight went his way, and Gwalchmei made ready; and many a suit of armour was offered him but he would have none save his own. Gwalchmei and Peredur accoutred themselves and followed after him, because of their fellowship and the great love they bore one another. But they kept not together, but each on his own.

Gwalchmei in the young of the day came to a valley, and in the valley he could see a rampart, and a great court within the rampart, and proud lofty towers round about it. And he could see a knight coming out to the gate to hunt, on a gleaming-black, wide-nostrilled, easy-paced palfrey, of proud and even tread, fast-stepping and unfaltering. He was the man who owned the court. Gwalchmei greeted him. 'God prosper thee, chieftain, and whence comest thou?' 'I come,' said he, 'from Arthur's court.' 'Art thou Arthur's man?' 'Aye, by my faith,' said Gwalchmei. 'I know good counsel for thee,' said the knight. 'I see thee tired and worn. Go to the court, and there shalt thou stay to-night if it seem good to thee.' 'Even so, lord, and God repay thee.' 'Take a ring as a token to the porter, and go on to the tower yonder. And there is a sister of mine there.'

And Gwalchmei came to the gate and showed the ring and made for the tower. And when he came, there was a big blazing fire alight, and a bright high smokeless flame from it, and a handsome majestic maiden sitting in a chair near the fire. And the maiden was glad to see him and made him welcome, and arose to meet him. And he went to sit one side of the maiden. They took their dinner, and after their dinner they turned to pleasant converse. And when they were thus, behold, a handsome hoary-headed man coming in to them. 'Alas, vile whore,' said he, 'didst thou but know how fitting it is for thee to play and sit with that man, thou wouldst not sit, and thou wouldst not play.' And he withdrew his head and away. 'Chieftain,' said the maiden, 'if thou wouldst do my counsel, for fear lest the man has a trap for thee, thou wouldst fasten the door,' said she. Gwalchmei arose, and when he came towards the door, the man, one of sixty, fully-armed, was making upwards for the tower. Gwalchmei made a defence with a gwyddbwyll board, lest any should come up, until the man came from hunting.

Thereupon, behold, the earl coming. 'What is this?' said he. 'An ugly thing,' said the hoary-headed man, 'that yonder vile woman is sitting and drinking till evening with the man who slew your father. And he is Gwalchmei son of Gwyar.' 'Leave off now,' said the earl, 'I will go inside.' The earl made Gwalchmei welcome. 'Chieftain,' said he, 'it was wrong of thee to come to our court if thou knewest thou hadst slain our father. Even though we cannot avenge it, God will avenge it upon thee.' 'Friend,' said Gwalchmei, 'as for that, this is how it is: it was neither to confess to killing your father, nor to deny it, that I came. I am going on a quest for Arthur and myself. Nevertheless, I ask a year's respite until I come from my quest, and that then, upon my oath, I come to this court to do one of two things: admit or deny it.' The respite he got willingly. And he was there that night. On the morrow he set forth, but under that head the story says no more of Gwalchmei than that.

And Peredur went on his way. Peredur wandered the Island to seek tidings of the black maiden, but he found them not. And he came to a land he knew not in a river valley. And as he was traversing the valley he could see a rider coming towards him, with the mark of a priest upon him. And he asked for his blessing. 'Alas, poor wretch,' said he, 'thou hast no right to receive blessing, and it will avail thee nothing, for donning arms on a day as exalted as this day.' 'And what day is to-day?' asked Peredur. 'To-day is Good Friday.' 'Blame me not. I did not know that. A year from to-day I departed my country.' And then he dismounted and led his horse in his hand. And he travelled a length of the high road until a by-way met him, and along the by-way through the forest. And the far side of the forest he could see a towerless castle, and he could see signs of habitation about the castle. And he came towards the castle, and at the castle gate there met him the priest who had met with him earlier. And he asked for his blessing. 'God's blessing upon thee,' said he, 'and it is more fitting to journey thus. And thou shalt be with me to-night.' And Peredur tarried that night.

On the morrow Peredur sought leave to depart. 'It is no day to-day for any to journey. Thou shalt be with me to-day and to-morrow and the day after. And I will give thee the best guidance I can concerning that which thou seekest.' And the fourth day Peredur sought leave to depart, and asked the priest to give him guidance concerning the Castle of Wonders. 'As much as I know, I will tell thee. Cross the mountain yonder, and the far side of the mountain there is a river, and in the river valley there is a king's court; and the king was there at Eastertide. And if thou art to get tidings anywhere of the Castle of Wonders, thou wilt get them there.'

And then he went on his way and came to the river valley,

and there met him a company of men going to hunt, and he could see amongst the company a man of high rank. And Peredur greeted him. 'Choose, chieftain, whether thou go to the court or whether thou come along with me to hunt. And I will send one of the retinue to give thee in keeping to a daughter of mine that is there, to take meat and drink until I come from hunting. And if thy errands be such as I can obtain, thou shalt obtain them gladly.' And the king sent a short yellow-haired youth along with him. And when they came to the court the lady had arisen and was going to wash. And Peredur came forward, and she greeted Peredur joyfully and made room for him at her side. And they took their dinner. And whatever Peredur said to her, she would laugh loudly, so that every one in the court might hear. And then the short yellow-haired youth said to the lady, 'By my faith,' said he, 'if thou hadst ever a man, 'tis this squire thou hadst. And if thou hast not had a man, thy mind and heart are set on him.'

And the short yellow-haired youth made after the king, and said that he thought it most likely that the squire who had met with him was his daughter's man. 'And if not her man, I think it likely he will be her man here and now, unless thou guard against him.' 'What is thy counsel, youth?' 'My counsel is that brave men be set upon him, and that he be held until thou know of that for certain.' And he set men upon Peredur to seize him and to put him in gaol. And the maiden came to meet her father, and asked him why he had had the squire from Arthur's court imprisoned. 'Faith,' he replied, 'he will not be free to-night or to-morrow or the day after, and he shall not come from where he is.' She made no demur to the king at what he said, and came to the squire. 'Is it tiresome for thee, to be here?' 'I should not mind though I were not.' 'Thy bed and thy state shall be no worse than the king's, and the best songs in the court thou shalt have at thy command. And were it more pleasant for thee than before that my bed be here for conversing with thee, thou shouldst have it gladly.' 'I will not gainsay that.' He was in prison that night. And the maiden held by what she had promised him.

And on the morrow Peredur could hear an uproar in the town. 'Alas, fair maiden, what uproar is this?' 'The king's host and his power are coming to this town to-day.' 'What would they then?' 'There is an earl near here, with two earldoms to his name, and he is as powerful as a king. And there will be an encounter between them to-day.' 'I beg thee,' said Peredur, 'to get me a horse and arms to go and look upon the encounter, on my pledge to return to my prison.' 'Gladly,' she replied, 'I will get for thee a horse and arms.' And she provided him with a horse and arms, and a pure red surcoat over his armour, and a yellow shield on his shoulder. And he came to the encounter, and those of the earl's men that met with him that day he threw them all to the ground. And he came back to his prison. She asked tidings of Peredur, but he spoke not one word to her. And so she went to ask tidings of her father, and she asked who had been best of his following. He replied that he knew him not: he was a man with a red surcoat over his armour and a yellow shield on his shoulder. And she smiled and came to where Peredur was. And in high regard was he held that night.

And three days on end Peredur slew the earl's men, and or ever any one might know who he was he would come back to his prison. And on the fourth day Peredur slew the earl himself. And the maiden came to meet her father and asked tidings of him. 'Good tidings,' said the king. 'The earl has been slain,' said he, 'and the two earldoms are now mine.' 'Dost know, lord, who slew him?' 'I do,' said the king. 'The knight of the red surcoat and the yellow shield slew him.' 'Lord,' said she, 'I know who that is.' 'For God's sake,' he replied, 'who is he?' 'Lord, he is the knight thou hast in prison.' Then he came to where Peredur was, and greeted him, and told him he would repay him the service he had done even as he himself would wish. And when they went to meat, Peredur was placed on the king's one hand, and the maiden on the other side of Peredur. And after meat the king said to Peredur, 'I will give thee my daughter to wife, and half my kingdom with her; and the two earldoms I will bestow on thee as a gift to thee.' 'May the Lord God repay thee. I came not hither to take a wife.' 'What dost thou seek then, chieftain?' ''Tis seeking tidings I am of the Castle of Wonders.' 'Loftier are the chieftain's thoughts than we expect to find,' said the maiden. 'Tidings of the castle thou shalt have, and men to guide thee through my father's dominion, and ample provision. And thou, chieftain, art the man I love best.' And then she said to him, 'Cross yonder mountain and thou wilt see a lake, and a castle within the lake, and that is called the Castle of Wonders. But we know naught of its wonders, save that it is so called.'

And Peredur came towards the castle, and the gate of the castle was open. And when he came to the hall, the door was open. And as he came inside he could see gwyddbwyll in the hall, and each of the two sets playing against the other. And the one he would support lost the game, and the other set up a shout just as though they were men. He grew angry, and caught up the pieces in his lap, and threw the board into the lake.

And as he was thus, lo, the black maiden coming in and saying to Peredur, 'God's welcome be not to thee. Thou dost oftener harm than good.' 'What is thy charge against me, black maiden?' asked Peredur. 'That thou hast made the empress lose her board, and she would not wish that for her empire.' 'Is there a means whereby the board might be recovered?' 'There is, wert thou to go to the Castle of Ysbidinongyl. There is a black man there laying waste much of the empress's dominion; and kill him, thou wouldst recover the board. But if thou go there, thou wilt not come back alive.' 'Wilt thou be a guide to me there?' asked Peredur. 'I will show thee a way there,' said she.

He came to the Castle of Ysbidinongyl and fought with the black man. And the black man asked quarter of Peredur. 'I will grant thee quarter. See that the board is in the place where it was when I came to the hall.' And then the black maiden came and said to him, 'Aye,' said she, 'God's curse upon thee for thy pains, for leaving alive the plague that is laying waste the empress's dominion.' 'I left him his life,' said Peredur, 'in order to get the board.' 'The board is not where thou didst first find it. Go back and slay him.'

Peredur went and slew the black man. And when he came to the court the black maiden was at the court. 'Maiden,' said Peredur, 'where is the empress?' 'Between me and God, thou wilt not see her now unless thou kill a plague that is in the forest yonder.' 'What kind of plague is it?' 'A stag is there, and it is swift as the swiftest bird, and there is one horn in its forehead, the length of a spear-shaft, and it is as sharp of point as aught sharpest-pointed. And it browses the tops of the trees and what herbage there is in the forest. And it kills every animal it finds therein. And those it does not kill, die of hunger. And worse than that, it comes every night and drains the fish pond in its drinking, and leaves the fish exposed, and most of them die before water comes thereto again.' 'Maiden,' said Peredur, 'wilt thou come and show me that animal?' 'Not so. No mortal has dared go to the forest for a year. There is the empress's lapdog, and that will raise the stag and bring it to thee. And the stag will make a rush at thee.'

The lapdog went as a guide to Peredur and raised the stag, and brought it to the place where Peredur was. And the stag made a rush at Peredur, and he let its charge go past him, and struck off its head with a sword. And as he was gazing at the stag's head, he could see a lady on horseback coming towards him, and taking up the lapdog in the sleeve of her cape and the head between her and her saddlebow, and the collar of red gold that was about the stag's neck. 'Chieftain,' said she, 'discourteously hast thou acted, slaying the fairest jewel that was in my dominion.' 'That was requested of me. And is there a way I might win thy friendship?' 'There is. Go to the breast of yonder mountain, and there thou wilt see a bush. And at the foot of the bush there is a stone slab, and do thou there ask for a man to joust, three times. Thou wouldst then have my friendship.'

Peredur went on his way and came to beside the bush and asked for a man to joust. And a black man rose up from under the slab, and a bony horse under him, and huge rusty armour upon him and upon his horse, and they fought. And as Peredur would throw the black man to the ground, he would leap back into his saddle. And Peredur dismounted and drew his sword. And thereupon the black man disappeared, and Peredur's horse and his own horse with him, so that he got no second glimpse of them.

And Peredur walked along the mountain. And the far side of the mountain he could see a castle in a river valley, and he came towards the castle. And as he came inside the castle, he could see a hall, and the hall door open. And in he came, and he could see a lame grey-headed man sitting at the end of the hall, and Gwalchmei sitting on his one hand, and Peredur's horse he could see in the same stall as Gwalchmei's horse. And they made Peredur welcome, and he went to sit the other side of the grey-headed man. And a yellow-haired youth went on his knee before Peredur and besought Peredur's friendship. 'Lord,' said the youth, 'I came in the guise of the black maiden to Arthur's court, and when thou didst throw away the board, and when thou slewest the black man from Ysbidinongyl, and when thou slewest the stag, and when thou didst fight against the black man of the slab; and I came with the head all bloody on the salver, and with the spear that had the stream of blood from its tip to the handgrip along the spear. And the head was thy cousin's, and it was the witches of Caer Loyw that had slain him. And 'twas they that lamed thy uncle. And thy cousin am I, and it is prophesied that thou wilt avenge that.'

And Peredur and Gwalchmei resolved to send to Arthur and his war-band, to ask him to come against the witches. And they began to fight with the witches. And one of the witches slew a man of Arthur's before Peredur's eyes, and Peredur bade her desist. And a second time the witch slew a man before Peredur's eyes, and a second time Peredur bade her desist. And the third time the witch slew a man before Peredur's eyes, and Peredur drew his sword and smote the witch on the crest of her helm, so that the helm and all the armour and the head were split in two. And she raised a shout, and bade the other witches flee, and said that it was Peredur, the man who had been with them learning knighthood, and who was destined to slay them. And then Arthur and his war-band fell upon the witches, and the witches of Caer Loyw were all slain. And thus is it told of the Castle of Wonders.

GEREINT SON OF ERBIN

It was Arthur's custom to hold court at Caer Llion on Usk, and he held it continually for seven Easters and five Christmasses. And once upon a time he held court there at Whitsuntide; for Caer Llion was the most accessible place in his dominions, by sea and by land. And he gathered about him to that place nine crowned kings who were vassals of his, and along with them earls and barons; for those would be his guests at every high festival unless sore straits prevented them. And when he would be at Caer Llion holding court, thirteen churches would be occupied with his Masses. This is how they would be occupied: a church for Arthur and his kings and his guests, and the second for Gwenhwyfar and her ladies; and the third would be for the steward and the suitors, and the fourth for Odiar the Frank and the other officers; nine other churches would be between nine captains of the war-bands, and for Gwalchmei above all, for he by excellence of renown for feats of arms and dignity of noble birth was chief of the nine captains of the war-bands. And there might not be contained in any one church more than we have mentioned above.

Glewlwyd Mighty-grasp was head porter to him; but he would have nothing to do with the office save at one of the three high festivals; but seven men who were in office under him would share the year between them, namely, Gryn and Penpingion and Llaesgymyn and Gogyfwlch, and Gwrddnei Cat-eye who could see as well by night as by day, and Drem son of Dremhidydd, and Clust son of Clustfeinydd, who were warriors of Arthur's.

And Whit Tuesday as the emperor was sitting at his carousal, lo, a tall auburn-haired youth coming in, with a tunic and sur-coat of ribbed brocaded silk upon him, and a gold-hilted sword about his neck, and two low boots of cordwain upon his feet; and he came before Arthur. 'All hail, lord,' said he. 'God prosper thee,' he replied, 'and God's welcome to thee. And hast thou fresh tidings?' 'I have, lord,' he replied. 'I know thee not,' said

Arthur. 'Now I marvel thou dost not know me. And a forester of thine am I, lord, in the forest of Dean. And Madawg is my name, son of Twrgadarn.' 'Tell thy tidings,' said Arthur. 'I will, lord,' said he. 'A stag have I seen in the forest, and I never saw the like of it.' 'What is there about it,' asked Arthur, 'that thou shouldst never have seen its like?' 'It is pure white, lord, and it goes not with any animal for presumption and pride, so exceeding majestical it is. And it is to ask counsel of thee, lord, that I am come. What is thy counsel concerning it?' 'I shall do what is most fitting,' said Arthur; 'go to hunt it to-morrow in the young of the day, and have that made known to-night to each one from the lodgings, and to Rhyferys (who was head huntsman to Arthur) and to Elifri (who was Arthur's head groom), and to every one besides those.' And on that they determined; and he sent the groom on ahead.

And then Gwenhwyfar said to Arthur, 'Lord,' said she, 'wilt thou give me leave to go to-morrow and see and listen to the hunting of the stag that the youth spoke of?' 'I will, gladly,' said Arthur. 'Then I shall go,' said she. And with that Gwalchmei said to Arthur, 'Lord,' said he, 'were it not meet for thee to permit him to whom it should come in his hunting to cut off its head and give it to the one he would wish, either to his own lady-love or to his comrade's lady-love, whether it come to a rider or to one on foot?' 'I grant it, gladly,' said Arthur, 'and on the steward be the blame if every one be not ready in the morning to go a-hunting.'

And they spent the night with temperate indulgence in songs and entertainment and stories, and service a-plenty. And when they each of them thought it time to go to sleep, they went.

And when day came on the morrow they awoke. And Arthur called on the chamberlains who guarded his bed, none other than four squires. These were they: Cadyrieith son of the porter Gandwy, and Amhren son of Bedwyr, and Amhar son of Arthur, and Goreu son of Custennin. And those men came to Arthur and greeted him and arrayed him. And Arthur marvelled that Gwenhwyfar had not awoke, and had not turned in her bed. And the men desired to wake her. 'Wake her not,' said Arthur, 'since she had rather sleep than go to see the hunting.'

And then Arthur went on his way, and he could hear two horns sounding, one near the lodging of the head huntsman and the other near the lodging of the head groom. And a full muster of all the hosts came to Arthur, and they set out towards the forest. And through Usk they came to the forest, and they left the high road and travelled land high and lofty till they came to the forest.

And after Arthur had gone from the court, Gwenhwyfar awoke and called her maidens and was apparelled. 'Maidens,' said she, 'I had leave last night to go and see the hunting; and let one of you go to the stable, and let her have brought what horses are there that are suitable for women to ride.' And one of them went, and there were found in the stable two horses only. And Gwenhwyfar and one of the maidens set off on the two horses. And they came through Usk, and followed the trail of men and horses and their tracks. And as they were travelling in this wise they could hear a mighty great commotion. And they looked back and could see a horseman on a young willow-grey charger of immense size, and a young auburn-haired bare-legged knight of princely mien upon it, and a gold-hilted sword on his thigh, and a tunic and surcoat of brocaded silk about him, and two low boots of cordwain upon his feet, and over that a mantle of blue-purple, and an apple of gold at each of its corners. And the horse stepped out high-mettled, brisk and lively, with short even tread. And he overtook Gwenhwyfar. And he greeted her. 'God prosper thee, Gereint,' she made answer, 'and I knew thee when first I saw thee now, and God's welcome to thee. And why didst thou not go to hunt with thy lord?' 'Because I knew not when he went,' said he. 'I too marvelled,' said she, 'how he might go without letting me know.' 'Aye, lady,' he said, 'for my part I slept so that I knew not when he went.' 'And thou art the very best companion for me,' said she, 'of a young man, to have my companionship, in the whole dominion. And there could be as much pleasure from the hunting for us as for them, for we shall hear the horns when they are sounded, and we shall hear the dogs when they are loosed and when they start to bay.'

And they came to the edge of the forest and there they halted. 'We shall hear from hence,' said she, 'when the dogs are loosed.'

And with that they heard a commotion. And they looked back towards the commotion, and they could see a dwarf riding a big sturdy horse, wide-nostrilled, ground-devouring, strong-mettled. And in the dwarf's hand there was a whip; and near the dwarf they could see a lady on a handsome pale white horse, of proud even pace, and a royal robe of brocaded silk about her, and near to her a knight on a great mud-stained charger, and heavy shining armour on him and his horse. And certain were they that they had never seen man and armour more remarkable for size than they; and each one of them near to the other.

'Gereint,' said Gwenhwyfar, 'dost know yonder big knight?' 'Not I,' he answered; 'yonder huge outlandish armour permits neither his face nor his expression to be seen.' 'Go, maiden,' said Gwenhwyfar, 'and ask the dwarf who the knight is.' The maiden went to meet the dwarf. The dwarf waited for her, when he saw her coming towards him. And the maiden asked the dwarf, 'Who is the knight?' said she. 'I will not tell thee,' said he. 'Since thy manners are so bad,' said she, 'that thou wilt not tell me that, I will ask him in person.' 'Thou wilt not, by my faith,' replied he. 'Why?' said she. 'Because thine is not the dignity of a person for whom it is fitting to speak with my lord.' Then the maiden turned her horse's head towards the knight. With that the dwarf struck her with a whip that was in his hand, across her face and eyes, till the blood streamed forth. The maiden, for pain of the blow, returned to Gwenhwyfar, bemoaning her pain. 'Most churlishly,' said Gereint, 'did the dwarf deal with thee. I will go,' said Gereint, 'to find out who the knight is.' 'Go thou,' said Gwenhwyfar.

Gereint came to the dwarf. Said he, 'Who is the knight?' 'I will not tell thee,' said the dwarf. 'I will ask it of the knight in person,' he answered. 'Thou wilt not, by my faith,' said the dwarf. 'Thou art not of dignity enough to have a right to speak with my lord.' 'I have spoken with a man who is as good as thy lord,' said Gereint, and he turned his horse's head towards the knight. The dwarf overtook him and struck him in the same place as he had struck the maiden, till the blood stained the mantle that was on Gereint. Gereint set his hand to the hilt of his sword, and debated in his mind, but considered how it was no vengeance for him to slay the dwarf and the armed knight take him cheaply and without armour. And he came back to the place where Gwenhwyfar was.

'Wisely and prudently didst thou act,' said she. 'Lady,' said he, 'I shall again go after him, with thy leave, and he will come at last to an inhabited place where I may provide myself with armour, either on loan or against surety, so that I may pit my strength against the knight.' 'Go then,' said she, 'but go not too close to him until thou art provided with good armour. And great anxiety shall I feel for thee,' said she, 'till I have tidings of thee.' 'If I am alive,' said he, 'by nones to-morrow evening thou shalt hear tidings, if I escape.' And with that he set off.

The way they went was below the court in Caer Llion, and at the ford on Usk they crossed over and travelled fair level land, high and lofty, until they came to a walled town. And at the town's end they could see a stronghold and a castle. And to the town's end they came. And as the knight proceeded through the town, the people of every house would arise to greet and welcome him. And when Gereint came to the town he looked in every house to seek to recognize any of those he might see. But he knew no one, nor any one him, so that he might have the favour of arms, either on loan or against surety. And he could see every house full of men and arms and horses, and shields being polished, and swords furbished, and armour burnished, and horses shod.

And the knight and the lady and the dwarf made for the castle that was in the town. Every one in the castle made them welcome, and on the battlements and on the gates and in every direction they were breaking their necks to greet them and make them welcome. Gereint stood and looked to see whether he would tarry in the castle. And when he knew for certain that he was staying, he looked about him and could see, a short way from the town, an old ruined court and in it a broken hall. And because he knew no one in the town he went towards the old court, and after he had come to the court he could see hardly any thing, but an upper chamber he saw, and a stairway of marble coming down from the chamber. And on the stairway he saw sitting a hoary-headed man with old tattered clothes about him. Gereint looked at him closely for a long while. The hoary-headed man said to him, 'Youth,' said he, 'what thoughts are thine?' 'I am thoughtful,' he replied, 'because I know not where I am to go this night.' 'Wilt thou come on hither, chieftain,' said he, 'and thou shalt have the best that can be got for thee?' 'I will,' he replied, 'and God repay thee.' And he came forward and the hoary-headed man went on to the hall before him. And he dismounted in the hall and left his horse there, and came forward to the upper chamber, he and the hoary-headed man. And in the chamber he saw an exceeding old woman seated on a cushion, with old tattered garments of brocaded silk upon her; and when she had been in the flush of her youth he believed that no one had seen a woman fairer than she. And a maiden was to be found near beside her, and about her a shift and a mantle, very old and growing threadbare. And certain was he that he had never beheld any maiden more fully endowed with beauty, grace and comeliness than she. And the hoary-headed man said to the maiden, 'There is no groom for this youth's horse to-night, save thee.' 'The best attendance I can,' said she, 'I will give, both to him and his horse.' And the maiden drew off the young man's boots, and then supplied the horse with straw and corn. And she made for the hall as before, and came back to the upper chamber. And then the hoary-headed man said to the maiden, 'Go to the town,' said he, 'and the best provision thou canst manage of meat and drink, have it brought here.' 'I will, gladly, lord,' said she. And the maiden came to the town. And they conversed whilst the maiden was in the town. And presently, lo, the maiden coming and a man-servant with her, and a bottle on his back full of bought mead, and a quarter of a young ox; and in the maiden's hands there was a helping of white bread, and one manchet loaf in her mantle. And she came to the upper chamber. 'I failed,' said she, 'to get better provision than this, nor would I be given credit for better than this.' 'Well enough,' said Gereint; and they had the meat boiled. And when their food was ready they went to be seated, that is, Gereint sat between the hoary-headed man and his wife. And the maiden waited upon them; and they ate and drank.

And when they had finished eating Gereint began to converse

with the hoary-headed man and asked him whether it was he who first owned the court that he was in. 'I am he, to be sure,' said he, 'who built it, and I owned the city and the castle thou hast seen.' 'Alas, man,' said Gereint, 'why didst thou lose it then?' 'I lost a great earldom along with it,' he replied, 'and this is why I lost them. I had a nephew, my brother's son, and his dominions and my own I took unto me. And when he came to his strength he laid claim to his dominions. I withheld his dominions from him. He then made war on me and conquered the whole of what was in my hands.' 'Good sir,' said Gereint, 'wilt thou tell me what coming was that of the knight who came to the city a while ago, and the lady and the dwarf? And why there is the preparation I saw by the making ready of arms?' 'I will tell thee,' said he. 'It is a preparation against to-morrow for a game that the young earl has, namely, to set up two forks in a meadow that is there, and on the two forks a silver rod, and a sparrowhawk will be set upon the rod. And there will be a tournament for the sparrowhawk, and the throng thou sawest in the whole town of men and horses and arms will come to the tournament. And the lady he loves best will accompany each man, and that man will not be permitted to joust for the sparrowhawk with whom there is not the lady he loves best. And the knight thou sawest has won the sparrowhawk two years; and if he win it the third it will be sent to him every year thereafter, and he will not himself come thither, and Knight of the Sparrowhawk will the knight be called henceforth.'

'Good sir,' said Gereint, 'what is thy counsel to me concerning that knight, about an injury I received from the dwarf, and a maiden of Gwenhwyfar, Arthur's wife, received?' And Gereint told the hoary-headed man the story of his injury. 'It is not easy for me to give thee counsel, for there is neither woman nor maiden thou dost avow, so that thou might go to joust with him. Those arms there that were mine, thou couldst have, and, wert thou to prefer him, my horse instead of thine own.' 'Good sir,' he replied, 'God repay thee. My own horse is good enough for me, I am used to him, together with thine arms. And wilt thou not permit me, good sir, to avow yonder maiden, who is thy daughter, at the appointed hour to-morrow? And if I come from the tournament alive, my loyalty and love will be to the maiden so long as I live. If, however, I come not away, the maiden will be as chaste as before.' 'Gladly will I do that,' said the hoary-headed man, 'and since thou art settled upon that plan, thou must needs when it is day on the morrow have thy horse and thy arms ready, for then the Knight of the Sparrowhawk will make proclamation, that is, he will ask the lady he loves best to take the sparrowhawk, since it becomes her best. "And thou hadst it," he will say, "last year, and the last two. And if there is any one who denies it thee to-day, by force will I defend it for thee." And for that reason,' said the hoary-headed man, 'thou must needs thyself be there when it is day; and we three will be with thee.' And upon that they determined; and at that hour of the night they went to sleep.

And before day they arose and dressed them. And by the time it was day they were all four standing on the meadow bank. And the Knight of the Sparrowhawk was then making proclamation and asking his lady-love to fetch the sparrowhawk. 'Fetch it not,' said Gereint. 'There is a maiden here who is fairer and more comely and of nobler lineage than thou, and has a better claim to it.' 'If thou maintain the sparrowhawk as her due, come forward to joust with me.' Gereint came forward to the meadow's end, furnished with a horse and heavy rusted mean outlandish armour upon him and his horse; and they bore down upon each other. And they broke a set of spears, and broke the second, and broke the third set, and that every other, and they broke them even as they were brought them. And when the earl and his troop could see the Knight of the Sparrowhawk with the upper hand, then there would be a shout of exultation and joy from him and his troop; and the hoary-headed man and his wife and daughter would be sad. And the hoary-headed man served Gereint with spears even as he broke them, and the dwarf served the Knight of the Sparrowhawk. And then the hoary-headed man came to Gereint. 'Chieftain,' said he, 'see here the spear that was in my hand the day I was ordained an ordained knight; and from that day till this I have not broken it; and there is a right good point to it. For not one spear of thine avails thee.' Gereint took the spear, with thanks to the hoary-headed man therefor. Thereupon, lo, the dwarf coming to his lord, and with him too a lance. 'See thou too here a spear that is not worse,' said the dwarf, 'and bear in mind that no knight ever withstood thee as long as this has stood.' 'Between me and God,' said Gereint, 'unless sudden death take me, he will be none the better for thy help.' And far off from him Gereint spurred his horse and bore down upon him, with a warning to him, and struck him a keen-piercing, cruel-hard blow in the strong part of his shield, so that his shield was split and his armour broken fronting the blow, and so that his girths broke and he too and his saddle were over his horse's crupper to the ground. And Gereint quickly dismounted, and was fired with rage, and drew his sword, and fell upon him with impetuous might. The knight too arose and drew another sword against Gereint, and they fought on foot with swords until either's armour was shivered by the other, and the sweat and blood were taking away the light of their eyes. And when Gereint would have the upper hand, the hoary-headed man and his wife and daughter would rejoice; and when the knight would have the upper hand, the earl and his party would rejoice. And when the hoary-headed man saw that Gereint had received a mighty painful blow he quickly drew nigh to him and said to him, 'Chieftain,' said he, 'remember the injury thou didst receive from the dwarf. And was it not to seek to avenge thine injury thou camest here, and the injury done to Gwenhwyfar, Arthur's wife?' And there came to Gereint remembrance of the dwarf's words to him, and he summoned up his strength and raised his sword and smote the knight on the crown of his head so that all his head armour was broken, and all the flesh and skin broken, and into his pate, and so that it gave a wound to the bone and the knight fell on his knees and threw his sword from his hand and asked quarter of Gereint. 'And too late,' said he, 'have my false presumption and my pride permitted me to ask quarter. And if I do not gain respite to make my peace with God for my sins, and to talk with a priest, I shall be none the better for quarter.' 'I will grant thee quarter on this condition,' said he, 'that thou go to Gwenhwyfar, Arthur's wife, to make her amends for the injury done to her maiden by thy dwarf. Sufficient for me, however, is that which I have done to thee for what injury I received of thee and thy dwarf. And thou art not to dismount from the time thou goest hence into the presence of Gwenhwyfar to make amends to her even as will be appointed in Arthur's court.' 'And I will do that gladly. And who then art thou?' asked he. 'I am Gereint son of Erbin. And thou too, say who thou art.' 'I am Edern son of Nudd.' And he was then thrown on to his horse, and he came straight to Arthur's court, and the lady he loved best before him, and his dwarf, and a great lamentation with them. (His story so far as that.)

And then the young earl and his troop came to where Gereint was, and greeted him and invited him along with him to the castle. 'Not I,' said Gereint. 'There where I was last night will I go this night.' 'Then since thou wilt not be invited for now, thou shalt have abundance of what I can have prepared for thee there where thou wast last night; and I will have a bath prepared for thee, and do thou rid thee of thy weariness and fatigue.' 'God repay thee,' said Gereint, 'and I will go to my lodging.' And in this wise Gereint came, and earl Ynywl and his wife and daughter. And when they came to the upper chamber, the young earl's chamberlains had come to the court with their service and were making ready all the living quarters and supplying them with straw and fire, and in a short while the bath was prepared. And Gereint went thereto, and his head was washed.

And thereupon the young earl came, one of forty ordained knights, what with his own men and guests from the tournament. And then he came from the bath, and the earl bade him go to the hall to eat. 'Where is earl Ynywl?' said he, 'and his wife and daughter?' 'They are in the upper chamber yonder,' said the earl's chamberlain, 'putting on the raiment which the earl has had brought to them.' 'Let not the maiden,' said he, 'wear any thing save her shift and mantle until she come to Arthur's court, for Gwenhwyfar to dress her in whatever raiment she will have.' And the maiden did not dress herself.

And then they came each one to the hall, and they washed and went to sit and eat. This is how they sat: on one side of Gereint sat the young earl, and then earl Ynywl; on the other side of Gereint were the maiden and her mother, and thereafter each one as his dignity gave precedence. And they ate, and had unstinted service and abundance of divers kinds of dishes. And they conversed, that is, the young earl invited Gereint for the morrow. 'Not I, between me and God,' said Gereint. 'To Arthur's court will I go with this maiden to-morrow. And long enough I reckon the time that earl Ynywl has been in penury and tribulation; and mainly it is to seek to enhance his substance that I go.' 'Chieftain,' said the young earl, 'it is not through injustice of mine that earl Ynywl is without dominion.' 'By my faith,' said Gereint, 'he will not be without his dominion unless sudden death take me.' 'Chieftain,' said he, 'concerning what discord there has been between me and Ynywl, I will gladly abide by thy counsel, since thou art impartial as to justice between us.' 'I do not ask,' said Gereint, 'that he be given any thing save what is rightfully his, and his various deprivations from the time he lost his kingdom till this very day.' 'And I will gladly do that for thy sake,' said he. 'Aye,' said Gereint, 'let all those that are here who should be vassals of Ynywl do him homage here and now.' And all the men did so, and that settlement was agreed on. And his castle and his town and his dominion were made over to Ynywl, and all that he had lost down to the least jewel he had lost.

And then Ynywl said to Gereint, 'Chieftain,' said he, 'the maiden thou didst avow the day the tournament was, is ready to do thy bidding; and here she is in thy power.' 'I desire naught,' said he, 'save that the maiden be as she is until she come to Arthur's court. And I would have Arthur and Gwenhwyfar be bestowers of the maiden.' And on the morrow they set out on their way to Arthur's court. (Gereint's story so far as this.)

Now this is how Arthur hunted the stag. They apportioned the hunting stations for the men and dogs, and loosed the dogs upon it; and the last dog that was loosed upon it was Arthur's favourite dog. Cafall was his name. And he left all the dogs behind and caused the stag to turn; and on the second turn the stag came to Arthur's hunting station. And Arthur set upon it, and or ever a man might kill it Arthur had cut off its head. And then the horn was sounded for the kill; and then they all assembled together. And Cadyrieith came to Arthur and said to him, 'Lord,' said he, 'yonder is Gwenhwyfar, and no one with her save one maiden.' 'Then do thou ask,' said Arthur, 'Gildas son of Caw and all the clerics of the court to proceed with Gwenhwyfar towards the court.' And that they did.

And then they set forth each one, and they debated concerning the stag's head, to whom it should be given; one desiring to give it to the lady he loved best, another to the lady he for his part loved best, and each one of the household and the knights bickering sharply over the head. And with that they came to the court. And Arthur and Gwenhwyfar heard the bickering over the head, and Gwenhwyfar said then to Arthur, 'Lord,' said she, 'this is my counsel concerning the stag's head, that it be not given until Gereint son of Erbin come from the quest he has gone on.' And Gwenhwyfar told Arthur the reason for the quest. 'Let that be done, gladly,' said Arthur. And that was determined on.

And on the morrow Gwenhwyfar caused watchers to be on the rampart against Gereint's coming. And after mid-day they could see a hump of a little man on a horse, and behind him a woman or a maiden, as they thought, on a horse, and behind her a big bowed knight, with his head hanging low, exceeding sad, and broken worthless armour upon him. And before they came near the gate, one of the watchers came to where Gwenhwyfar was and told her the kind of folk they could see and the kind of appearance that was upon them. 'I know not who they are,' said he. 'I know,' said Gwenhwyfar; 'that is the knight Gereint went after, and I think it likely it is not of his own free will that he comes. And if Gereint has overtaken him, he has avenged in full the injury done to the maiden.' And thereupon, lo, the porter coming to where Gwenhwyfar was. 'Lady,' said he, 'there is a knight at the gate, and no man has ever seen a sight so dreadful to look upon as he: there are broken worthless pieces of armour on him, and the colour of his blood upon them getting the better of their own colour.' 'Knowest thou who he is?' asked she. 'I do,' he answered. 'He is Edern son of Nudd,' said he, 'but I know him not.'

And then Gwenhwyfar came to the gate to meet him, and in

he came. And it grieved Gwenhwyfar to see the sight she saw on him, did he not permit along with him the dwarf, so ill-mannered as he was. Thereon Edern greeted Gwenhwyfar. 'God prosper thee,' said she. 'Lady,' said he, 'greetings to thee from Gereint son of Erbin, the best and bravest of men.' 'Did he encounter thee?' she asked. 'Aye,' said he, 'and not to my advantage; but the fault of that was not his, but mine, lady. And greetings to thee from Gereint; and in greeting thee he has compelled me to this place to do thy bidding for the hurt done to thy maiden by the dwarf. But he has forgiven the hurt done him because of what he has done to me, for he thought I was in peril of my life, and a strong, forceful, firm and warrior-like compulsion did he impose upon me unto this place to do thee justice, lady.' 'Alas, sir, where did he overtake thee?' 'In the place where we were jousting and contending for a sparrow-hawk, in the town that is now called Caerdyf. And with him there was nothing of a retinue save three persons, very poor and mean in appearance, namely, an exceeding old hoary-headed man and an aged woman and a fair young maiden, with old tattered clothes upon them. And by Gereint's avowing the love of the maiden, he took part in the tournament for the sparrow-hawk, and declared that maiden had better claim to the sparrowhawk than the maiden there, who was with me. And for that reason we jousted. And even as thou seest, lady, did he leave me.' 'Sir,' said she, 'when dost thou think Gereint will come here?' 'To-morrow, lady, I think he will come, and the maiden.'

And then Arthur came to him, and he greeted Arthur. 'God prosper thee,' said Arthur. And Arthur gazed a long while upon him and marvelled to see him thus. And he thought he recognized him, and asked him, 'Art thou Edern son of Nudd?' 'I am, lord,' said he, 'having met with exceeding great affliction and unbearable wounds.' And he told Arthur the whole of his misadventure. 'Aye,' said Arthur, 'it is right for Gwenhwyfar to be merciful to thee, from what I hear.' 'Whatever mercy thou wilt, lord,' said she, 'I will show him, for it is as much an insult to thee, lord, for me to be put to shame as for thee thyself.' 'The best justice in the matter,' said Arthur, 'is to permit the man to have healing till it is known whether he will live. And if he live, let him make amends as the nobles of the court shall decide, and do thou take sureties to that end. But if he die, too much will be the death of a youth so excellent as Edern in atonement for a maiden's hurt.' 'I am content with that,' said Gwenhwyfar. And then Arthur went as surety for him, and Cradawg son of Llŷr, and Gwallawg son of Llennawg, and Owein son of Nudd, and Gwalchmei, and many a man besides. And Arthur had Morgan Tud summoned to him. Chief of physicians was he. 'Take to thee Edern son of Nudd, and have a chamber prepared for him, and seek a cure for him as good as thou wouldst have it for me were I wounded. And let none into his chamber to disturb him, save thyself and thy disciples who will be about his cure.' 'I will do that gladly, lord,' said Morgan Tud. And then the steward said, 'Where is it right, lord, to give the maiden into keeping?' 'To Gwenhwyfar and her handmaidens,' he replied. And the steward gave her into keeping. (Their story so far.)

On the morrow Gereint came to the court, and Gwenhwyfar had watchers on the rampart lest he should come unawares. And the watcher came to where Gwenhwyfar was. 'Lady,' said he, 'I think I see Gereint and the maiden with him. And he is on horseback, but with a walking garb upon him. The maiden, however, I see her very white, and like to a linen garment do I see about her.' 'Make ready, all my women, and come to meet Gereint, to welcome him and wish him joy.' And Gwenhwyfar came to meet Gereint and the maiden. And when Gereint came to where Gwenhwyfar was he greeted her. 'God prosper thee,' said she, 'and a welcome to thee. And a profitable, prosperous, well-blessed and praiseworthy venture hast thou been on. And God repay thee,' said she, 'for having amends made me so handsomely as thou hast.' 'Lady,' said he, 'it was my desire to have amends made thee according to thy wish. And here is the maiden because of whom thou hast been freed from thy disgrace.' 'Aye,' said Gwenhwyfar, 'God's welcome to her, and it is not improper to welcome her.'

They came inside and dismounted, and Gereint went to where Arthur was and greeted him. 'God prosper thee,' said

Arthur, 'and God's welcome to thee. And even though Edern son of Nudd has come by affliction and wounds at thy hand, a prosperous venture hast thou been upon.' 'Not on me the blame for that,' said Gereint, 'but the arrogance of Edern son of Nudd himself, that he would not declare his name. Nor would I leave him till I knew who he was, or till the one should vanquish the other.' 'Sir,' said Arthur, 'where is the maiden whom I have heard thou dost avow?' 'She is gone with Gwenhwyfar to her chamber.'

And then Arthur came to see the maiden. And Arthur and his companions and every one from the whole court welcomed the maiden. And each of them was certain that if the provision made for the maiden should be in keeping with her beauty, they had seen never any better endowed than she. And Arthur bestowed the maiden upon Gereint; and the bond that was at that time made between two persons was made between Gereint and the maiden; and a choice of all Gwenhwyfar's raiment for the maiden. And whoever might see the maiden in that raiment, he would see in her a fair, seemly and beauteous sight. And that day and that night they spent with songs a-plenty and abundance of dishes, and diverse kinds of drink and profusion of games. And when they thought it time to go to sleep, they went. And in the chamber where was Arthur and Gwenhwyfar's bed, a bed was prepared for Gereint and Enid. And that night for the first time they slept together. And on the morrow Arthur satisfied the suitors on Gereint's behalf with ample gifts. And the maiden acquainted herself with the court, and companions were brought to her of men and women till there was better report of no maiden in the Island of Britain than of her.

And then Gwenhwyfar said, 'Rightly did I hit the mark,' said she, 'concerning the stag's head, that it should be given to no one until Gereint came, and this is a proper occasion to give it to Enid daughter of Ynywl, the maiden of most fame. And I do not believe any one will begrudge it her, for there is naught between her and any, save what there is of love and fellowship.' That was approved by all, and by Arthur too, and the stag's head was given to Enid. And from that time forth her fame increased thereby, and her companions, more than before. Gereint from that time forth loved tournament and stern combats, and he would come victorious from all. And a year was he thus, and two and three, until his fame had spread over the face of the kingdom.

And once upon a time when Arthur was holding court in Caer Llion on Usk at Whitsuntide, lo, coming towards him wise, prudent, and most learned and eloquent messengers, and greeting Arthur. 'God prosper you,' said Arthur, 'and God's welcome to you. And whence do you come?' 'We come, lord,' said they, 'from Cornwall, and we are messengers from Erbin son of Custennin, thy uncle. And our message is to thee, and greetings to thee from him, even as an uncle should greet his nephew and as a vassal should greet his lord, and to inform thee that he is growing heavy and enfeebled and is drawing near to old age, and that the men whose lands border on his, knowing that, encroach upon his boundaries and covet his lands and dominions. And he beseeches thee, lord, to send Gereint his son unto him to defend his dominions and to know his boundaries. And to him he represents that it would be better for him to spend the flower of his youth and his prime defending his own boundaries than in tournaments which bring no profit though he win fame therein.' 'Aye,' said Arthur, 'go to change your garments and take your meat and rid you of your weariness, and before you go hence you shall have an answer.' They went to meat.

And then Arthur considered how it would not be easy for him to let Gereint go from him, or from the same court as him. Neither was it pleasant nor fair to him to keep his cousin from defending his dominions and boundaries since his father was unable to maintain them. Not less were Gwenhwyfar's anxiety and longing and those of all the ladies and all the maidens, for fear lest the maiden should go away from them. That day and that night they spent with abundance of every thing; and Arthur made known to Gereint the meaning of the mission and the messengers' coming from Cornwall to him there. 'Aye,' said Gereint, 'whatever advantage or disadvantage come to me, lord, thereby, I will do thy will concerning that mission.' 'Here is counsel for thee in that matter,' said Arthur, 'though thy going will be painful to me: that thou go to settle into thy dominions and to defend thy boundaries. And take with thee the company thou desirest, and those thou lovest best of my liegemen to bring thee on thy way, and of thine own kinsmen and fellow knights.' 'God repay thee, and that will I do,' said Gereint. 'What murmuring,' said Gwenhwyfar, 'do I hear from among you? Is it of men to bring Gereint on his way towards his country?' 'Aye,' said Arthur. 'I too,' said she, 'must think of companions on the way and provision for the lady who is with me.' 'Thou dost well,' said Arthur.

And that night they went to sleep. And on the morrow the messengers were let depart and were told that Gereint would come after them. The third day thereafter Gereint set out. This is the company that went with him: Gwalchmei son of Gwyar, and Rhiogonedd son of the king of Ireland, and Ondiaw son of the duke of Burgundy, Gwilym son of the ruler of France, Howel son of Emyr Llydaw, Elifri Anaw Cyrdd, Gwyn son of Tringad, Goreu son of Custennin, Gweir Big-breadth, Garannaw son of Golithmer, Peredur son of Efrawg, Gwyn Llogell Gwŷr, elder of Arthur's court, Dyfyr son of Alun Dyfed, Gwrei Interpreter of Tongues, Bedwyr son of Bedrawd, Cadwri son of Gwrion, Cei son of Cynyr, Odiar the Frank, steward of Arthur's court. 'And Edern son of Nudd,' said Gereint, 'of whom I hear that he is able to ride, I would have come with me.' 'Why,' said Arthur, 'it is not seemly for thee to take that man with thee, though he be well, until peace be made between him and Gwenhwyfar.' 'Gwenhwyfar would be able to permit him with me upon sureties.' 'If she permit him, let her permit him freely, without sureties, for afflictions and hurt enough are upon the man for the injury done to the maiden by the dwarf.' 'Aye,' said Gwenhwyfar, 'what thou seest to be right in that matter, thou and Gereint, I shall do willingly, lord.' And she then permitted Edern to go freely; and plenty more went to bring Gereint on his way.

And they set out and went on their way, the fairest company that any one had ever seen, towards the Severn. And on the far side of the Severn were the best men of Erbin son of Custennin, and his foster-father at their head, receiving Gereint gladly, and many of the ladies of the court with his mother too, to meet Enid daughter of Ynywl, his wife. And every one of the court and of the whole dominion felt exceeding great joy and gladness at the coming of Gereint, so great the love they bore him, and so great the fame he had won since he went from them, and because he was minded to come and take possession of his own dominion and maintain his boundaries.

And they came to the court. And for them in the court there was a rich amplitude of divers kinds of dishes and an abundance of drink and unfailing service, and divers kinds of songs and games. And in honour of Gereint all the nobles of the dominion were invited that night to appear before Gereint. And that day and that night they spent with convenience of ease. And on the morrow in the young of the day Erbin arose and summoned Gereint to him, and the noblemen who had come to bring him on his way, and he said to Gereint, 'I am a man heavy with age,' said he, 'and so long as I was able to maintain the dominion for thee and for myself, maintain it I did. But thou art a young man, and in the flower of thy manhood and thy youth art thou. Maintain now thy dominion.' 'Why,' said Gereint, 'of my own will thou hadst not for the present given authority over thy dominions into my hands, and thou hadst not yet fetched me from Arthur's court.' 'Into thy hands I now give it, and further, receive to-day the homage of thy men.'

And then Gwalchmei said, 'It is best for thee to satisfy the suitors to-day, but receive the homage of thy dominions to-morrow.' And then the suitors were summoned to one place. And then Cadyrieith came to them to weigh their intent and to ask each one of them what was their request. And Arthur's retinue began to make gifts; and straightway there came the men of Cornwall, and they too gave. And it was not for long that they were giving, such was the eagerness of each one of them to give. And of those who came there to ask for gifts, not one went away thence save with his desire. And that day and that night they spent with convenience of ease.

And on the morrow in the young of the day Erbin bade Gereint send messengers to his men to ask them whether it was convenient for them that he should come to receive their homage, and whether they felt grievance or offence for any thing they might have against him. Then Gereint sent messengers to the men of Cornwall to ask them that. They made answer that they had each one naught save fullness of joy and exaltation at Gereint's coming to receive their homage. And then he received homage of such of them as were there. And they were there together the third night. And on the morrow Arthur's retinue asked leave to depart. 'Too hard is it for you to depart yet. Stay with me until I shall have received the homage of those of my best men who purpose to come to me.' And they stayed until he had done so. And they set out towards Arthur's court, and then Gereint went to bring them on their way, both he and Enid, as far as Dyngannan; and then they parted. And then Ondiaw son of the duke of Burgundy said to Gereint, 'First traverse,' said he, 'the bounds of thy dominion, and mark well and closely thy dominion's limits. And if oppression weigh on thee, make it known to thy comrades.' 'God repay thee,' said he, 'and that will I do.' And then Gereint made for the bounds of his dominions, and skilled guidance with him of the best men of his dominions. And the furthest limit that was shown to him he bore in mind.

And as had been his custom whilst he was in Arthur's court he frequented tournaments, and he pitted himself against the bravest and strongest men until he was renowned in that region as in the place he was in aforetime, and till he enriched his court and his companions and his noblemen with the best horses and the best suits of armour, and the best and most noteworthy jewels. And he did not cease therefrom until his fame spread over the face of the kingdom. And when he knew that, he began to love ease and leisure, for there was none who was worth his fighting against him. And he loved his wife and peace in his court and songs and entertainment, and he settled thereto for a while. And thereafter he loved dalliance in his chamber and with his wife, so that naught save that was pleasing to him, until he was losing his noblemen's hearts and his hunting and his pleasure, and the hearts of all the retinue of the court, and until there was a secret murmuring and scoffing at him by the people of the court because he was so utterly forsaking their company for love of a woman. And those words reached Erbin's ears; and when Erbin had heard of it he told it to Enid, and asked her whether it was she who was causing that in Gereint and instigating him to forsake his household and retinue. 'Not I, by my confession to God,' said she, 'and there is nothing more hateful to me than that.' But she knew not what to do, for it was not easy for her to confess that to Gereint, nor was it easier for her to listen to what she heard without warning Gereint thereof. And she felt great grief within her because of that.

And one morning in the summer-time they were in bed and he on the outer edge. And Enid was without sleep in a chamber of glass, and the sun shining on the bed; and the clothes had slipped from his breast and arms, and he was asleep. She looked upon the great beauty and majesty of the sight she saw in him, and said, 'Woe is me,' said she, 'if it is through me that these arms and this breast are losing fame and prowess as great as was theirs.' And thereupon her tears flowed freely, so that they fell on to his breast. And that was one of the things that woke him, together with the words she had just spoken. And another thought distressed him, that it was not out of care for him that she had spoken those words, but because she was meditating love for another man in his stead, and desired dalliance apart from him. And with that Gereint lost his peace of mind, and called upon a squire, and he came to him. 'Have,' said he, 'my horse and armour speedily prepared, and that they be ready, and do thou,' said he to Enid, 'arise and dress thee and have thy horse accoutred, and bring with thee the worst dress to thy name, to go riding. And shame on me,' said he, 'if thou come here till thou know whether I have so utterly lost my strength as thou reckonest, and further, whether it will be as pleasant for thee as was thy desire to seek dalliance with him thou wert thinking of.' And she arose and dressed in a simple dress. 'I know nothing of thy thoughts, lord,' said she. 'Nor shalt thou know them as yet,' said he.

And then Gereint went to see Erbin. 'Good sir,' said he, 'there is a quest I go on, and I do not know when I shall come again. And do thou, sir,' said he, 'see to thy dominion until I come again.' 'I will,' said he, 'but I marvel how suddenly thou goest. And who will travel with thee, seeing that thou art not a man to travel the land of Lloegyr alone?' 'None comes with me save one other person.' 'Now God counsel thee, son,' said Erbin, 'and many a man with his claim upon thee in Lloegyr.'

And Gereint came to where his horse was, and his horse was accoutred with heavy shining outlandish armour. And he then bade Enid mount her horse and travel ahead and keep a good lead. 'And for aught thou seest and for aught thou hearest,' said he, 'concerning me, turn not back. And unless I speak to thee, speak not one word either.' And they went on their way. But it was not the pleasantest and most frequented road that he caused to travel, but the wildest road and that wherein it was likeliest there would be thieves and robbers and venomous wild beasts. And they came to the high road and followed it, and they could see a great forest ahead of them; and they came towards the forest. And coming from the forest they beheld four armed knights, and these looked at them, and one of them said, 'This is a good place for us,' said he, 'to take the two horses yonder and the armour and the woman too, and those we shall have without effort so far as yonder solitary heavy-headed, dejected, lumpish knight is concerned.' And Enid heard those words, but knew not what to do for fear of Gereint, whether she should tell or hold her tongue. 'God's vengeance on me,' said she, 'if I had not rather death at his hand than at the hand of an other. And though he slay me I shall tell him, lest he be seen slain unawares.' And she waited for Gereint until he was close to her. 'Lord,' said she, 'dost hear the words of yonder men concerning thee?' He raised his face and looked on her in anger. 'There was no need for thee,' said he, 'save to observe the order that was given thee, which was to hold thy tongue. Thy loving care is naught to me, and is no warning. And though thou long to see my death, and see me slain by yonder men, there is no fear in me.' And thereupon the foremost of them couched his spear and bore down upon Gereint. And he received him, and not as a weakling, and let his thrust go past, and he then thrust at the knight in the middle of his shield, so that his shield was split and his armour broken, and so that there was a full forearm's length of the shaft in him and he was the length of Gereint's spear over his horse's crupper to the ground. And the second knight made at him in wrath at the slaying of his comrade. And with one thrust he overthrew him and slew him like the other. And the third made at him, and him he slew likewise. And likewise too he slew the fourth. Sad and sorrowful was the maiden to see that. Gereint dismounted and drew off the slain men's suits of armour and placed them in their saddles, and he tied the reins of the horses and mounted on his horse. 'See what thou must do,' said he, 'take the four horses and drive them before thee, and go on in front, as I bade thee a while back. And speak not one word to me till I speak to thee. By my confession to God,' said he, 'if thou wilt not do so, thou shalt not go unpunished.' 'I shall do what I can of that, lord,' said she, 'according to thy bidding.'

They travelled on to a forest, and they left the forest and came to a great level plain, and in the middle of the plain there was a thickset tangled copse. And they beheld three knights coming from it towards them, furnished with horses, and armour about them to the ground and about their horses. The maiden watched them closely; and when they drew near, the words she heard from them were, 'This is a good find for us,' said they; 'without effort, four horses and four suits of armour. And so far as yonder drooping knight is concerned, we shall get them cheaply. And the maiden too will be in our power.' 'That is true,' said she, 'the man is fatigued after contending with the knights just now. God's vengeance on me if I do not warn him,' said she. And the maiden waited for Gereint until he was close to her. 'Lord,' said she, 'dost thou not hear the words of yonder men concerning thee?' 'What are they?' said he. 'They are saying amongst themselves that they will get this booty cheaply.' 'Between me and God,' said he, 'more irksome to me than what the men say is that thou wilt not hold thy tongue for me, nor abide by my direction.' 'Lord,' said she, 'it is lest thou be taken unawares that I act thus.' 'Now hold thy tongue, and thy loving care is naught to me.' And thereupon one of the knights couched his spear and made at Gereint and thrust at him to good purpose, as he supposed, but Gereint took the thrust lightly and sent it glancing aside, and then he made for him in turn and thrust at his very middle, and what with the onrush of man and horse, all his armour availed not, so that the spear-head and a length of the shaft was out through him, and so that he too was his arm and his spear's length over the horse's crupper to the ground. The other two knights came, each in turn, and their onset was no better than the other. The maiden, standing and looking thereon, was anxious on the one hand for thinking that Gereint would be wounded contending with the men, and on the other hand for joy to see him getting the upper hand. Then Gereint dismounted and bound the three suits of armour in the three saddles, and tied the reins of the horses together, so that there were then in all seven horses with him.

And he mounted his own horse and ordered the maiden to drive the horses. 'And it is no better for me,' said he, 'to tell thee than to be silent, since thou wilt not abide by my direction.' 'I will, lord, so far as I can,' said she, 'save that I cannot conceal from thee the dire hateful words that I hear concerning thee, lord, from outlandish folk that travel the wilderness, such as those.' 'Between me and God,' said he, 'thy loving care is naught to me. And from now on hold thy tongue.' 'I will, lord, so far as I can.' And the maiden went on her way, and the horses ahead of her, and she kept her distance. And coming from the copse which was even now spoken of above, they traversed open. country, lofty and fair, level and high and beautiful. And some distance from them they could see a forest, and except for seeing the edge nearest them they could see thereafter neither edge nor limit to the forest. And they came towards the forest. And coming from the forest they beheld five knights, impetuous, head-strong and powerful, on chargers strong, thickset, big-boned, ground-devouring, wide-nostrilled and mettled; and armour a-plenty upon the men and upon their horses. And after they had drawn near, the words Enid heard from the knights were, 'See here a good find for us, cheaply and without effort,' said they; 'all these horses and suits of armour we shall have, and the woman too, so far as yonder solitary, moping, lumpish, dejected knight is concerned.'

The maiden was greatly troubled at hearing the men's words, so that she knew not what in the world to do; but at last she made up her mind to warn Gereint and turned her horse's head in his direction. 'Lord,' said she, 'hadst thou heard the talk of yonder knights as I have heard it, thy care would be greater than it is.' Gereint gave a sour, vexed, and bitter jeering laugh and said, 'I hear thee,' said he, 'going against every thing that I forbid thee; and maybe thou shalt yet repent it.' And there and then, lo, the men encountering them, and Gereint, victoriously exultant, had the upper hand of the five men. And he placed the five suits of armour in the five saddles, and tied the reins of the twelves horses together and made them over to Enid. 'And I know not,' said he, 'what good it is for me to give thee orders, but this once, as a warning to thee, orders will I give thee.' And the maiden went on her way to the forest, and she kept her distance as Gereint bade her. And painful had it been for him to see trouble as great as that with the horses for a maiden so excellent as she, had anger permitted him. And they made for the forest; and deep and vast was the forest, and night came upon them in the forest. 'Maiden,' said he, 'it avails us not to try and proceed.' 'Aye, lord,' said she, 'whatever thou wilt, we shall do.' 'It is best for us,' said he, 'to turn aside into the forest to rest, and wait for day to proceed.' 'Let us, gladly,' said she. And that they did.

And he dismounted and lifted her to the ground. 'I cannot for aught,' said he, 'but sleep for weariness. And do thou watch the horses, and sleep not.' 'I will, lord,' said she; and he slept in his armour. And the night was passed, and at that season it was not long. And when she saw the dawn of day show its light, she looked around her to see whether he was waking. And with that he was waking. 'Lord,' said she, 'I had been wanting to wake thee for some time.' He was silent towards her with annoyance, for he had not bidden her speak. And then he arose and said to her, 'Take the horses,' said he, 'and go on thy way, and keep thy distance as thou didst keep it yesterday.'

And a while into the day they left the forest and came to a most clear open plain, and there were meadows to one side of them, and men with scythes mowing the meadows; and they came on to a river, and the horses bent down and drank of the water, and they climbed from the river to a lofty hill side. And then there met them a young slender lad with a towel about his neck, and they could see a package in the towel, but knew not what it was, and a small blue pitcher in his hand, and a cup on the mouth of the pitcher. And the youth greeted Gereint. 'God prosper thee,' said Gereint, 'and whence comest thou?' 'I come,' he replied, 'from the town that is there before thee. Lord,' said he, 'would it displease thee to be asked whence thou too comest?' 'It would not,' said he; 'I am come through the forest yonder.' 'It is not to-day thou art come through the forest?' 'Not so,' said he, 'it was in the forest that I was last night.' 'I venture,' the youth replied, 'that thy state there last night was not good, and that thou hadst neither meat nor drink.' 'No, between me and God,' replied he. 'Wilt thou do my counsel,' asked the youth, 'to take of me thy meal?' 'What kind of meal?' he asked. 'A breakfast I was taking to the mowers yonder, naught else than bread and meat and wine. And if thou wilt, good sir, they shall have naught.' 'I will,' said he, 'and God repay thee.'

And Gereint dismounted, and the youth lifted the maiden to the ground. And they washed and had their meal. And the youth sliced the bread and gave them drink and waited on them in all. And when they had finished the youth arose and said to Gereint, 'Lord, with thy leave I will go to fetch food for the mowers.' 'Go first to the town,' said Gereint, 'and procure me a lodging in the best place thou knowest, and the most commodious for the horses. And thou,' said he, 'do thou take any one horse thou choosest, and its armour along with it, as payment for thy service and provision.' 'God repay thee,' said the youth, 'and that would be payment sufficient for a service which might be greater than that I have done thee.' And the youth went to the town and took the best and most comfortable lodging he knew of in the town. And after that he went to the court, and his horse and its armour along with him; and he came to where the earl was and told him all his adventure. 'And I will go, lord, to meet the knight and show him his lodging,' said he. 'Go, gladly,' he replied, 'and a joyous welcome will he get here, should he desire it, gladly.' And the youth came to meet Gereint and told him that he would have a joyous welcome from the earl in his own court. But he wished for nothing save to go to his own lodging. And he got a comfortable chamber with plenty of straw and coverings, and a roomy comfortable place for his horses, and the youth had ample provision made ready for them.

And after they had eased their garments, Gereint said to Enid, 'Get thee,' said he, 'to the far end of the chamber and come not to this end of the house. And summon the woman of the house to thee, if thou wilt.' 'I will, lord,' said she, 'even as thou sayest.' And thereupon the man of the house came to Gereint and bade him welcome. 'Chieftain,' said he, 'hast thou eaten thy dinner?' 'I have,' he replied. And then the youth said to him, 'Wilt thou have,' said he, 'drink or aught else before I go to see the earl?' 'I will, in faith,' replied Gereint. And thereupon the youth went into the town and fetched them drink. And they took drink. And straightway after that Gereint said, 'I cannot help but sleep,' said he. 'Aye,' said the youth, 'whilst thou sleepest I will go to see the earl.' 'Go, gladly,' he replied, 'and come back hither when I bade thee come.' And Gereint slept, and Enid slept.

And the youth came to where the earl was, and the earl asked him where was the knight's lodging, and he told him. 'And I must go presently,' said he, 'to wait upon him.' 'Go,' he replied, 'and greet him from me and tell him I will go to call on him presently.' 'I will,' he replied. And the youth came when it was time for them to awake; and they awoke and walked abroad. And when they thought it time to take their food, they took it. And the youth waited upon them. And Gereint asked the man of the house whether he had company he would like to invite to him. 'Aye,' he replied. 'Then bring them hither, to have their fill at my charge of whatever is best that may be found for sale in the town.' The best company that the man of the house had he brought there to have their fill at Gereint's charge.

Thereupon, lo, the earl coming one of twelve ordained knights to call upon Gereint. And Gereint arose and bade him welcome. 'God prosper thee,' said the earl. They went to sit, each one as his dignity entitled him. And the earl conversed with Gereint and asked him what journey he was on. 'I have in mind,' said he, 'only to look for adventures and to perform quests that please me.' The earl then looked on Enid with a close gaze, and he felt certain that he had never beheld a maiden

fairer than she, nor better endowed, and he set his heart and
mind on her. And he asked Gereint, 'Have I leave of thee to go
to yonder maiden and converse with her? I see her as it were
estranged from thee.' 'Thou hast, gladly.' And he came to where
the maiden was and said to her, 'Maiden,' said he, 'it is not
pleasant for thee on this journey with yonder man.' 'It is not
unpleasant,' said she, 'for me to journey now the way he journeys.' 'Thou hast neither menservants nor maidens,' he replied,
'to attend on thee.' 'Why,' said she, 'it is pleasanter for me to
follow yonder man than were I to have menservants and
maidens.' 'I know good counsel for thee,' he replied. 'I will give
my earldom into thy power, and do thou stay with me.' 'I will
not, between me and God,' said she. 'To yonder man did I first
of all pledge my troth, and I will not break faith with him.'
'Thou dost wrong,' he replied. 'If I slay yonder man I shall have
thee as long as I will, and when I want thee not I will turn thee
away. But if thou wilt do this for me of thine own free will, there
will be unbroken eternal harmony between us so long as we live.'

She pondered what he was telling her, and in her heart she
determined to encourage him in what he asked. 'This is what is
best for thee, chieftain,' said she, 'lest I be accused of faith-
lessness past telling, that thou come hither to-morrow to take
me away as though I knew nothing of it.' 'That I will,' said he;
and thereupon he arose and took his leave and went away, he
and his men. And at the time she told Gereint nothing of the
man's conversation with her, lest there arise anger or anxiety in
him, or distress.

And they went to sleep at the proper time. And at the beginning of the night she slept a little. But towards midnight she
awoke and set to rights all Gereint's arms, that they might be
ready to put on. And in fear and trembling she came to the side
of Gereint's bed, and quietly and softly she said to him, 'Lord,'
said she, 'awake and array thee, and this is the earl's conversation
with me, lord, and his thoughts concerning me,' said she. And
she told Gereint his whole conversation. And though he was
angry with her, he took warning and arrayed himself; and when
she had lit a candle as a light for him to dress, 'Leave the candle
there,' said he, 'and bid the man of the house come hither.' She

went, and the man of the house came to him, and then Gereint asked him, 'Dost know what sum I owe thee?' 'I think it little thou owest, good sir,' said he. 'Then whatever I owe thee, take thou the eleven horses and the eleven suits of armour.' 'God repay thee, lord,' said he, 'but I have not spent on thee the worth of one of the suits of armour.' 'What matters it to thee?' he asked; 'thou wilt be all the richer. Friend,' said he, 'wilt thou come as a guide to me out of the town?' 'I will,' said he, 'gladly. And in what direction art thou minded?' 'In a direction other than the place where I came into the town I would wish to go.'

The man of the lodging brought him on his way until he had all the guidance needed. And then he bade the maiden take up a distance in front, and she took it, and went on ahead, and the inn-keeper came home; and he had only just entered the house when, lo, the greatest commotion that any one had heard coming upon the house. And when he looked out, lo, he could see around the house fourscore knights fully armed, and the Dun Earl was at their head. 'Where is the knight that was here?' asked the earl. 'By thy hand,' said he, 'he is a good way off from here, and he went from here a good while since.' 'Why, villain,' said he, 'wouldst thou let him go without telling me?' 'Lord,' he replied, 'thou didst not give him into my keeping. Hadst thou so given him, I had not let him go.' 'What direction,' he asked, 'dost thou think that he went?' 'I know not,' he replied, 'but it was the high road that he took.'

They turned their horses' heads for the high road, and they observed the tracks of the horses and followed the tracks and came to a great high road. And the maiden looked back when she saw the light of day, and she could see behind her a great haze and mist, and she saw it nearer and nearer to her. And she was perturbed thereat, and thought that the earl and his host were coming after her. With that she could see a knight appearing out of the mist. 'By my faith,' said she, 'I will warn him though he slay me. I had rather my death at his hand than see him slain without his being warned. Lord,' said she, 'dost thou not see the man bearing down upon thee, and many other men along with him?' 'I do,' he replied, 'and however much thou art bidden to hold thy tongue, hold thy tongue thou never wilt.

Thy warning is naught to me. And hold thy tongue!' And he turned upon the knight and at the first thrust threw him to the ground under his horse's feet. And so long as one of the four-score knights was left, at the first thrust he threw each one of them. And from good to better they came at him, save for the earl. And last of all the earl came at him, and broke a spear, and broke a second. Then Gereint turned upon him and thrust with a spear at the thick of his shield, so that his shield was split and all his armour broken at that point, and so that he himself was over his horse's crupper to the ground and was in peril of his life. And Gereint drew near him, and what with the noise made by his horse the earl came to his senses. 'Lord,' said he to Gereint, 'thy mercy!' And Gereint showed him mercy. And what with the exceeding hardness of the ground where the men were thrown, and the exceeding fury of the thrusts they received, not one of them took himself off without a mortal-bitter, grievous-hurtful, mighty-bruising fall from Gereint.

And Gereint went his way on the high road he was on, and the maiden kept her distance. And near them they could see the fairest valley that any one had ever seen, and a great river along the valley. And they could see a bridge over the river and the high road coming to the bridge, and above the bridge on the other side of the river they could see a walled town, the fairest any one had ever seen. And as he was making for the bridge he saw a man coming towards him through a small thick copse, on a huge tall even-paced horse, mettled but tractable. 'Knight,' said Gereint, 'whence comest thou?' 'I come,' he replied, 'from the valley below.' 'Why, sir,' said Gereint, 'wilt thou tell me who owns this fair valley and the walled town yonder?' 'I will, gladly,' he replied. 'Gwiffred Petit the French and the English call him, and the Welsh call him Y Brenhin Bychan.'[1] 'And I am going,' said Gereint, 'to the bridge yonder, and to the lower high road below the town.' 'Go not,' said the knight, 'on to his land past the bridge unless thou wouldst encounter him, for it is his way that there comes no knight on to his land whom he does not seek to encounter.' 'Between me and God,' said Gereint, 'I shall

1 Y Brenhin Bychan: The Little King.

go my way despite him.' 'I hold it most likely,' said the knight,
'if thou do so, that thou wilt come by shame and humiliation.'

Right wroth and hot-hearted Gereint proceeded along the
road as was his intention before. And it was not the road that
made for the town from the bridge that Gereint travelled, but a
road that made for the ridge of the rough land, lofty, exceeding
high, with a wide prospect. And as he was journeying thus, he
could see a knight following him upon a powerful stout charger,
strong-paced, wide-hoofed and broad-chested. And he had
never seen a man smaller than him he saw on the horse; and
armour a-plenty upon him and his horse. And when he came
up with Gereint he said to him, 'Say, chieftain,' said he, 'was it
of discourtesy or in presumption that thou wouldst have me lose
my privilege and break my custom?' 'Not so,' said Gereint, 'I did
not know the road was forbidden to any.' 'Since thou didst not
know,' said he, 'come with me to my court to make me amends.'
'I will not, by my faith,' he replied. 'I would not go to thy lord's
court unless Arthur be thy lord.' 'Now by Arthur's hand,' said
he, 'I will have redress of thee, or I shall get exceeding great hurt
from thee.' And without more ado they set upon each other, and
a squire of his came to serve him with spears as they broke. And
each of them gave the other heavy painful strokes till the shields
lost all their colour. And it was ugly for Gereint to do battle
with him, so very small was he, and so very difficult it was to
mark him, and so exceeding hard were the strokes he dealt. And
they did not weary of it before their horses were brought to
their knees, and at long last Gereint threw him headlong to the
ground. And then they set them to fight on foot, and each of
them gave the other blows grievous-swift, painful-heavy, bitter-
strong, and they pierced the helms and broke the mailcaps and
battered the armour until their eyes were losing their light for
sweat and blood. And at last Gereint was fired with rage, and
summoned up his strength, and felon-hearted, bravely-swift,
cruelly and mightily, he raised his sword and struck him on
the crown of his head a blow mortal-keen, venomous-sharp,
grievous-bitter, until all the head armour was broken, and the
skin and the flesh, and there was a wound to the bone, and so
that his sword was out of the Little King's hand to the verge of

the field away from him. And then in God's name he begged for Gereint's quarter and mercy. 'Thou shalt have quarter,' said Gereint, 'but thy manners were not good, nor wert thou just – on condition that thou hold with me and go not against me a second time, and if thou hear of distress upon me, that thou relieve it.' 'Thou shalt have that, lord, gladly.' And he took his word thereon. 'And, lord,' said he, 'thou shalt come with me to my court yonder, to rid thee of thy weariness and fatigue.' 'I will not, between me and God,' he answered.

And then Gwiffred Petit looked on Enid where she was, and it grieved him to see such a press of afflictions on a woman of such noble presence as she. And with that he said to Gereint, 'Lord,' said he, 'thou dost wrong not to refresh thyself and take thine ease. And if hardship meet thee in that condition it will not be easy for thee to get the better of it.' Gereint wished for nothing save to go on his way, and he mounted his horse, bloodstained and uneasy. And the maiden kept her distance ahead.

And they journeyed towards a forest which they could see some way from them. And the heat was great, and the armour sticking to his flesh with sweat and blood. And after they had come to the forest he halted under a tree to shun the heat, and he was then more mindful of the pain than when he had received it. And the maiden halted under another tree. And with that they could hear horns and a mustering. And this was the meaning of it: Arthur and his company were dismounting in the forest. He pondered which way he might go to avoid them, and thereupon, lo, a man on foot perceiving him. This was a servant of the steward who was there, and he came to the steward and told him how he had seen even such a man as he had seen in the forest. Thereat the steward had his horse saddled and caught up his spear and shield and came to where Gereint was. 'Knight,' said he, 'what dost thou there?' 'I am standing under a cooling tree, and shunning the ardour and heat of the sun.' 'What journey art thou on, and who art thou?' 'Looking for adventures and journeying the way I would.' 'Well,' said Cei, 'come with me to see Arthur who is here close by.' 'I will not, between me and God,' replied Gereint. 'Thou wilt be made to come,' said Cei. And Gereint knew Cei, but Cei did not know Gereint. And Cei made at him as best he could. And Gereint grew angry, and with the haft of his spear he struck him under the chin so that he was headlong to the ground. But he had no wish to do worse to him than that.

And wildly fearful Cei arose and mounted his horse and came to his lodging. And then he made his way to Gwalchmei's pavilion. 'Why, man,' said he to Gwalchmei, 'I have heard tell from one of the servants that a wounded knight has been seen in the forest above, and mean armour upon him. And if thou dost what is right, thou wilt go and see whether that be true.' 'I mind not if I go,' said Gwalchmei. 'Then take thy horse,' said Cei, 'and some of thy armour; I have heard tell he is none too courteous to any who come his way.'

Gwalchmei caught up his spear and shield, and mounted his horse and came to where Gereint was. 'Knight,' said he, 'what kind of journey art thou on?' 'I am going about mine errands, and looking for adventures.' 'Wilt thou tell who thou art, or wilt thou come to see Arthur who is here close by?' 'I will not tell thee who I am, and I will not go to see Arthur,' said he. And he knew Gwalchmei, but Gwalchmei did not know him. 'It shall never be told of me,' said Gwalchmei, 'that I let thee get away from me before I learn who thou art.' And he bore down upon him with a spear and thrust at him into his shield so that the shaft was splintered in pieces and the horses forehead to forehead. And he then looked closely at him, and knew him. 'Alas, Gereint,' said he, 'is it thou who art here?' 'I am not Gereint,' said he. 'Gereint! between me and God,' he replied, 'and this is an ill-advised sorry venture.' And he looked about him and perceived Enid, and greeted her and welcomed her. 'Gereint,' said Gwalchmei, 'come thou and see Arthur. He is thy lord and first cousin.' 'I will not,' he replied, 'I am not in a state to go and see any one.' And thereupon, lo, one of the squires coming after Gwalchmei to have word with him. Gwalchmei sent him to tell Arthur how Gereint was there wounded and would not come to see him, and that it was pitiful to see the state he was in; and that without Gereint knowing, and in a whisper between him and the squire. 'And request Arthur,' said he, 'to shift his pavilion near to the road, for he will not come to see him of his own free will, and it would not be easy to compel him in the condition he is in.'

And the squire came to Arthur and told him that. And he removed his pavilion to the side of the road. And then was the maiden's heart gladdened, and Gwalchmei enticed Gereint along the road to the place where Arthur was encamped, and his squires pitching a tent at the side of the road. 'Lord,' said Gereint, 'all hail!' 'God prosper thee,' said Arthur, 'and who art thou?' 'This is Gereint,' said Gwalchmei, 'and of his own free will he would not have come to see thee to-day.' 'Aye,' said Arthur, 'he lacks counsel.' And thereupon Enid came to where Arthur was and greeted him. 'God prosper thee,' said Arthur. 'Let some one lift her to the ground.' And one of the squires lifted her. 'Alas, Enid,' said he, 'what journey is this?' 'I know not, lord,' said she, 'save that I needs must journey the way he journeys.' 'Lord,' said Gereint, 'with thy leave, we will be on our way.' 'Whither will that be?' asked Arthur. 'Thou canst not go at present unless thou go to complete thy death.' 'He would not suffer me to bid him stay,' said Gwalchmei. 'He will suffer me,' said Arthur, 'and further, he shall not go hence till he is whole.' 'It would please me best, lord,' said Gereint, 'if thou gave me leave to depart.' 'I will not, between me and God,' he replied. And then he had a maiden called to take Enid and lead her to Gwenhwyfar's bower. And Gwenhwyfar and all the other ladies made her welcome, and then the riding habit was drawn from off her and another placed upon her. And he called on Cadyrieith and bade him pitch a tent for Gereint and his physicians, and charged him to have ready plenty of every thing, as it might be requested of him. And Cadyrieith did so, even as he was bidden in all. And he brought Morgan Tud and his disciples to Gereint.

And then Arthur and his company spent close on a month healing Gereint. And when Gereint's flesh was strong, he came to Arthur and asked leave to go his way. 'I know not whether thou art yet quite well.' 'In faith I am, lord,' said Gereint. 'It is not thou that I will believe in that matter, but the physicians who have tended thee.' And he summoned the physicians to him and asked them whether that was true. 'True enough,' said Morgan Tud.

On the morrow Arthur gave him leave to depart, and he went to finish his journey. And that day Arthur went thence. And Gereint bade Enid travel in front and keep her distance ahead, as she had done before. And she went her way and followed the high road. And as they were thus they heard, close to them, the hoarsest shriek in the world. 'Stay here,' said he, 'and wait, and I will go and see the meaning of the shriek.' 'I will,' said she. And he went and came to a clearing that was near the road. And in the clearing he could see two horses, the one with a man's saddle and the other with a woman's saddle upon it, and a knight with his armour on him, dead; and standing over the knight he saw a young damsel with her riding habit about her, and shrieking. 'Ah, lady,' said Gereint, 'what has befallen thee?' 'Here was I travelling, I and the man I loved best, and with that there came three giants upon us, and without regard for any justice in the world towards him, they slew him.' 'Which way were they going?' asked Gereint. 'That way, along the high road,' said she. He came to Enid. 'Go,' said he, 'to the lady who is there below, and wait for me there, if I come.' Sad was she that that was bidden her, but even so she came to the maiden, and it was pitiful to hear her. And she was certain that Gereint would never come.

He went after the giants and overtook them. And each one of them was bigger than three men, and a mighty club was on the shoulder of each of them. He bore down upon one of them and pierced him through his middle with a spear, and drew his spear out of him and pierced another of them as well; but the third turned on him and struck him with his club so that his shield was split and his shoulder stayed the blow, and so that all his wounds opened and all his blood was running from him. With that he drew his sword and made at him and struck him a painful-sharp, terrible, mighty-powerful blow on the crown of his head, so that his head and throat were split right to his shoulders, and he fell down dead. And in this wise he left them dead and came to where Enid was. And when he saw Enid he fell to the ground for dead from his horse. Enid gave a terrible, sharp-piercing shriek and came and stood over him in the place where he fell.

And thereupon, lo, coming in answer to the shriek, earl Limwris and a troop that was with him, who were travelling the road. And because of the shriek they crossed the road, and then the earl said to Enid, 'Lady,' said he, 'what has befallen thee?' 'Good sir,' said she, 'there has been slain the one man that ever I loved best and ever shall.' 'And thou,' he asked of the other, 'what has befallen thee?' 'He whom I loved best has been slain likewise,' said she. 'What killed them?' asked he. 'The giants,' said she, 'slew the man I loved best; and the other knight,' said she, 'went after them, and he came away from them even as thou seest him, and his blood running past measure. And I think it likely,' said she, 'that he came not away without having slain some of them, or all.' The knight that had been left dead the earl had buried, but he thought there was still some life in Gereint and had him brought along with him in the hollow of his shield and on a bier, to see whether he would live.

And the two maidens came to the court. And after they had come to the court, Gereint was placed after that fashion on the bier on a head-table in the hall. They all drew off their outdoor clothes, and the earl begged Enid to change and put on another dress. 'I will not, between me and God,' said she. 'Why, lady,' he replied, 'be not so unhappy.' 'Very difficult it is to advise me in that matter,' said she. 'I will so deal with thee that there will be no need for thee to be unhappy, whatever be the fate of yonder knight; whether he live or die. There is here a good earldom; thou shalt have it in thy power, and me too with it,' said he, 'and be joyous and of good cheer henceforth.' 'I will not be joyous henceforth, by my confession to God,' said she, 'as long as I live.' 'Come and eat,' said he. 'I will not, between me and God,' said she. 'Thou shalt, between me and God,' he replied. And he led her with him against her will to the table, and time and time again he bade her eat. 'I will not eat, by my confession to God,' said she, 'until he who is on yonder bier shall eat.' 'Thou canst not make that good,' said the earl; 'yonder man is well nigh dead.' 'I shall try to,' said she. He offered her a cup full of drink. 'Drink this cup,' said he, 'and it will give thee other thoughts.' 'Shame on me,' said she, 'if I drink aught until he drink.' 'Indeed,' said the earl, 'it is of no more avail for me to be courteous to thee than to be discourteous.' And he gave her a box on the ear. She gave a great sharp-piercing shriek, and made outcry far greater than before, and it came into her mind that were Gereint alive she would not be boxed on the ear so. With that Gereint came to himself at the echoing of her shriek, and he rose up into a sitting posture and found his sword in the hollow of his shield, and hastened to where the earl was and struck him a keen-forceful, venomous-painful, mighty impetuous blow on the crown of his head, so that he was cloven, and so that the table stayed the sword. Every one then left the tables and fled out. And it was not fear of the living man that was greatest upon them, but the sight of the dead man rising up to slay them. And then Gereint looked on Enid and a double grief came over him: the one to see how Enid had lost her colour and her mien, and the other was that he knew then she was in the right. 'Lady,' said he, 'dost thou know where our horses are?' 'I know,' said she, 'where thine own went, but I know not where went the other. To yonder house thy horse went.' He then came to the house and fetched out his horse, and mounted upon it, and raised Enid up from the ground and set her between him and the saddlebow. And away he went.

And whilst they were journeying in this wise, as though between two hedges, and night vanquishing the day, lo, they could see between them and the firmament spear-shafts following them, and they could hear the clatter of horses and the clamour of a host. 'I hear a following after us, and I shall place thee the other side of the hedge.' And he placed her. And thereupon, lo, a knight making at him and couching his spear, and when she saw that she said, 'Chieftain,' said she, 'what glory wilt thou win by slaying a dead man, whoever thou art?' 'Alas, God,' he replied, 'is this Gereint?' 'Aye, between me and God. And who art thou?' 'I am the Little King,' said he, 'coming to thine aid, after hearing how there was distress upon thee. And hadst thou done my counsel, there would not have befallen thee what distress there has.' 'Naught may be done,' said Gereint, 'with what God wills. Many a good,' he added, 'comes of counsel.' 'Aye,' said the Little King, 'I know good counsel for thee even now, that thou come with me to the court of my brother-in-law who is here close by, to have thyself healed by the best that is to be had in the kingdom.' 'Let us go, gladly,' said Gereint. And Enid was placed on the horse of one of the Little King's squires, and they came on to the baron's court, and a welcome was given them there and they received care and attendance. And on the morrow physicians were sent for, and the physicians were found, and in a little while they came. And then Gereint was tended till he was quite whole. And while he was being tended, the Little King had his armour repaired until it was as good as it had ever been at its best. And a fortnight and a month were they there.

And then the Little King said to Gereint, 'We shall go now towards my own court, to rest and take our ease.' 'Were it thy pleasure,' said Gereint, 'we would journey one day more and then return.' 'Gladly,' said the Little King; 'go thou.' And in the young of the day they journeyed, and more joyously and gladly than ever did Enid fare along with them that day. And they came to a high road, and they could see it branch into two. And along one of these they could see a man on foot coming to meet them; and Gwiffred asked the man on foot whence he was coming. 'I come from doing errands in the country.' 'Say,' said Gereint, 'which road of these two is it best for me to travel?' 'It is best for thee to travel that,' said he; 'if thou go this, thou wilt never come back. Down below there is a hedge of mist, and within it there are enchanted games, and each and every man that has gone thither has never come back. And the court of earl Ywein is there, and he permits none to lodge in the town save those who come to him at his court.' 'Between me and God,' said Gereint, 'we shall proceed to the road below.'

And they came along it until they came to the town, and in what they considered to be the fairest and the choicest place in the town they took lodging. And as they were thus, lo, a young squire coming to them and greeting them. 'God prosper thee,' said they. 'Good sirs,' said he, 'what purpose is yours here?' 'To take lodging,' they replied, 'and stay the night.' 'It is not that man's custom who owns the town to permit any to lodge therein of gentle folk, save they that come to him in person to his court. And do you come to the court.' 'Let us go, gladly,' said Gereint. And they went along with the squire, and were made welcome at the court. And the earl came to the hall to greet them, and bade the tables be prepared, and they washed and went to sit down. This is how they sat: Gereint was one side of the earl, and Enid the other side. Next to Enid the Little King, then the countess next to Gereint; all thereafter as was proper for them.

And thereupon Gereint thought about the game, and imagined that he would not be permitted to go to the game, and he stopped eating by reason thereof. The earl looked on Gereint, and thought and imagined that it was because of going to the game that he was ceasing to eat, and it grieved him that he had ever instituted those games, though it were only to avoid losing so excellent a youth as Gereint. And if Gereint had requested him to desist from that game he would have desisted from it gladly for ever. And with that the earl said to Gereint, 'What thoughts are thine, chieftain, that thou dost not eat? If thou art dubious of going to the game, it shall be granted thee that thou go not, and that no man shall ever go thereto, in honour of thee.' 'God repay thee,' said Gereint, 'but I wish for nothing save to go to the game and to be directed thereto.' 'If that pleases thee best, thou shalt have it gladly.' 'Best, in faith,' he replied. And they ate, and they had ample attendance and an abundance of dishes and profusion of drink. And when meat was over they arose, and Gereint called for his horse and armour and arrayed him and his horse. And all the hosts came until they were close by the hedge, and not lower was the hedge they could see than the highest point they could see in the sky. And on every stake they could see in the hedge there was a man's head, save for two stakes; and many indeed were the stakes in the hedge and throughout it. And then the Little King said, 'Will any be permitted to go with the chieftain, save himself alone?' 'He will not,' said earl Ywein. 'In what direction,' asked Gereint, 'does one proceed here?' 'I know not,' said Ywein, 'but in the direction most easy for thee to go, go thou.'

And fearlessly, without delay, Gereint went forward into the mist. And when he left the mist he came to a great orchard, and he could see a clearing in the orchard, and a pavilion of brocaded silk with a red canopy he could see in the clearing, and the entrance of the pavilion he could see open. And there was an apple tree over against the entrance of the pavilion, and on a branch of the apple tree was a big hunting-horn; and with that he dismounted and came inside the pavilion. And there was no one inside the pavilion save a solitary maiden sitting in a golden chair, and another chair over against her, empty. Gereint sat in the empty chair. 'Chieftain,' said the maiden, 'I counsel thee not to sit in that chair.' 'Why?' asked Gereint. 'The man who owns that chair has never suffered another to sit in his chair.' 'I care not,' said Gereint, 'even though he take it ill that one sit in his chair.' And thereupon they could hear a great commotion near the pavilion. And Gereint looked to see what was the meaning of the commotion, and saw a knight outside on a wide-nostrilled, mettled, high-spirited, strong-boned charger, and a cloak in two halves about him and his horse, and armour enough thereunder. 'Say, chieftain,' said he to Gereint, 'who bade thee sit there?' 'I myself,' he replied. 'It was wrong of thee to do me shame so great as that, and disgrace; and do thou arise thence, to make me amends for thine own indiscretion.' And Gereint arose, and without more ado they went to do battle, and they broke a set of spears, and broke the second set, and broke the third set, and each of them dealt the other bitter-hard, swift-telling blows. And at last Gereint was fired with rage, and spurred his horse and made at him and thrust at him in the strongest part of his shield, so that it was split and the head of the spear was into his armour, and all his saddle-girths broken, and he himself was over his horse's crupper the length of Gereint's spear and the length of his arm headlong to the ground. And swiftly he drew his sword, intending to cut off his head. 'Alas, lord,' said he, 'thy mercy, and thou shalt have what thou wilt.' 'I wish for nothing,' he replied, 'save that this game never be here, nor the hedge of mist, nor the charm nor the enchantment that has been.' 'That thou shalt have gladly, lord.' 'Then do thou see to it,' said he, 'that the mist disappear from the place.' 'Sound yonder horn,' said he, 'and the moment thou dost sound it, the mist will disappear. And until a knight who had overthrown me should sound it, the mist would never disappear from thence.'

And sad and anxious was Enid in the place where she was, with anxiety for Gereint. And then Gereint came and sounded the horn, and the moment he blew one blast thereon the mist disappeared. And the company came together, and peace was made between each one of them and his fellow. And that night the earl invited Gereint and the Little King and on the morrow early they parted and Gereint went towards his own domain. And he ruled it from that time forth prosperously, he and his prowess and valour continuing with fame and renown for him and for Enid from that time forth.

TEXTUAL NOTES

These Notes show departures from the diplomatic editions referred to on page xxxi of the Introduction. WM = *The White Book Mabinogion*; RM = *The Red Book Mabinogion*; B = *Bulletin of the Board of Celtic Studies*, University of Wales Press, Cardiff; IW = Professor Sir Ifor Williams; JLL-J = Professor J. Lloyd-Jones.

Page 3, line 27, brownish-grey. WM *llwyt tei*, RM llwyttei. IW emends *llwytlei*.

Page 6, line 5, as by himself. WM —, RM —. IW inserts *ac idaw ynteu*.

Page 9, line 38, than if he went at a walking pace. WM *nochynt bei ar y gam*, RM *nochyn bei ar y gam*. Emend *no chyt bei ar y gam*.

Page 23, line 8, Penarddun. WM, RM *Penarddim*.

Page 25, line 20, Anarawd. WM, RM *Anarawc*. Emend *Anarawt* (and so below, 30, 10).

Page 26, line 8, as thick as his little finger. WM —, RM —. IW inserts *ae uys bychan*.

Page 27, line 24, brigand. WM *anorles*, RM *auorles*. Correct reading WM MS *anorlos*. This we regard as a form of *anorloes* < *an* (intensive) + *gor* + *lloes*.

Page 33, line 34, Dogs of Gwern, beware of Morddwyd Tyllion! WM, RM *Guern gwngwch uiwch uordwyt tyllyon*. IW emends *Guerngwn gwchuiwch uordwyt tyllyon*.

Page 35, lines 21–2, and even as they began. WM, RM *Ac y dechreuyssant*. IW emends *Ac[y gyt ac] y dechreuyssant*.

Page 50, line 14, and Gwydion son of Dôn. WM *o a euyd uab Don o*, RM *Ac eueyd uab Don*. Emend *a guyd[yon] uab Dono*.

Page 50, line 15, would go. WM —, RM —. IW inserts *a aei*.

Page 51, line 34, right good. WM *lawn da*, RM *llawnda*. Emend *iawnda* (T. J. Morgan, B ix 126).

Page 53, lines 25–6, in Math son of Mathonwy's bed. WM *yguelei uath uab mathonwy*, RM *y gwelei uath uab mathonw*. Emend *yguele math uab mathonwy*.

Page 54, line 30, Maen Tyriawg. WM, RM *maen tyuyawc*. Emend *maen tyryawc*.

Page 60, line 15, Cefyn Clun Tyno. WM *geuyn clutno*, RM *geuyn clútno*.

Page 65, line 37, Nor rain wets it, nor heat melts. WM *nis gwlych glaw nis mwy/ tawd*, RM *nys gwlych glaw nys mw y tawd*. Emend *nis gwlych glaw nis mwy tawd [tes]*.

Page 65, line 38, hath he suffered. WM *aborthes*, RM *a borthes*. JLL-J emends *porthes*.

Page 66, line 5, The sanctuary of a fair lord. WM *mirein medur ym ywet*, RM *mirein medur ym ywet*. IW emends *mirein modur ynyuet*.

Page 81, line 18, Yet the first plague was open and manifest. RM —, Shirburn MS 113 *Ac eyssoes kyhoed oed ac amlwg er ormes kyntaf*.

243

Page 83, line 15, through his magic. RM *tew yw y hut*. Shirburn MS 113 *trwy y hut*.

Page 85, line 1, wellborn. WM *kynmwyd*, RM *kynmwyt*. JLL-J emends *kymmwyd*.

Page 86, line 34, a battle-axe. WM, RM *Gleif penntirec*. We consider *gleif* to be originally a gloss, later incorporated in the text, and possibly misplaced.

Page 87, line 1, and a ... buckler. WM *achroys*, RM *a chroes*. Correct reading WM MS *ac yays* (the first *y* has a cancel mark through it).

Page 87, line 3, boss. WM *lloring*, RM *llugorn*. Following Foster *llering* (B viii 21–3), we emend *llerig* (? derived from Old English *lærig*).

Page 87, line 13, and his stirrups. WM, RM *ae warthafleu sangnarwy*. We consider *sangnarwy* to be in error for *sangharwy* (derived from *sang + rwy*), itself a gloss on *gwarthafleu*. B xiii 17.

Page 87, lines 14–15, stirred upon him. WM *Ny chwynei ... arnaw*, RM *Ny chrymei ... y danaw*. Emend WM *Ny chwyuei ... arnaw*.

Page 87, line 35, for thee. WM *in*, RM *inn*. Emend *itt*.

Page 88, line 4, Dinsel. WM, RM *dinsol*. Foster (B viii 24–5) emends *Dinsel*, identifying it with Denzell. The phrase 'in the North' originally meant in the North of Cornwall.

Page 88, line 23, Nine-teeth. WM *naw nawt*, RM *naw nawd*. JLL-J emends *naw nant*.

Page 89, line 20, Rhongomyniad. WM *ron gom yant*, RM *rongomyant*.

Page 90, line 3, son of Roch. WM, RM *m. poch*.

Page 90, line 16, Gofyncawn. WM *gonyn cawn*, RM *gouynkawn*. Correct reading WM MS *gouyn cawn*.

Page 90, line 33, and Gofan. WM, RM *Ac ouan*. Emend *A Gouan*.

Page 91, line 17, Cut-beard. WM *uaryf twrch*, RM *varyf twrch*. Emend *uaryf trwch*.

Page 92, line 7, Gwynnan. WM, RM *gwynhan*.

Page 93, line 12, the Island of Britain. WM, RM *teir ynys prydein*. Delete *teir* (and so below, 96, 1–2, and 116, 10).

Page 94, line 10, until. WM, RM *pan*. Emend [*hyt*] *pan*.

Page 95, lines 3–4, son ... son ... son. WM, RM *merch ... merch ... merch*. Emend *mab ... mab ... mab*. We presume that an abbreviation *m.* (= *mab*) was misunderstood in an earlier text. B xiii 13–14.

Page 95, line 5, Half-wit. WM *keudawc pwyll hanner dyn*, RM *keudawt pwyll hanner dyn*. We consider *pwyll* to be a gloss on *keudawt*.

Page 97, line 27, Quoth they. WM *am keudawt*, RM *ac y dywedassant wrthaw*. Read *amkeudant* (and so below, 100, 35 and 101, 12).

Page 97, lines 34–5, and because ... my ruin. WM *ac am uym priawt ym ryamdiuwynwys uym priawt yspadaden penkawr*, RM *ac am vympriawt ym rylygrwys vym brawt yspadaden pen kawr*. Delete the second *uym priawt* in WM.

Page 99, line 8, We pledge it. WM *As redwn*, RM *Rodwn*. Emend *As rodwn*.

Page 99, line 35, gatemen. WM *keithawr*, RM *porthawr*. Correct reading WM MS *porthawr*.

Page 101, line 2, and hurled it. WM, RM *ac odif*. Correct reading WM MS *ae odif*.

Page 101, line 13, us. WM *ui*, RM *ni*. Correct reading WM MS *ni*.

Page 101, line 15, who is told to seek. WM *y dywir vrthaw erchi*, RM *yssyd yn erchi*. Emend *y dyw[ed]ir vrthaw erchi*.

Page 101, line 27, so that the cinders and ashes thereof be its manure. WM *hyt pan hydeclo hwnnw. ae luda a uo teil itaw*, RM *hyt pan uo yn lle teil idaw*. Correct reading WM, MS *hyt pan vo glo hwnnw*, etc.

Page 105, line 33, the Bearded. WM *varchawc*, RM *uarchaw*. Emend *varuawc*.

Page 107, line 9, Neued. WM *uynet*, RM *vynet*.

Page 112, line 14, and still he fought with the men. RM *Ac ymlad ar gwyr ualkynt ar gwyr*. The scribe has written *ar gwyr* twice.

Page 114, line 14, Pen. RM *openn*.

Page 114, line 32, Ledewig. RM *lewic*. Emend *le[de]wic*.

Page 114, line 36, went after. RM *yd aeth*. Emend *yd aeth [yn ol]*.

Page 115, line 2, Cadw. RM *kaw* (as elsewhere).

Page 115, line 6, Ysbaddaden. RM *yspaden*.

Page 115, line 12, mean. RM *salwen*. Emend *salwett*.

Page 117, lines 1–2, glittered. RM *llithrei*. Emend *llathrei*.

Page 118, line 5, Peluniawg. RM *pelumyawc*. Emend *pelunyawc*.

Page 118, line 10, Glyn Ystun. RM *glynn ystu*. Emend *glynn ystū* (= ystun).

Page 119, lines 1–2, Garth Grugyn. RM *garth gregyn*. Correct reading RM MS *garth grugyn*.

Page 119, line 2, Grugyn. RM *llwydawc*. Clearly an error.

Page 122, line 18, in Hallictwn. RM *ymallictwn*.

Page 122, line 18, as far as. RM *ver*. Emend *vet*.

Page 122, line 20, And. RM *ar*. Emend *ac*.

Page 122, line 22, as far as Didlystwn. RM *hyt yn nillystwn*. Emend *hyt yn nitlystwn*.

Page 123, line 8, on the other dais. RM *ar y parth arall . . . ar y parth*. Delete the second *ar y parth*.

Page 124, line 2, and the like of. RM *a chrynhebrwyd*. Emend *a chynheb[yg]rwyd*.

Page 124, line 6, green. RM *las*. Emend *[yn] las*.

Page 125, lines 18–19 5, I . . . have been. RM *bun*. Emend *bum*.

Page 127, line 19, Marini. RM *mariui*.

Page 128, line 21, doomed. RM *diuethaf*. Emend *diuetha*.

Page 128, line 24, to the centre. RM — . Insert *yr kanol*.

Page 129, lines 20–1, red-topped. RM *penngech*. Emend *penngoch*.

Page 129, line 26, over. RM *uchaf*. Emend *[ar] uchaf*.

Page 131, line 30, And Arthur's amazement was as great. RM *a chan aruthret uu gan arthur*. Emend *a chyn . . .*

Page 132, line 3, fleecy. RM *ewyrdonic*. Emend *gwyrdonic*.

Page 132, line 10, the rider. RM *milwr*. Emend *marchawc*.

Page 132, line 12, red with the blood. RM *gan waet*. Emend *[yn goch] gan waet*.

Page 132, line 14, Arthur. RM *arthurthur*.

Page 133, lines 33–4, And Owein bade Gwres son of Rheged. RM *Ac yd erchis y owein wers uab reget*. Emend *Ac yd erchis owein y wres uab reget*.

Page 134, line 11, Osla. RM *ossa*.

Page 134, line 21, son of Custennin. RM *custennin*. Emend [*uab*] *custennin*.

Page 134, line 23, Big-hip. RM *uordwyt twyll*. Emend *uordwyt twll*.

Page 134, line 30, Greidiawl. RM *greidyal*.

Page 134, line 32, Cawrda. RM *Hawrda*. Emend *Kawrda*.

Page 134, line 33, Cadyrieith. RM *karieith*. Emend *ka*[*dy*]*rieith*.

Page 135, line 4, more mighty RM *wrdarch*. Emend *wrdach*.

Page 145, line 1, I came. WM, RM, *adyuot*. Emend *dyuot*.

Page 147, line 31, even though. WM, RM *kany*. Emend *kyn*[*n*]*y*.

Page 149, line 1, he could see. WM —, RM —. Insert *a welei*.

Page 149, line 33, a table. WM —, RM —. Insert *bwrd*.

Page 150, lines 8–10, not to come … of thee. WM *pryt na delut y edrych y gofut a uu arnaf i. ac a oed itti. ac ys gwneuthum i dyti yn gyfoethawc. Ac a oed kam itti na delut y edrych y gofut a uu arnaf i. Ac oed kam itti hynny*, RM *pryt na delut y edrych y gofut a uu arnaf i. Ac a oed itti. ac ys gwneuthum i dy ti ẏ gyfoethawc. Ac a oed kam itti. na delut y edrych y gofut a uu arnaf i. Ac oed kam itti hynny.* Emend *pryt na delut y edrych y gofut a uu arnaf i. ac ys gwneuthum i dyti yn gyfoethawc. Ac oed kam itti hynny.*

Page 150, line 24, whether. WM, RM *a*. Emend *ae*.

Page 156, line 3, throbbing. WM *llanui*, RM *llawn*. Correct reading WM MS *llamu*.

Page 165, lines 24–5 and in everything … mother was. Transposed from WM col. p. 120, 7–9, where it occurs at the end of (our) next paragraph. RM, p. 195, 9–11, confirms the change

Page 180, line 19, the exceeding whiteness of her flesh. Insert *y chnawt* after *gwynhet*.

Page 181, line 19, he happened to be. WM *ac ydoeth ydydoed*, RM *ac yd yttoed*. Emend WM *ac adoeth* (= *attoeth*) *ydydoed*.

Page 183, line 21, though. WM *kanys*, RM *kannys*. Emend *kyn*(*n*)*ys*

Page 186, line 3, perilous. WM, RM, *hyt*. Emend *byt* (:*pyt*, 'danger').

Page 192, lines 17–18, and a robe of gold brocaded silk. WM *ac emwisc o bali*, RM *ac eur wisc o bali*. Correct reading WM MS *ac eurwisc o bali*.

Page 198, lines 4–5, And I will send. WM, RM *ae*. Emend *a*.

Page 208, line 31, and one manchet loaf. WM *ac ouuyt/coesset*, RM *ac un coesset*. Correct reading WM MS *ac un dor*[*th*] *coesset*.

Page 211, line 26, the dwarf's words. WM, RM *ymadrawd y gwr*. Emend *ymadrawd y corr*.

Page 225, lines 29–30, a-plenty. WM *dgynder*, RM and Pen. 6 *dogynder*. Correct reading WM MS *docy*[*nder*].

Page 231, line 14, the men. WM, RM *y gwr*. Emend *y gwyr*.

SUPPLEMENTARY TEXTUAL NOTES, 1974

Page 36, line 2, he was older. WM, RM *y uot yn hynny o amser.* Emend *y uot [yn hyn] yn hynny o amser.* (B xvii 269–70).

Page 76, line 11, Gadeon. WM, RM *ac adeon.* Emend *a Gadeon* (and so below, 78, 25; 78, 25).

Page 90, line 6, Cadwy. WM, RM *ac adwy.* Emend *a Cadwy* (and so below, 134, 24).

Pages 108–9, lines 38–1, And there was great debate ... came inside the fort. WM *Sef a wnaeth ef ae gedymdeithon a glyn wrthaw mal nat oed vwy no dim ganthunt mynet dros y teir catlys a wnaethant.* Delete *a wnaethant.* RM *Dadleu mawr a uu gan y gwyr a oed allan am dyuot bedwyr a chei y mywn. A dyuot gwas ieuanc oed gyt ac wynt y mywn. vn mab custennin heussawr. Sef a wnaeth ef ae gedymdeithon yg glyn wrthaw dyuot dros y teir katlys hyt pann yttoed y mywn y gaer.*

Page 243, Note to 81, 18. For Shirburn MS 113 read Llanstephan MS 1 (and so below, 83, 15).

BRYNLEY F. ROBERTS

INDEX OF PROPER NAMES

This book is set in CASLON, designed and engraved by William Caslon of WILLIAM CASLON & SON, Letter-Founders in London, around 1740. In England at the beginning of the eighteenth century, Dutch type was probably more widely used than English. The rise of William Caslon put a stop to the importation of Dutch types and so changed the history of English typecutting.